305113004H

WITHDRAWN

International Library of Psychology
Philosophy and Scientific Method

Judgment and Reasoning
in the Child

International Library of Psychology Philosophy and Scientific Method

GENERAL EDITOR . C. K. OGDEN, M.A. (*Magdalene College, Cambridge*)

* *Asterisks denote that other books by the same author are included in this series.
A complete list will be found at the end of the volume.*

Judgment and Reasoning in the Child

By

JEAN PIAGET

Doctor of Science, Director of the Institut Rousseau
and Professor at the University of Geneva
Author of *Language and Thought of the Child*

In collaboration with

MLLES E. CARTALIS, S. ESCHER, A. HANHART, L. HAHNLOSER,
O. MATTHES, S. PERRET,

And

M. ROUD

ST. EDMUND HALL
LIBRARY
OXFORD

LONDON
ROUTLEDGE & KEGAN PAUL LTD
BROADWAY HOUSE: 68-74 CARTER LANE, E.C.4

First published in England 1928
Reprinted 1951
Reprinted 1962

Translated by
MARJORIE WARDEN

Printed in Great Britain by
Lowe & Brydone Printers Limited, London, N.W.10

CONTENTS

vii

CHAPTER I

GRAMMAR AND LOGIC

CONJUNCTIONS EXPRESSING CAUSAL, LOGICAL, AND DISCORDANT RELATIONS, AS USED BY CHILDREN BETWEEN THE AGES OF THREE AND NINE.[1]

WE have endeavoured to show in an earlier work that thought in the child is ego-centric, *i.e.* that the child thinks for himself without troubling to make himself understood nor to place himself at the other person's point of view. We tried, above all, to show that these ego-centric habits have a considerable effect upon the structure of thought itself. Thus it is chiefly because he feels no need to socialize his thought that the child is so little concerned, or at any rate so very much less concerned than we are, to convince his hearers or to prove his point.

If this be the case, we must expect childish reasoning to differ very considerably from ours, to be less deductive and above all less rigorous. For what is logic but the art of proof ? To reason logically is so to link one's propositions that each should contain the reason for the one succeeding it, and should itself be demonstrated by the one preceding it. Or at any rate, whatever the order adopted in the construction of one's own exposition, it is to demonstrate judgments by each other. Logical

[1] With the collaboration of Mlle Olga Matthes.—We wish to take the opportunity of expressing our warmest thanks to M. Dottrens and the staff of the school in which we worked, for the kindness and hospitality that were shown to us.

reasoning is always a demonstration. If, therefore, the child remains for a long time ignorant of the need for demonstration, this is bound to have an effect upon his manner of reasoning. As we have already pointed out (L.T.,[1] Chap. III, § 5), the child is not really aware of the necessity of arranging his sentences in logical order.

But how are we to enquire into the nature of logical relations in children, while retaining our hold upon reasoning as revealed in direct psychological observation, and yet avoid making use of the necessarily artificial framework of the logicians ?

We may begin by a method, tentative but natural, which consists in seeing how the child behaves when confronted with those conjunctions which denote causality or logical relations (because, for, therefore, etc.) and with those expressing antithetical relations (in spite of, even though, although, etc.). In this connexion two courses seem to be indicated. The first consists in inducing the child, by means of appropriate experiments, to make use of these conjunctions, to make him understand or invent, for example, sentences in which the required conjunctions are used. The second consists in noting in the child's spontaneous talk all the sentences in which the said conjunction is used. For instance, in studying the conjunctions of causality as used between the ages of 6 and 7 we shall have to note down every ' because,' every ' since,' and every ' why ' occurring in the corresponding questions.

In one of the chapters of our last volume we made a certain contribution to this question by analysing, not the conjunctions of causality in the child, but the questions corresponding to these conjunctions (the ' whys '). The analysis of these ' whys ' yielded as a first important result the fact that before the age of 7 there seems to be no pronounced desire for logical justification. What the ' whys ' bear witness to is a need to explain and justify

---

[1] The initials " L.T. " refer to the author's *The Language and Thought of the Child*, uniform with this volume.

material phenomena, human actions, the rules of school and society, etc., far rather than a wish to justify judgments, *i.e.* a wish to deduce or demonstrate anything. The present chapter is partly intended to confirm the following conclusion : if the absence or rarity of " whys of logical justification " really has the significance which we have attributed to it, we must expect to find in childish idiom on the one hand a correspondingly rare occurrence of the " because of logical justification," and on the other a persistent difficulty on the part of the child in finding the correct justification for simple propositions which he is asked to demonstrate. This is what we shall try to establish.

Now, if such are the habits of childish thought, childish idiom ought to display a discontinuous and chaotic character in contrast to the deductive style of the adult, logical relations being omitted or taken for granted. In a word, there will be ' juxtaposition ' and not relating of propositions. The study of juxtaposition will therefore constitute the second object of this chapter.

The phenomenon of juxtaposition is very frequent in child thought. A well-known and particularly striking example has been signalled in the case of children's drawings, and has been referred to as ' synthetic incapacity.' [1] M. Luquet has pointed out that one of the most universal characteristics of these children's drawings is the inability shown by their authors to portray the relations existing between the different parts of the model. The thing is not there as a whole, the details only are given, and then, for lack of synthetic relations, they are simply juxtaposed. Thus an eye will be placed next to a head, an arm next to a leg, and so on.

This synthetic incapacity covers more ground than one would think, for it is really the mark of the whole of childish thought up to a certain age. We have already observed it (L.T., Chap. III) in connexion with understanding between children. We have tried to show that

[1] Luquet, *Les Dessins d'un enfant*, Paris, Alcan., 1913.

occasions abound when, instead of expressing the relation between two propositions by the word ' because ' (as had been done in the corresponding adult communication) or in any other way, the child was content to juxtapose these propositions without any further ado, whether or no he had been conscious of any causal connexion between them. Now, in three-quarters of such cases, the child who was spoken to did not realize that such a connexion was in question, and could therefore see nothing more than two statements which were independent of each other.

Juxtaposition is therefore, in a certain sense, the converse of the process which we studied under the name of ' syncretism.' Syncretism is the spontaneous tendency on the part of children to take things in by means of a comprehensive act of perception instead of by the detection of details, to find immediately and without analysis analogies between words or objects that have nothing to do with each other, to bring heterogeneous phenomena into relation with each other, to find a reason for every chance evènt ; in a word, it is the tendency to connect everything with everything else. Syncretism is therefore an excess of relating while juxtaposition exhibits a deficiency in the same function. The two seem in complete opposition to each other. In drawing, children give only the detail and neglect the synthesis, but childish perceptions seem to be formed by general schemas rather than by analysis. In thinking, the child is ignorant of logical justification, he juxtaposes propositions instead of connecting them, but he is able to give a reason for everything, to justify every phenomenon and every coincidence. How exactly are these contradictory phenomena related to each other ? This is the question to which we must find an answer.

To sum up, the object of this chapter will be 1° to form an introduction to the study of childish reasoning by means of an analysis of the types of relation involved in the conjunctions of causality, of logical connexion, and of discordance ; 2° to draw from this study an analysis of the phenomenon of juxtaposition ; and 3° to show the relations existing between juxtaposition and syncretism.

I. CONJUNCTIONS OF CAUSALITY AND LOGICAL RELATIONS.

The method we have adopted is extremely simple. In the first place, we are in possession of a number of records of the actual conversation of children of different ages who were under observation for about a month each (see L.T., Chap. I). We have selected from these records the sentences which contain conjunctions, and we have analysed them from the point of view which concerns us at present. In the second place, we have made experiments in the Elementary schools of Geneva, which consist in asking the children to invent or to complete sentences containing the word 'because' or other causal conjunctions.

To do this, you begin by asking the child if he knows how to invent sentences with a given word (table, etc.). When he has understood he is asked to invent a phrase containing the word 'because,' etc. Sometimes the child is bored, in which case you pass straight on to the second part of the experiment. You tell the subject that you are going to give him an unfinished sentence : " Then you must make up the end yourself, so that it should go nicely with the beginning, so that the sentence should be true, etc." You then give a list of sentences to complete after the following pattern : " The man fell off his bicycle because . . .," and the child must make up an ending. As a rule this game is quite popular to begin with. You can also take the child's answer as a new starting-point. For instance, if the subject answers, " Because he slipped," you ask : " And he slipped because . . .," and so on, as long as it makes sense. You must at the same time try to avoid boredom or automatism.

B

In order to study the use of the conjunction ' because '
we used this method to experiment on about 40 children
from 6 to 10 who were examined individually. In addition
to this, we carried out a collective enquiry on 200
children from 7 to 9 by writing the sentences to be completed on the black-board. The simultaneous use of
collective enquiry and personal examination is a method
that has much in its favour in the experiments in question :
the first supplies one with statistical data in a short time,
and the second enables one to check the results by analysis.
In this way we collected about 500 sentences by means
of personal interrogatory, and about 2000 by means of
collective enquiry.

§ I. Types of Relation expressed by the Conjunction 'Because.'—Before describing our results we
must begin by distinguishing between the two main types
of relations which are denoted by the conjunction 'because'
[parce que], viz. the relation of cause and effect, or causal
relation, and the relation of reason and consequent or the
logical relation.

The causal ' because ' is the mark of a relation of
cause and effect between two phenomena or two events.
In the sentence which we gave to the child, " The man
fell off his bicycle because . . .," the ' because ' calls for
a causal relation, since it is a question of connecting an
event (a fall) with another event (e.g. " someone got in
his way "), and not of connecting one idea with another.

The logical ' because,' on the other hand, denotes a
relation, not of cause and effect, but of ' implication,' of
reason and consequent ; what the ' because ' connects here
is no longer two observed facts, but two ideas or two judgments. For instance, " Half 9 is not 4, because 4 and 4
make 8." Or, " That animal is not dead, because (or
since) it is still moving."

Difficulties, from the logical point of view, undoubtedly
face us at this juncture, but we shall try to exclude them
from these purely genetic studies. When does implication
begin and when does the causal relation end ? Have

not the relations just mentioned the same right to be named causal as those that were given first ? Or at any rate, is not the half of a number as much a datum of empirical observation for the child as is a fall from a bicycle ? But to take such a standpoint is to forget that in order to explain why half 9 is not 4, we have to appeal to definitions and relations which are not causes, but logical relations, whereas to explain a bicycle accident there is really no need to appeal to anything beyond facts. It is therefore primarily in virtue of the type of explanation which they admit of that these two kinds of explanation differ ; the one is (*logical*) *demonstration*, the other (*causal*) *explanation*.

This criterion, which naturally raises difficulties in its turn, is nevertheless justifiable on psychological and not only on logical grounds. It is clear to observation that logical justification or proof appears at a much later date than causal explanation. When you ask him to complete the sentence : " The man fell off his bicycle because . . .," the child experiences no difficulty. When you ask him : " Half 9 is not 4 because . . .," the question strikes him as absurd. He is even tempted to give a causal explanation as an answer : " because he can't count." The distinction we are making here does obviously refer to something. It may even be said to depend upon a very universal law of mental development, viz. that the desire to check results comes very much later in point of time than the faculty for inventing explanations.

In addition to this, it is necessary to distinguish a third type of relation, which may be considered as intermediate between the last two, and which we shall call the *relation of motive for action* or the *psychological relation*. The ' because ' which denotes this relation establishes a relation of cause and effect, not between any two facts, but between an action and an intention, between two psychological actions. For instance : " I slapped Paul's face, because . . . he was laughing at me." The relation here is empirical in a sense, since it is a question of two facts and of a causal explanation. In another sense, however, it is logical, since it introduces a reason, an intelligent motive as cause. We have here as much a justification as an explanation.

We have distinguished this third type because children have a tendency to replace logical by psychological relations. We gave an example of this just now. " Half 9 is not 4, because he can't count."

It was necessary to bring in these distinctions since it is our intention in this chapter to point to some of the difficulties which a child experiences in establishing correct relations. These difficulties will of course vary considerably according as we are dealing with one type of relation or another. An excellent reason, moreover, for allowing the utility of these distinctions is the good work which they did in connexion with the ' whys ' of children (L.T., Chap. V). To each one of our classes of ' because ' there will be seen to correspond a class ' whys ' : the ' whys of causal explanation ' ("Why do boats stay on the water ? "), the ' whys of motivation ' ("Why are you going ? "), the ' whys of logical justification ' ("Why is it a dog and not a wolf ? "). Now, both the respective appearance and the functional importance of these three kinds of question are subject to singular variations, as we have already shown at some length. Hence the desirability of keeping to this classification.

Finally, it may be wondered in connexion with each of our experiments, what is the exact relation which subsists between language and reasoning. When a child fails to complete one of our sentences, is it because he does not know the conjunction, or because he cannot handle the mental relation which it presupposes ? It is impossible to settle this question a priori. We shall see later, with regard to the conjunctions of discordance, that some of them, such as ' although,' may not be understood, even though the relation of discordance is understood when other words are used. The matter is not the same when it comes to ' because.' Between the years of

6 and 9, when the relation indicated by 'because' is incorrect, one can always assume that reasoning has been at fault ; the word 'because' [*parce que*] is used spontaneously by the child from the age of 3 to 4 onwards.

§ 2. HYPOTHESES [1] DRAWN FROM THE ANALYSIS OF CHILDREN'S TALK.—Before passing on to the examination of such experiments as we have made, it will be well to take our stand upon actual observation, and to ask ourselves in what sense and how often children make use of the conjunction 'because.' The results obtained in this way will constitute very useful hypotheses, which will serve to guide us in the interpretation of later material.

To help us in this task we have at our disposal eight homogeneous samples of observation. Three of them are familiar to us—the language of Lev and of Pie at the age of 6 and the language of Lev at the age of 7 (language dealt with in Chapter I of the volume L.T.). Since then Mlles Buerguer, Fiaux and Gonet have taken a record, according to the same method, of a collection of remarks, of which mention will be found in the Appendix.

We are now in possession of nearly 10,000 remarks taken down in identical circumstances from eight children only, it is true (counting Lev and Ad who were each studied on two separate occasions as four), but scattered between the ages of 3 and 7 in such a manner as to yield at least a few working hypotheses.

The first question to be asked is that of the absolute frequency of 'because.' To these statistics may be added the few occasions on which use was made of 'since' [*alors*], and which number 3 out of the 1500 sentences spoken by Dan (age 3) and 1 out of the 1500 spoken by Ad (age 4). Here is the table which we obtained. The combined numbers of 'because' and 'since' are expressed in percentages, *i.e.* relatively to the number of sentences constituting our material. Thus 1·2% means that out of 100 remarks 1·2 contain the term 'because.'

[1] *See* note on p. 61.

	'Because' and 'Since.'	Coefficient of Ego-centrism.
Dan, age 3 . . .	1·2%	0·56
Jan, age 3 . . .	1·5%	0·56
Ad, age 4 . . .	1·2%	0·60
Ad, age 5 . . .	2%	0·46
Pie, age 6 . . .	2%	0·43
Lev, age 6 . . .	2·4%	0·47
Clau, age 7 . .	3·5%	0·30
Lev, age 7 . . .	6·1%	0·27

Such a table undoubtedly enables us to make three hypotheses subject to verification by wider statistics and other methods which we shall develop later on.

The first is that the number of appearances of 'because' and 'since' increases with age and seems to increase considerably round about 7, after having been more or less stationary just before. In other words, if the phenomenon of 'juxtaposition' is defined as the lack of explicit relation between propositions which imply such a relation, there are strong reasons for assuming that juxtaposition is sufficiently present up till the age of 7 to 8 (Lev being a child 6 months or a year in advance of the normal) for it to diminish after that age. As this is a conclusion which we have already reached in another way (L.T., Chap. III), we may be permitted to retain it with a certain degree of confidence.

The second hypothesis is that 'because' and 'since' increase in number with the socialization of thought, or if it is preferred, that juxtaposition diminishes as the child emerges from ego-centrism. This point of view has already been made known to us elsewhere.[1] It must be admitted that the evolution undergone by Lev speaks in favour of this hypothesis; his coefficient of ego-centrism passes from 0·47 to 0·27 in a year, while the number of 'because' and 'since' increases from 2·4% to 6·1%. But it goes without saying that the only way of really

[1] L.T., Chap. III, §§ 4 and 5.

verifying it would be to look for the correlation between these two kinds of coefficients in a large number of children of the same age.

Our third hypothesis is concerned with the nature of juxtaposition. It seems permissible to ask whether egocentrism of thought does not necessarily involve a certain incoherence or, as Bleuler calls it, a certain 'absence of direction' in the succession of images and judgments. If this were so, juxtaposition would be explained. Now M. Bleuler has shown in his well-known studies on psychoanalysis that a connexion exists between the degree of socialization and the degree of ' direction,' or let us say of conscious direction of thought. Dreams, delirium, or even day-dreaming, in short, every manifestation of 'autistic' or incommunicable thought appear to us as 'undirected' in this sense, that the images and ideas which succeed one another in consciousness seem to lack any connecting links, any implication, even any causal relation (dreams have no way of explaining causality except by juxtaposition). Now what is the origin of this lack of conscious direction ? Is it some deep and genuine disharmony ? Not at all. For analysis shows that the various images and ideas which seem so disconnected are in reality grouped together by one and the same tendency or by one and the same desire. Thus there is always direction in thought, but in cases like these the direction is unconscious and is more akin to simple motor or affective tendencies than to willed and conscious direction. If, therefore, there is an apparent lack of direction, this means that autistic thought does not take cognizance of the motives which guide it. But this ignorance is precisely the result of the autistic character of thought; it is because it is not detached from the ego that this sort of thinking does not know itself. Only by means of friction against other minds, by means of exchange and opposition does thought come to be conscious of its own aims and tendencies, and only in this way is it obliged to relate what could till then remain juxtaposed. This is why every act of socialized intelligence implies not only consciousness of a definite thought direction (as, for instance, of problem) but also consciousness of the successive statements of a narrative (relations of implication) or of those between successive images of the objects of thought (causal relations).

This, then, is how we can make clear to ourselves the connexion between ego-centrism and juxtaposition. There is nothing in ego-centrism which tends to make thought conscious of itself (since this self - consciousness only arises through some shock with another mind), and this unconsciousness enables the objects of thought to succeed one another in an unrelated fashion. Juxtaposition is therefore the result of absence of direction in the successive images and ideas, and this absence of direction is itself the outcome of that lack of self-consciousness which characterizes all ego-centric thought.

Let us turn to the analysis of ' because ' and ' since ' as they were noted in the talk of those few children. Out of the 134 relations shown by Jan, Dan, Ad, Pie and Lev at 6 years old, 112 are psychological, 10 causal, and 12 logical.

The frequent appearance of the psychological ' because ' is particularly striking. Here are some examples :

" *Look, he's laughing!*—Why ?—*Because he wants to catch the apple* " (Dan). " *I don't want them to open that because it would be a pity* " (Dan). " *But René isn't here yet, he'll be late . . . because he always comes slowly, he plays on the way* " (Dan).

" *Look out there, 'cos it goes round* " (Ad). " *I want to make a stove.*—Why ?—*Because for [parce que pour] the heating* " (Ad). " *I must hurry up, because Mummy is coming* " (Ad).

" *I'm going to sit here, because my drawing is here* " (Pie). " *I say, Ez ! Come here, because we'll both have the same thing* " (Pie).

It will have been noticed that the psychological ' because ' sometimes gives a genuine psychological explanation ("he's laughing . . . because . . .") and sometimes expresses the motive of an action or of a command (" I don't want to . . . because "). There are many intermediate forms between these two, hence the name *relations of motivation* which can be used in this connexion. As a rule it is easy to distinguish between logical justification and motivation. The former always gives the motive for a judgment or statement, the latter for a desire, a command, or an act. Thus the first alone constitutes a proof, the second is only subjective motivation.

The genuinely causal ' because ' is rare. This, as we have seen (L.T., Chaps. I and III), is due to the fact that there is very little attempt on the part of children to socialize their search for the causal explanation of external phenomena. This does not mean that they do not feel the need for explanation ; on the contrary, an examination of the questions asked by children shows that at the age of 6, 18% of the questions refer to physical causality (L.T., Chap. V).

Here are some examples of this way of relating : " [It is broken *because it wasn't properly stuck.*" (Dan). " *The train can't get past there. . . . Because there is too much sand up there*" (Ad). " *One of them would like to get into the nest, but he can't, because it* (the nest) *is too small* " (Pie), etc.

Logical relations number only 12 out of 134, which is a useful confirmation of the result obtained from our study of ' why ' (L.T., Chap. V). These relations can be easily recognized by the fact that they constitute neither causal explanations nor subjective motivations but always *proofs* or the beginnings of proof. Here are some examples :

" *No, it's a boat, because it hasn't any wheels* " (Dan). " *It's badly done* [a staircase].—Why ?—*Because you don't make them that way, you make them this way* " (Dan). [Dan sets out some Loto cards.] " *Yes, it's that one, since it's at the bottom.*"

" How can you tell that they are going to school ?— *Going to school ? Because the satchel is behind* " (Pie).

It may be noticed that in some cases the 'because' is not spontaneous, but is given in answer to an adult's question. Be that as it may, the problem remains as to how the need for justification develops with age. In the following table we shall place Jan, Dan and Ad in one group, Ad, Lev, and Pie at 5 and 6 in the other, and we shall add the results of 100 instances of 'because' taken at random from the table-talk of two adults in the course of a few consecutive days. The numbers show the proportion of times when 'because' expresses a logical relation to the total number of occasions on which the word 'because' is used at all.

Jan, Dan and Ad . . .	0·04	Age, 3–4
Ad (age 5), Pie and Lev .	0·10	Age, 5–6
Clau and Lev . . .	0·18	Age, 7
X and Y	0·33	Adult

We must, of course, beware of forming any hasty conclusion from statistics which cover, it is true, nearly 10,000 childish sentences, but are drawn from the talk of eight children only. But we repeat once more that our only object is to frame hypotheses which shall be tested later on by a different method of procedure. And it is the mark of a sound method that the hypotheses which guide its experiments should have been born of the crude facts of observation such as those which make up the body of the statistics given above.

These data seem to point to some period in time—between the ages of 7 and 8—as that after which the chief development of logical justification sets in. And we shall see later on in connexion with our collective enquiry that the unfinished sentences were successfully completed in a proportion of cases which increased rapidly from the age of 7–8.

If this is so, then we are warranted in making the hypothesis that the need for logical justification is concomitant with the decline of ego-centrism on the one hand

and with the diminution of juxtaposition in general on the other, since we have already shown that it is during his seventh year that Lev's coefficient of ego-centrism goes from 0·47 to 0·27, and that his ' because ' goes from 2·4% to 6·1%. This solitary but closely observed case seems therefore to indicate that the decline of ego-centrism, that of juxtaposition in general, and the development of logical justification are all of a piece.

It will be easy enough to see how this mutual dependence works out, if the sequel proves it to exist. We have on many occasions stressed the point that the need for checking and demonstration is not a spontaneous growth in the life of the individual ; it is on the contrary a social product. Demonstration is the outcome of argument and the desire to convince. Thus the decline of ego-centrism and the growth of logical justification are part of the same process (cf. in particular, L.T., Chap. II). On the other hand, we saw just now that ego-centrism entails a certain lack of direction in thinking, owing to the fact that there is nothing here which tends to make thought conscious of itself and consequently to systematize or ' direct' its successive judgments. It is therefore no mere coincidence that all these phenomena should group themselves around the age of 7–8, which forms a definite stage in the development of the socialization of thought.

But once again, these are only hypotheses. Let us now try to verify them by experiment.

§ 3. JUXTAPOSITION AND THE EMPIRICAL ' BECAUSE.'— We have shown what is to be understood by juxtaposition in childish idiom ; it is the fact that the successive judgments which constitute the child's talk are not connected by explicit relations but are simply stuck together. If this phenomenon really lasts up till the age of 7-8, we must expect to find, even at this age, that when the children are asked to complete a sentence which implies a definite relation, there is a certain amount of confusion between the various possible relations. Only this element of confusion will prove that the relation was not implicit in the child's mind, and that the child was really incapable of establishing the correct relation.

For we must beware of confusing juxtaposition with mere ellipsis. We do not ourselves express every ' because ' that enters into our explanations, and it is even the mark of good style to bring out causal relations by a mere string of statements : " It is raining. The thunder has ionized the air, and the ions have brought about the formation of rain-drops." But this style is the result of art. It is only after having become conscious of causal relations that we can omit them, and our own elliptical style does not deceive us. In the same way an artist will contrive to express himself by means of a few pencil-strokes, juxtaposed like those of children who are labouring under ' synthetic incapacity ' ; but here again the apparent juxtaposition is the result of art.

Now, if the scarcity of the word ' because ' up till the age of 7–8 is really a proof that the child's mind is devoid of certain relations, experiment should reveal a whole series of confusions when the child is pressed to find the correct relation. And this, as a matter of fact, is what proves to be the case. The data show that up to the age of 7-8 the word ' because ' is occasionally an equivocal term which is used for all purposes, and covers a number of heterogeneous types of relation—causal, consecutive, and even finalistic, the child being apparently quite undisturbed by this heterogeneity. Sometimes there seems to be no need for the use of ' because ' at all ; it will be placed at the beginning of a proposition which bears no relation whatever except that of simultaneity to the principal proposition of the sentence. This is all the more significant in view of the fact that we are concerned here only with the ' because ' of empirical relation, leaving aside for the moment the logical ' because ' which offers additional difficulties of its own.

Here are some examples of these heterogeneous relations as made by children who are otherwise quite capable of handling the word ' because,' but who, in regard to our uncompleted sentences, use the word sometimes in a correct sense, sometimes in a sense akin to ' in such a manner that ' (consecutive relation), and sometimes in the sense of ' and.'

Ga (age 7), after having correctly invented such sentences as : " *There is a window broken, because a boy threw a stone,*" finishes other sentences in the following manner : " A man fell down in the street, *because he fell ill.*" [1] Now Ga does not mean that the man fell down because he was ill, but that he fell, and that was what made him ill : " *He fell down. They took him to the chemist's.*—Why did he fall?—*Someone had put some ice on the pavement.*" ' Because ' might here be replaced by ' and ' or by ' in such a manner that.' The causal relation seems to have been changed over into a consecutive relation.

Similarly, Sci (age 7 ; 2) : " A man fell down in the road, because *he broke his leg, he had a bit of wood stuck on* [a wooden leg]." Kel (8 ; 6) : " The man fell from his bicycle, *because he broke his arm.*" Brico (7 ; 6) and Je (8 ; o) : " because *he broke his leg.*"

Berne (6½) : " I teased that dog, because *he bit me.*" (Berne means : First I teased the dog, and then he bit me.)

Leona (7½) : " I had a bath, because *afterwards I was clean.*" " There was a draught because *the draught gave me a cold.*" " I went to the cinema, because *it was pretty.*" (We found out that he did not know it was pretty before going to the cinema ; he did not go *because* it was pretty, but he went *and* it was pretty.)

Don (age 6) : " I've lost my pen because *I'm not writing.*" " I went for a message yesterday, because *I went on my bike.*" " They are playing music (in the next room), because *you can hear it.*"

Mour (6 ; 10) : " That boy threw me a stone, because *he is in prison.*" " The man fell off his bicycle, because *afterwards he was ill and they picked him up in the street.*" Of course this does not prevent Mour from correctly completing other sentences such as : " I shan't go to school to-morrow, because *it is cold.*" Or " I hurt myself, because *I fell off my bicycle.*"

Berg (age 6), among many correct propositions, brings out such statements as : " He fell off his bike, because

[1] The sentence to be completed is in Roman type, the child's answer is in *italics.*

he fell and then he hurt himself." Mor (9 ; 1) [backward] tells us " I am not well, because *I'm not going to school."*

Finally, let us recall the point brought out earlier, that Dan (3½) in his spontaneous language, uses the word ' because ' sometimes correctly and sometimes as follows : *" I want to make a stove . . . because for the heating."* ' Because ' stuck in this way on to ' for ' or ' so that ' is frequently met with in the talk of children from 3 to 4 years old. One also meets with the expression " because because of." [1]

What interpretation are we to put on all this ? At first sight it would seem simply that the child is hesitating indefinitely between causal explanation and logical justification. His ' because ' seems at times to be a genuine ' because,' sometimes it resembles a ' since ' ; and the reason for this is that the child does not realize when he is being required to explain, and when to justify.

Roughly speaking, this interpretation is the true one, but it must be qualified by two additional remarks. In the first place, the child (as we have already seen and as we shall show in the following section) is in no way conscious of proving what he says or what is said to him. For instance, it is certainly not from any love of justification as such that the above answers were given to us ; they are due simply to the desire to make up a relation since the child has been asked for one, and in these cases, it turns out that the first relation which comes into his head refers to the consequence of the event, not to its cause, thus giving the impression that the child was trying to justify the sentence to be completed. After all, it is the consequence of an event which constitutes the logical justification of the judgment which affirms the event. The fact that he has broken his leg is both the consequence of the fact that the man fell off his bicycle and the justification of the judgment : " That man fell off his bicycle." (The French word for since, ' puisque,' is derived from

---

[1] French " parce qu' à cause " [Translator's note].

words which originally expressed nothing but sequence
' et puis . . . que '—' and then . . . that '.)

The simplest interpretation is therefore that the child,
realizing that there is a vague connexion between a
proposition such as " The man fell off his bicycle " and
another such as " He was ill afterwards," does not enquire
whether this connexion is causal, consecutive, or logical
(relation of justification) but simply expresses this relation
by ' because.'

Now, since we are concerned here with sentences to be
completed and not with material taken from the spontaneous talk of the child, the conclusion to be drawn from
these data is not that the child confuses cause and effect,
but rather that before the age of 7–8 he is perhaps incapable—whether in narrative, argument, or in any of his
relations with other people—of differentiating between
the various types of possible relations (cause, consequence, or logical justification), and of handling them to
good effect.

The best proof that this is no fanciful reading of the
facts is that the same phenomena are to be found in the
spontaneous idiom of children. When a child constructs
his own sentences instead of completing half-formed
sentences, inversions similar to those which we have
described may be observed, though naturally they occur
in a smaller proportion. We have already discussed this
matter in connexion with understanding between children
(L.T., Chap. III, § 5). For example, Pour (7 ; 6), instead
of saying : " The water stays there because the pipe is
so placed," or in his own style, " The water stays there
because the pipes can't get there," reverses the relation and
says : " *Because the water stays there, the pipes can't get
there.*" Mart (age 8), instead of saying : " Why does the
water run out there and not run out here ? Because the
tap is open there and shut here," says : " *Why is the tap
open there . . . etc. ?* [because] *the water runs out there,
and here . . . etc.*" See also in connexion with the turning of ' because ' into ' why,' Chapter V of vol. L.T.

(§ 5 to the end). In a word, these facts are exactly similar to those which we have just elicited by means of experiment.

But it is chiefly in interrogatories referring to natural phenomena or machines that one can note at every turn these inversions due to the lack of direction in thought. For example, Schnei (4½) tells that an engine which has been lighted before him goes because of the fire. The fire is put out: " *It's not going now*—Why is it not going any longer ?—*Because it has stopped.*—Why has it stopped ? —*Because it* [the wheel] *is not going round fast.*—But why is it not going round any longer ? . . .," etc. This type of answer is extremely frequent between the ages of 7 and 8. It cannot be due to any desire to justify the statements, since these are self-evident. Nor is it due to any difficulty in giving a causal explanation, since the child knows the cause in question. It is simply a case of lack of direction or order in thinking ; the different relations are interchangeable at any moment, because they have no fixed function in the subject's speech.

These phenomena of non-differentiation are probably connected with what was revealed by our examination of 'why.' We were able to show (L.T., Chap. V) that many of the ' whys ' of children under 7–8 bear witness to an undifferentiated state where cause is confused with reason, with motive, and hence, in a sense, with consequence.

The proof then of the true importance attaching to the phenomenon of juxtaposition would seem to lie in these apparent inversions of the causal relation : the habit which children have of merely juxtaposing their successive statements instead of binding them together betrays a genuine difficulty in the management of relations as they occur in speech. Originally, it would seem, the child refrains from voicing any explicit relations, because his experience is limited to what may be called ' relational feelings,' among which, however, he is incapable of distinguishing one kind from another. Then from among these vague relations those are gradually differentiated which we call causal, consecutive, and finalistic. And only once those three relations have been separately established (round about 7–8) would that of implication (logical justification) seem to have any claim to an autonomous and distinct existence.

We shall see, moreover, that the same thing holds good in the case of all conjunctions with which the child is unfamiliar. When he is asked to complete a sentence containing *e.g*, ' although,' the child, instead of saying that he does not know the word, feels that it must mean some sort of relation, and therefore chooses the simplest and most undifferentiated, that which could be rendered by a mere ' and.' Consequently, it is only natural that the same principle should hold for a long time in the case of ' because ' — occasionally in the child's spontaneous idiom (though rarely, since explicit relations are just those which the child does his best to eliminate from his idiom)—but chiefly in such experiments as those of the uncompleted sentences.

It might be claimed that mistakes such as we have been discussing are purely grammatical and have no concern with the child's thought. This reading of the facts could be maintained with regard to ' for ' and the conjunctions of discordance, but it falls to the ground as regards the spontaneous ' because ' in the talk of the child from 3–4. To examine this problem it is necessary to analyse children's concrete ideas of things, to get them to talk about nature, or arrange little experiments with them which they can discuss afterwards, etc. Whether or not there is in such cases any confusion between cause and effect, or between cause and logical reason, etc., is quite another matter. What we are examining now is simply the verbal expression of causality or rather the *narration* of causal sequences. All that we claim is that in such narration the child is incapable of differentiating clearly between relations of causality, of sequence and of justification (however clearly he may have distinguished them in concrete observation) ; which means

C

that he is incapable of assigning a fixed function in speech to each of these relations. In a word it comes to this, that the child cannot give an account of facts. He follows neither the order of logical demonstration nor that of causal sequence, but mixes the one up with the other. And this is exactly what we found to be the case with regard to the structure of the explanations which take place between one child and another (L.T., Chap. III, § 5).[1]

Finally, the question may be raised as to when we are to date the disappearance of this stage during which the child mixes up all empirical relations into one undifferentiated relation. In other words, from what age onwards are children able to complete a sentence correctly which contains an empirical ' because ' ? According to our qualitative analyses there would seem to be a diminution of juxtaposition at the age of 7 to 8. Is it possible to verify this hypothesis by means of a collective enquiry ? In order to carry this out we gave the two following sentences to 180 children of 7–8, taken from the Elementary schools in Geneva, and asked them to complete them in writing :

1. I shan't go to school to-morrow, because . . .

2. That man fell off his bicycle, because . . .

The first sentence was successfully finished by about 85% of the 7-year old boys and by 95% of the boys be-

---

[1] A possible way of verifying the hypothesis that ' because ' still indicates a relation of simple juxtaposition in the child might be to ask our subjects straight away what the word ' because ' means. But all definition presupposes the awareness of subconscious operations, and we know from M. Claparède's law of *prise de conscience* that the more automatically a relation is used, the more difficult it is to bring it into consciousness. We saw in the last paragraph, moreover, to what extent childish ego-centrism blocks the way to awareness of thought as such. These conclusions can easily be verified with regard to the word ' because.' When children from 7 to 9 are asked what the word ' because ' means in such sentences as " I shall not go to school to-morrow because I am ill," most of them answer : " It means that he is ill." Others maintain that " It means that he won't go to school." In short, these children have no idea of the definition of the word ' because,' in spite of the fact that they can manipulate it spontaneously, at any rate in the sense we have specified.

tween 8 and 9. It will be remembered that a test is said to have been successful when 75% of the children of a certain age can pass it. The second sentence is from this point of view not successfully completed at seven (70%), but is so with children of eight (77%).

It may therefore be assumed that on an average the correct use of the empirical ' because ' takes its start at the age of 7–8.[1]

§ 4. THE RELATION OF IMPLICATION AND THE LOGICAL ' BECAUSE ' AND ' SINCE.'—If the confusion with regard to the empirical relations denoted by the word ' because ' is really such as we have shown it to be, no correct management of the relation of implication can be expected to appear before the age of 7–8. For the implicative or logical relation connects not one fact with another, but reason with its consequent, or rather a judgment with its proof or logical antecedent. The hypothesis may therefore be advanced that logical implication has a double origin, or at any rate presents two complementary features.

On the one hand, as was shown by our examination of ' why ' (L.T., Chap. V) and of the empirical ' because,' the child, before reaching the age of 7–8, simply has a tendency to confuse logical and causal relations. He conceives the world as being the work of a human and entirely reasonable agency (excluding, for example, all

---

[1] We shall say nothing about the word ' for ' [Fr. ' car '] which belongs almost exclusively to written language and is, as such, used only to a very limited extent before the age of 7–8. The few experiments we made in connexion with it, however, gave results analogous to those which we have just been describing. Besides, ' for ' is occasionally not understood at all, in which case it signifies, according to the context, ' and ' or even ' but.' For example : " It is hot to-day, for *to-morrow it will be cold* " (Boz, age 7). " She is a very nice little girl, for *she has a bad fault* " (Guign, age 9), etc.

It is difficult, therefore, to separate logical and grammatical factors. In so far as it was possible for us to do so, we met with the same phenomena as in connexion with ' because,' and at an age when ' because ' was already used correctly (ages 8–10). This shifting of difficulties is perfectly natural. It often happens that a fresh obstacle resuscitates difficulties previously overcome in connexion with a different obstacle.

idea of chance, etc.) and he consequently draws no distinction between the causes of phenomena and the psychological or logical motives which would have actuated men if they had been the creators of these phenomena. It is therefore only after the age of 7–8, *i.e.* after the decline of this naïve realism has set in that the different types of relations come to be clearly distinguished, and that logical implication can become autonomous.

In the second place, logical implication arises mainly out of psychological motivation ; to justify a judgment is, after all, to give the motive for an act or at any rate for a certain kind of act, viz. that which consists in narrating the action instead of carrying it out. In this way the more conscious the child becomes of himself, the greater will be the importance of the ' because ' of justification as against the ' because ' of purely psychological motivation. Now we saw above that the decisive factor in causing a child to become conscious of himself was contact and above all contrast with the thought of others. Before society has administered these shocks, the child inclines to believe every hypothesis that comes into his head, feeling no need for proof and incapable if he did feel such a need of becoming conscious of the motives which really guided his thought.

To sum up, logical implication is doubly rooted in psychological motivation, whether, as is the case before the age of 7–8, the child attributes motives and intentions to nature and thus confuses causal with psychological relations, or whether, as is again the case before 7–8, the child's ego-centrism prevents the desire for objective proof (*i.e.* proof that is valid for all) to supplant that for simple subjective motivation.

If these deductions are right, the use of logical relations will be seen to develop after the age of 7–8 (as was shown to be the case in § 2 and also in Chapters II, III and IV of the volume L.T.), and analysis will show that this development coincides with that by which the child becomes aware of his thought-processes as such.

In order to verify the first of these assertions, let us
see at what age children are able to finish sentences which
imply logical justification. We experimented on the same
180 children mentioned in the last paragraph by means of
the two following propositions:

1. Paul says he saw a little cat swallowing a big dog.
His friend says that is impossible (or silly) because . . .

2. Half 9 is not 4 because . . .

	AGE 7.		AGE 8.	
	Boys.	*Girls.*	*Boys.*	*Girls.*
Sentence 1 .	36% (47)	38% (60)	50% (77)	54% (72)
Sentence 2 .	8% (41)	6% (44)	30% (57)	14% (46)
Together .	21% (44)	22% (52)	40% (67)	34% (59)

	AGE 9.			
	Boys.	*Girls.*	*Boys.*	*Girls.*
Sentence 1 .	88% (88)	61% (72)	88% (88)	61% (72)
Sentence 2 .	25% (62)	17% (48)	25% (62)	17% (48)
Together .	56% (75)	39% (60)	56% (75)	39% (60)

Alongside of the net percentages we have placed in
brackets the wider percentages which contain, in addition
to entirely correct answers, answers which are simply
incomplete but show signs, nevertheless, of implicit
logical justification. Later on we shall see what is the
nature of these answers.

This table therefore shows very clearly that logical
justification is a far more difficult matter than handling
the empirical ' because.' For example, the same boys
whose success was 80% in the case of the sentences mentioned in the last paragraph only achieved a success of
35% or 47% in the case of the first of our two sentences,
easy though it might appear to be. The table also shows
that progress between the ages of 7 and 9 is fairly rapid
from our present point of view. To what then are we to
attribute the peculiar difficulty with regard to logical
justification? The clue is to be found in an analysis
of the results obtained in individual examination.

The least satisfactory answers are of the following type :

Gue (age 6) tells us : " Ernest has 4 francs. He buys with his 4 francs 2 francs worth of chocolate and a ball that cost 3 francs. This is impossible, because *he had stolen them.*"

Tacc (age 9) : " Half 9 is not 4, because *he can't count.*" " Half 6 is 3, because *he divides it.*" " Paul says that 2 + 2 = 5. That's silly, because *he doesn't know how to count,*" etc.

Gue (age 6) : " Paul says he saw a little cat . . . etc. It's impossible, because *it isn't true.*"

Mour (age 6) : " Ernest has 4 francs. He buys, with these 4 francs, . . . etc. It's impossible, because *it's silly, because you could never do that.*" Maz (8 ; 0) : " Paul was given 12 apples to share with Jean. Paul will take 6, because *he's quite right.*" Aub (8 ; 2) : " Paul says 2 + 2 = 5. It's impossible, because *it's wrong.*" " Half 7 is not 4 because *it's not right.*" Mart (8 ; 10) : " Half 6 is 3, because *it's right.*"

We need not add any more examples, though the supply is abundant. The mechanism is always the same. In the simplest cases the child confines himself, by way of logical justification, to giving a psychological explanation of the action which he is asked to justify or invalidate : " he stole it," or " he can't count," or " he divides," etc. In such cases there is still obvious confusion between logical justification and psychological motivation. In the more advanced cases the child appeals not so much to individual as to collective motives : " it's right," " you can or you cannot do that," " he is quite right," etc. But there is clearly no considerable progress ; the child makes no attempt to analyse the ' why ' of the questions submitted to him. He invokes, not as yet a logical reason, but a collective reason, the *decus*, so to speak (a thing is ' done ' or is not ' done '), and in this way puts logical and social rules on an equal level. In Baldwin's words the child recognizes ' syndoxic ' but not yet ' synnomic ' laws. These children therefore justify their judgments in the same way as children under the age of 7–8 argue (L.T., Chaps. I–II), *i.e.* by simply affirming, or by appealing to authority, but never by really substantiating their statements.[1]

It is now perfectly easy to see why the logical reasons given by a child of 7-8 are incomplete. It is in no way because the child lacks the knowledge or information necessary for demonstration. For example, in the two sentences which we ·used for our collective enquiry it would be quite easy for the children to say with regard to the first sentence that "little animals don't eat big ones." It is less easy for them (and the statistics make this very clear) to say that 4 and 4 make 8, in order to prove that half 9 is not 4. But this does not mean that the notion of half is foreign to them. Other lines of investigation, it is true, have given rise to various difficulties connected with the idea of half, but all the Geneva children of 7, 8 and 9 know that half of 8 is 4 and half of 10 is 5, and that every half is the result of division into two equal parts. When we say that they ' know ' this, we mean that they know how to find half of a number, and are therefore able to handle certain notions as though they were conscious of their definitions. But this is just what they are not conscious of, and that is why, as soon as one tries, in connexion, for example, with some verbal expression, to make them conscious of such definitions, the attempt provokes all sorts of intellectual difficulties. One might say then that it is for lack of possessing definitions that the child can make no use of logical justification ; but that would involve us in a vicious circle, for it is just this need for logical justification that causes the mind to become conscious of the definition of notions which it previously was content merely to make use of.

In a word, it is not for lack of knowledge that the child fails to deal adequately with logical justification. The reason is far simpler and lies in the fact that owing to

---

[1] Note in this connexion expressions like " they say that " which are found in children who have discovered true logical relations. Gia (age 8) : " Half 6 is 3 because *they say that* 3 *and* 3 *make* 6." " Half 9 is not 4 because 4 *and* 4 *make* 8 *and you can't say that* 4 *and* 4 *make* 9."

his ego-centrism he does not realize the need for it. The examples given above show that the supreme appeal which children are tempted to make when asked to justify a statement is the appeal to public opinion. But as often happens in such cases the appeal to public opinion is always accompanied by the conviction that one is its mouthpiece ; the subject is ignorant of possible divergencies, and consequently has a tendency to avoid any analysis of the reasons, valid or invalid, which alone would make this public opinion legitimate. Chapter III of volume L.T. showed that children, in so far as they are ego-centric, always believe themselves to be in immediate agreement with every one else. They believe that the other person always knows what they are thinking about and is acquainted with their reason for doing so ; in a word, they always believe themselves to have been completely understood. This is why, in primitive arguments, each speaker confines himself to mere statement without motivation (L.T., Chap. II) or with only such embryonic and rudimentary motivation as leaves the essentials of the matter unsaid.

Highly instructive in this connexion are the justifications which we classified as ' incomplete ' when we sorted out the results of our collective enquiry. A separate analysis of these shows very clearly that each one contains implicitly a perfectly valid reason, but one which the child cannot express, just because it is not the kind of reason which he ever tries to give. Here are some examples :

Maz (age 8) : " Half 6 = 3, because *it has been divided.*" ' To be divided ' obviously means to be divided into two equal parts, but that is just what Maz forgets to say, so that he is really only repeating the original statement.

Ber (age 6) : " Half 6 = 3, because *half of six makes* 3." The same remark applies here. It should be noted that the few correct answers obtained are very clear (" because 3 and 3 make 6," etc.), which proves that they are not beyond the general level of the children in question.

Maz (age 8) : " Half 9 is not 4, because *there is one*

more." The answer is right, but once again it takes
for granted the argument : 4 and 4 make 8, "and there
is one more " wanted to make 9.

Bazz (age 8) : " Paul says he saw a little cat eating a
big dog. His friend says that's impossible, because *the
litte cat ate the big dog."* As we found out by talking to
him, Bazz has understood the problem, but he considers
the impossibility in question to be so much a matter of
course that he contents himself with repetition. Similarly,
Mor (7 ; 11) : " *Because the little cat is little, and the big
dog is big."*

The same Mor (7 ; 11) : " Paul says that the road from
his house goes down all the way to school and goes down
all the way back from school. Jean says that's impossible,
because *on the way there the road goes up."* The same
applies here : Mor states without justifying, because he
feels no need to do otherwise.

We need press the point no further. Even when the
child has reasoned correctly (and this is the only case that
we are concerned with now, in contrast to the cases dealt
with above), he cannot justify his reasoning, because he
is accustomed to take the essential point for granted.

We are now in a position to ask a question, the answer
to which will either confirm or destroy our hypothesis
that difficulty in handling logical justification arises
from inability to be conscious of one's own reasoning
process. That 'essential,' that logical reason which
always remains implicit because it is taken for granted—
is the child conscious of it himself ? Has he had clearly
in his mind the propositions " Little cats do not eat big
dogs," or " A road cannot go down both on the way there
and on the way back," or " Half 8 is 4, because 4 and 4
make 8 ? " It is obvious that he has not. The child
has been conscious only of the particular cases to which
his answer referred, and was unable to express the corresponding general laws. Now it goes without saying that if
a proposition cannot be expressed, we cannot be conscious
of it. When we say that the child can handle a notion
before having become conscious of it, what we mean is
that there has been gradually built up in the child's mind

(*i.e.* in his various forms of incipient activity a schema), (*i.e.* a unique type of reaction) which can be applied every time mention is made of a little cat, or of a half, or of a road, etc., but which does not yet correspond to a verbal expression. The verbal expression alone can bring this schema into consciousness and transform it into a general proposition or a definition. The conscious realization of one's own thought is dependent upon its communicability, and this communicability is itself dependent upon social factors, such as the desire to convince, etc.

To sum up, we claim to have substantiated, in so far as our present knowledge of the facts will allow, the hypotheses advanced in § 2. In the first place we showed in § 3 that juxtaposition came from the absence or poverty of ' direction ' in the child's mind, that is to say, from a lack of clear relations between successive judgments. In the second place, we have just shown that the incapacity for logical justification is definitely the outcome of a certain unconsciousness, an inability to attain conscious realization. And both absence of direction and difficulty in conscious realization are well known to be, if not the product (for many other factors intervene), at least the indirect result of childish ego-centricity.

§ 5. THE CONJUNCTIONS ' THEREFORE ' AND ' THEN.'[1]— We have still to deal with a problem closely related to those which have been occupying us, the problem of ' therefore ' [*donc*], which touches on the question of deductive reasoning and consequently on that of logical justification.

After all, if our hypotheses concerning juxtaposition and logical justification are correct, they must admit of verification by a study of the term ' therefore,' which is only an inversion of ' because.' ' Therefore,' instead of denoting like ' because,' the relation of cause to effect or

---

[1] The classifications of the grammarians are, in the confessed opinion of contemporary students of linguistics, extremely arbitrary. The reader must therefore not be surprised to see the word ' then ' placed among conjunctions, as it frequently fulfils the functions of such.

of reason to logical consequent, marks a relation of effect to cause or a relation of causal or logical sequence. " It is hot, *because* the sun is shining." " The sun is shining, *therefore* it is hot," or " Half 4 is 2 because 2 and 2 make 4." " 2 and 2 make 4, *therefore* half 4 is 2." But a great difficulty in studying this relation, which the adult denotes by the word ' therefore,' is that there is no word in the child's language which marks it in an unambiguous manner. The word ' therefore ' [*donc*] does not exist in childish idiom before an age which we cannot as yet determine statistically, but which our observations leads us to fix above 11–12, *i.e.* (*cf.* Chap. II) at the moment when formal thought makes its first appearance. The word ' then ' [*alors*] which in childish talk is the equivalent of ' therefore ' has, however, far too many different meanings to be regarded as synonymous with ' therefore ' and to serve in an experimental study of the relation indicated by this word. This will be shown in greater detail later on.

What we shall attempt to find out, however, is in the first place why the word ' therefore ' does not exist in the language of the child, and in the second place, in what sense it is that the child makes spontaneous use of the term ' then.'

The first of these questions is easy enough to answer. Whatever the particular shade of meaning indicated by ' therefore ' in the adult, it is almost invariably used in the establishment of a proof. At least it always serves to connect to an uncontested proposition, a proposition of which one was supposedly ignorant or of which one did not know the logical necessity. In the sentence : " The sun is shining, *therefore* it is hot," the relation indicated is certainly empirical (the heat is the result of the fact that the sun is shining), but it is also logical, because deduction, and even necessary deduction has taken place. The word ' therefore ' is a sign that we are in a position to prove that the sun always produces heat, etc. To turn a ' because ' into a ' therefore ' is consequently to add something to it, it is to add to the causal relation, the possibility of a deduction, and of a necessary deduction into the bargain. We are now in a position to see quite clearly why this word is absent from the language of the child. In the first place, up to the age of 7–8 the use of logical justification remains at a very imperfect stage, which is a very good reason why the word ' therefore ' should havé found no place. Secondly, between the moment when the need for proof is felt for the first time and the moment when necessary deduction can be properly handled there must be a long transitional period of learning. For in order to be necessary, a deduction must be formal or hypotheticodeductive, *i.e.* its conclusions must be held to be true only by reason of its premises and quite independently of the empirical truth of these premises. " If such and such a condition be admitted, . . . then such and such other conditions will necessarily follow." Now, as we have shown elsewhere,[1] and as the next chapter will prove, the possibility of such a train of thought does not appear till about the age of 11–12. This seems a sufficient explanation for the absence of the word ' therefore ' from the child's vocabulary until he has reached the stage of development acquired at the age of 11–12.

Even so, however, it is none the less interesting to enquire into the different meanings which children ascribe to the word. For, although they do not use it themselves, they are constantly hearing it used even by uneducated adults. One of us noticed, for example, that in the conversation of some Savoyard peasants who were arguing in a café, the word ' therefore ' (' donc ') appeared very frequently. All the more reason then for the word being used by the parents and more especially by the teachers of our school-children. A word heard frequently by children must come to stand in their minds for one or several more or less stable types of thought-relation, and this fact will free us from the charge of artificiality in employing

[1] J. Piaget, " Essai sur la multiplication logique et les débuts de la pensée formelle chez l'enfant," *Journ. de Psych.*, xix. (1922), p. 222.

the same method for studying ' therefore ' as we used in the case of ' because.' [1]

The results of this experiment proved highly suggestive. The different meanings which the children gave to the word ' therefore ' turned out to correspond exactly to the different meanings of ' because.' Just as the word ' because ' fluctuated between the relation of causality and that of consequence or implication, so in the same way we shall see that ' therefore ' fluctuates between the relation of consequence and, curiously enough, the actual causal relation. In other words, ' therefore,' instead of being for the child the symmetrical counterpart of ' because,' points on the contrary, like ' because,' to an ' and ' which originally stands for mere juxtaposition accompanied by a relation which is felt but not yet clearly differentiated.

Here, to begin with, are a few examples of ' therefore ' taken in the sense of ' and ' (simple juxtaposition) :

Mus (8 ; 4) : " Fernand has lost his pen, therefore *he had a lovely pen.*" (Now Mus is not completely incapable of understanding the word ' therefore,' as he often takes it in the adult sense, *i.e.* in the sense of ' consequently ' : " It will be fine to-morrow, therefore *I shall go for a walk.*") Bab (age 9) : " Fernand has lost his pen, therefore *it was a new one.*" (The same applies here. Some of the sentences are correct : " To-morrow I shall have a holiday, therefore *it will be Sunday.*")

Here are some more examples in which ' therefore ' indicates the continuation of the narrative, the relation of antecedent and consequent, but of a purely temporal kind, free from any admixture of causal or logical sequence :

" Fernand has lost his pen, therefore *he has found it* (again)." Schm. (7 ; 10). *Cf.* use of ' then ' : " Fernand has lost his pen, then *he has found it again.*" Mus (8 ; 4) ". . . . therefore *he hasn't found it again* (Ga, age 7), etc.

[1] For the difference between understood and spoken vocabulary, see Bovet, *Interm. des Educ.*, 1916 (Nos. 34–35), p. 35.

Finally, here are a few examples where ' therefore '
is made to show, not the consequence, but the explanation
of what is given. ' Therefore ' might here be replaced
by ' because,' so that these cases are strictly analogous
to the apparent inversions of ' because ' which we studied
in § 3.

Tacc (age 9) : " Fernand has lost his pen, therefore
he has given it to another kid, he has lost it in the play-room."
and " I can't ride my bicycle, therefore *it is broken*."
    Same example, Leo (age 8) : ". . . . therefore *it is*
broken."

These last sentences could naturally be regarded as
correct if they were not said by children who on other
occasions used the word ' therefore ' in a purely fanciful
sense. Indeed, for these children, ' therefore ' means either
nothing at all, or it means · because.'
    In conclusion, our study of ' therefore,' short as it is,
seems in no way to invalidate the results obtained from
our study of ' because.' Out of the 30 children between
6 and 9, whom we examined individually, not one proved
capable of handling the word ' therefore ' in unambiguous
manner nor of bringing out the particular relations which
are indicated by the adult use of the term. In a word, the
child possesses no special and unambiguous word for the
relation of consequence. (The expression ' in such a
manner that ' is naturally quite beyond him.)
    This lack of differentiation between the different mean-
ings of ' therefore ' will now enable us to understand why
the childish term which serves as an equivalent for ' therefore ' is the word ' then ' [alors]. For even in adult speech
the word ' then ' is still vague and undifferentiated. It
can express localization in time (" It was *then* eight
o'clock "); localization in discourse (" Let us *then* appeal
to the following reasons "); logical consequence (" All
x's are y's, *then* this x is a y ") ; psychological motivation
(" The weather is fine, *then* let us go for a walk ") ; logical
sequence (" The temperature is too low, *then* the reaction

cannot have taken place.") Sometimes the meaning is so vague as to be unclassifiable (" Oh bother, *then !* ").[1] But even when the relation indicated is classifiable, it is far vaguer than when it is expressed by ' therefore ' or ' consequently.'

This character of vagueness is naturally more pronounced in the child, and probably also explains why the use of the word ' then ' seems to be quite independent of age. Some children, even very young ones, use it for all purposes, and their talk is full of it, while others are far more sparing in their use of the term. Thus in the case of the five children who showed regular progress in the use of ' because,' the distribution of ' then ' seems to be haphazard.

	" Because " [*parce que*]	" Then " [*alors*]	Logical "thens" [*alors*]
Dan, age 3	1·2%	2·06	
Jan, age 3	1·5%	1·10	0·12%
Ad, age 4	1·2%	2·80	
Ad, age 5	2·0%	0·50	
Pie, age 6	2·0%	0·86	0·11%
Lev, age 6	2·4%	1·78	
Lev, age 7	6·1%	2·80	
Clau, age 7	3·9%	1·33	0·24%

As before, the number of ' thens ' is calculated in % ; thus 2·06 means that out of 100 sentences 2·06 on an average contain ' then '.

We tried, moreover, to pick out from among these different ' thens,' those which it would not be too arbitrary to interpret as ' therefores ' indicating logical sequence (the relation of implication in deduction). As will be seen, the number of these logical ' thens ' seems to increase after the age of 7.

In view of this proportion of logical ' thens ' it would seem that the child showed more aptitude than we were

---

[1] French, " Zut alors." This peculiar exclamatory use of ' alors ' has no counterpart in English and is only very feebly rendered by ' then ' [Translator's note].

willing to allow him for a certain degree of deduction. But we must avoid hasty conclusions and enquire more carefully into the nature of the deduction in question.

Here are the most clearly marked cases in which ' then ' expresses a ' therefore ' of logical implication.

Dan $(3\frac{1}{2})$: " *And where shall I go ?*—In the next room— *Then I shall be alone ?* " " [Turning over a sheet of paper] *Then that's on the wrong side.*" " [Drawing] *Why am I making smoke ? Then it's a train.*" " *A name has been torn up there*—It is Denise—*Then it is her desk.*" Ad $(4\frac{1}{2})$: " *Is that yours ?*—No—*Then it's mine.*" Pie (age 6) : " *Then for* 22 *you must have* . . . *you must have* 2.—*For* 22 *you must have* 2 *and* 2." Lev (age 6) : " *If you lose one, then there's one left.*" " *No, it's not mine* [that pencil], *because it has No.* 2 *and that writing. Then I've lost mine.*" " [He turns a drawing round] : That's the way !—*Then that's the head.*" Lev (age 7) : " He is tiny—*Like me then.*" [He is searching a box for something he cannot find] : " *Then it must be in that box there. I saw it in a big box.*"

These implications, which are the most explicit deductions we came across in the 6700 sentences spoken by children, are obviously of a significant type. The very first glance at them reveals the fact that the deductions in question are applied only to individual cases ; the conclusion proceeds from one particular to another by means of immediate relations and without any appeal to the general case. This is a feature of childish deductions which has often been noted ; and which Stern takes as the characteristic mark of *transduction*. Transduction would then proceed from particular to particular, just as induction proceeds from particular to general and deduction from general to particular. But the whole formulation of deduction and induction is notoriously in need of revision. The adult often deduces from particular to particular, as M. Goblot has maintained in connexion with mathematical reasoning. But even if M. Goblot's claim be admitted, general propositions still play an important part as rules for deduction. For though we may be comparing two diagrams or two equations, or reasoning in a general way about particular objects, we are still, in deduction, constantly appealing to previously established laws or definitions, which are in fact general propositions. And this is just what is lacking in our childish transductions ; at no point do they ever appeal to proofs of this kind, nor require any awareness of general propositions.

The problem of childish transduction is a big one, and will be dealt with later on in the book (Chap. IV, § 5) ; for the moment we must content ourselves with the conclusion that the child's use of the word ' then ' is extremely elastic, and in no way implies the use of necessary deduction. And this confirms the results reached earlier in connexion with the ' because of logical justification.'

II. Conjunctions of Discordance.

We are now in a position to prove, from another angle, what we have been demonstrating in the preceding paragraphs, and the conjunctions we shall study for this purpose are not those which assert, but those which deny relations of logical implication, causality, or sequence. These are, of course, the conjunctions ' although,' ' even though,' ' in spite of the fact that,' ' all the same,'[1] ' but,' etc. The relation which these conjunctions express is generally known as ' concession ' or ' restriction.' We prefer the term ' discordance ' which we owe to M. Baley, because it emphasizes the antithesis between these conjunctions and those of causality. For the word ' although ' [quoique] expresses a discordance and not a positive relation between cause and effect. A proposition like " The level of the lake has not risen, although it has been raining for

---

[1] The French equivalents, quoique, bien que, malgré, quand même, contain shades of meaning which cannot be rendered by a single word in English. Throughout this section we shall make use principally of the term ' although ' followed in brackets by whichever of the French conjunctions was used in the original [Translator's note].

D

a week," means that there is normally a relation of cause
and effect between the amount of rain fallen and the
particular level of the lake, but that for once the rain
has not brought about a rise, and that there has been
discordance between cause and effect. The notion of
discordance stands, therefore, for a complication in the
notion of causality and introduces the idea of exceptions
to causal or logical relations. The reader will easily
grasp how interesting it would be for us to carry out a
study of this relation parallel with our investigation of
the nature of causal and logical relations. For we are
meeting here not only with a new problem—the study of
which will prove highly suggestive for the psychology of
reasoning in the child—but also, in a sense, with a new
question which will show itself to be complementary
to those with which we have been dealing. If indeed the
notion of discordance is to be found only in a completely
rudimentary state in the child, the question may be
raised whether this is not a new indication in favour of
our hypothesis that the consciousness of relations and
the need for verification are still very imperfect in the
child. For the sense of exceptions, as exemplified by
the use of discordance, is, after all, derivative from the
sense of logical and causal rules, and here as everywhere
else the absence of exceptions simply proves the absence
of fixed rules.

Before passing on to the examination of our material
we must touch upon a question of method. Conjunctions of
discordance are, as we shall see, very little understood
before the age of 11–12. What part are we to assign to
language and what to thought in our interpretation of this
lack of understanding ? In the solution of such a question
as this we may often be prejudiced by the very method of
investigation adopted, and it is important to reach some
agreement upon the matter before dealing with the actual
facts.

In the first place we may adopt, in regard to conjunctions of discordance, the same method of approach

as that which was followed in dealing with 'therefore.'
Even if children do not use these conjunctions, they are
constantly hearing them in the language of the adults
with whom they live. And though we may grant that
in the language of the people the use of *quoique* and
bien que is more restricted, it cannot be denied that
quand même and *malgré que*, etc., are in current usage.
The problem may therefore be expressed negatively :
why do children exercise choice in the language which
surrounds them and exclude from their own talk the
terms expressing discordance ? And above all, why do
they not understand these terms ? Clearly, the problem
is not merely linguistic but primarily one of genetic logic.

But we can narrow the problem down. We can try
to find out whether there is any uniformity in the manner
in which the children understand the different terms of
discordance, and in this way we can isolate the mental
from the verbal factors. Our procedure was as follows.
First we found out which was the best understood of the
conjunctions of discordance. This was done by the same
method as before : sentences given to be completed,
analysis of the answer with the child (each being examined
personally), and a collective enquiry on about 200 children
between the ages of 7 and 9. On the whole, *quand même*
proved to be the best understood conjunction. We then
tried to find out what meanings were attributed to
this word when it was not understood, and we ascertained
that the self-same meanings were to be found in connexion
with *malgré quoique*, and *bien que*, which are understood
in diminishing proportions. Such uniformity in degree
of understanding undoubtedly carries with it a two-fold
conclusion.

The first is that in the child's manner of distorting the
conjunctions of discordance there is an element of verbal
intelligence (whether positive or negative in its results
need not concern us here), which is something more than
mere deficiency in verbal understanding. The second
conclusion is that we must, nevertheless, take the actual

word into account, since certain words are better understood than others. Here again different factors may intervene, such as the language spoken around the child, which might tend to explain why *quand même*, for example, should be simpler to understand than *quoique*. We shall endeavour to give due weight to these different factors in the course of our analysis.

§ 6. NUMERICAL RESULTS AND TYPES OF MISTAKE.—In our collective enquiry we made use of the 9 following sentences (in the given order).

1. Ernest is playing in the street, even though (*malgré que*). . . .
2. I have some big friends, even though (*quand même*). . .
3. He slapped my face, although (*quoique*). . . .
4. I have given John my bicycle, though (*bien que*). . . .
5. I ate another roll, although (*bien que*). . . .
6. It is hot to-day, although (*malgré que*). . . .
7. He bathed yesterday, although (*quand même*). . . .
8. I didn't get wet yesterday, although (*quoique*). . . .
9. That man fell off his horse, although (*bien que*). . . .

If it be granted that a test has been passed when 75% of the children of a given age have answered correctly, then we must allow that at the age when our children were examined discordance was not yet understood. The statistical results were as follows :

	AGE 7.	AGE 8.		AGE 9.	
	Boys.	Boys.	Girls.	Boys.	Girls.
Bien que . . .	0%	16%	10%	13%	7% (?)
Quoique . . .	9%	18%	16%	21%	17%
Malgré que . .	18%	42%	32%	43%	42%
Quand même . .	22%	44%	39%	50%	50%

We do not claim to state at what age these conjunctions are understood. The whole enquiry needs to be continued between the years of 8-9 and 11-12. We have no precise data as to how discordance is dealt with during this second stage, except that in a class of girls of 13 our sentences were successfully completed by 93% of the subjects for *bien que ;* 96% for *malgré que* and *quand même ;* and 100% for *quoique.* On the strength of several individual examinations, however, we believe that the claim may be put forward that discordance begins to be correctly used round about the age of 11–12. On the other hand, if we consider, not explicit discordance such as is indicated by although (*quoique*) but implicit discordance such as is expressed by certain uses of ' but,' or by *quand même* (used as an adverb not a conjunction), then its appearance may be situated round about the years 7–8.

In the conversation at the *Maison des Petits*, for example, we only found three cases of *quand même*, taken adverbially in the sense of discordance, in the whole of our material, and all three cases were supplied by Lev at 6½ (none at 7). Undoubtedly the word *quand même* occurs earlier than this. Mlle Descœudres has noted it in a child of 2 whose vocabulary she studied, but not at 5 or at 7. But in such cases it is taken in quite a different sense, which is that of an exclamation. Here are some of these primitive forms of *quand même* in a little girl of 2 :[1]

Nel (age 2 ; 9) : " *Je crois j'en vois le gros train. Quand même !* (–What a noise it makes !) " " *Il fait chaud quand même sur ce banc !* " " *Oh, tite fleur jolie, elle est gentil quand même. Et pis celle-là !* " *Oh, les tites fleurs, y sont gentils quand même.*"

It is true that with Nel the word *quand même* almost looks like a term of discordance.

" *C'est une peau de lapin, ça qui est dans l'eau. Il est mort quand même ce lapin,*" and " *Ces bonnes graines* [some blackberries] *i sont mûrs quand même. J'en veux goûter ils sont mûrs* " (and so they were).

But such discordance as this is very vague and in the second example even unintelligible. As to the first example, does the child mean : the rabbit is dead even

---

[1] As this example is practically in baby-talk, we have thought it best to give it in the original French [Translator's note].

though [*quand même*] his skin is there ? It is not for us to say. More probably we have here simply another case of an exclamatory *quand même*. We may therefore say that with Nel discordance either cannot be expressed or is completely absent.

Here are the three examples taken from Lev at 6½ :

"I say, I'm six—*I am the strongest all the same [quand même]*." "*It hurt me too, but it doesn't matter, I'll put my hand there all the same [quand même].*" *Every one else has come in, but Mlle L. will go out all the same [quand même].*"

But these three cases of *quand même* are clearly more related to psychological motivation than to any intellectual preoccupation. They show ' concession ' rather than discordance. They do not therefore constitute a proof of the use of implicit discordance in simple statements before the age of 7–8. At the same time it can be shown that from this age onwards the right use is understood.

We must now decide upon some method of genetic grouping of the various types of mistake which we have met with in connexion with explicit discordance.

We might to begin with distinguish two types of discordance : empirical (*i.e.* physical and psychological), and logical. But at the age of our subjects in whom logical relations are only beginning to appear, logical discordance is still completely foreign to the child's mind. We shall therefore concern ourselves only with empirical discordance.

The mistakes found from this point of view may be classed into three groups : error by juxtaposition, confusion of discordance with causality, and discordance reduced to ' but.'

The most primitive mistakes arise from the fact that the child, totally ignorant as he is of the relation of discordance, completes the sentences which are given to him anyhow, and therefore chooses the simplest relation available, which is precisely the relation of juxtaposition.

Or else, because he is looking for the proposition which will best fit the given sentence, he will come to substitute the relation of causality for that of discordance. These two types of mistakes are contemporaneous ; they are found in the same children and indicate, one as much as the other, a failure to understand discordance. On the other hand, from the moment that there is, if not understanding, at least a feeling of discordance, a third type of mistake appears, analogous to that which we described in connexion with causality. In the child's talk of causality there is spontaneous substitution of a simple ' and ' for the conjunction ' because.' Conversely, when he is required to complete sentences containing ' because,' what happens is that the child finishes them as though ' because ' were an ' and,' as though causality could be replaced by a vague relationship simply meaning ' going with.' Similarly, with regard to discordance there is no term in the child's language that indicates this relation (with the exception of *quand même* taken adverbially during the age of 6–8), but a sort of primitive implicit discordance finds expression in the term ' but ' [*mais*]. Now we shall show later on that ' but ' stands to ' although ' in the same relation as ' and ' to ' because.' Moreover, and here the parallelism is complete, when the child is given sentences to finish containing although (*quoique* and *malgré que*), what happens is that he finishes them as though ' although ' meant ' but.'

Let us now turn to these three types of answer.

§ 7. FAILURE TO UNDERSTAND DISCORDANCE.—Some children give obviously fantastic answers to all the sentences submitted to them :

Mour (age 6) : " Jean has gone away, even though [*malgré*] *he has gone to the mountain.*" " Emile is playing in the street, even though [*malgré*] *not to be run over by the motors.*" Ber (age 6) : " I bathed, even though [*malgré*] *so you don't hurt yourself.*" " That boy slapped my face, even though [*malgré*] *it did hurt me.*" This last phrase means " and it hurt me," as we afterwards ascertained.

At this stage it is difficult to know if ' even though '
[*malgré*] means ' and ' or ' because.' The children really
answer completely at random.

With our subjects, however, the child's meaning is
quite clear. In these cases it can be observed that the
term of discordance sometimes means ' and,' sometimes
' because,' and sometimes is used correctly. Given such
a mixture of answers, we are naturally justified in concluding that in such cases discordance is not yet understood.
Here are some examples :

Leo (age 8) : " Emile is playing in the street, even
though [*quand même*] *it is cold* " (correct). " It is not
yet dark, even though [*malgré que*] *it is still day* " (=and
or because). " I have some big friends, even though
[*malgré*] *they are nice* " (=but). " He fell out of the
cart, even though [*malgré*] *it does hurt* " (=and). " He
fell out of the cart, although [*quand même*] *he didn't hurt
himself* " (=but or *quand même* taken adverbially : " he
didn't hurt himself all the same "). " It is not dark yet,
even though [*quand même*] *it is day* " (=and or because).

Thus even the word *quand même* does not possess for
Leo a completely unequivocal meaning.

Ral (age 8) : " Emile is playing in the street, even though
[*quand même*] *he is enjoying himself* " (=and). " It is
hot to-day even though [*quand même*] *it is raining* "
(correct). " René is going away to the mountains, even
though [*quand même*] *he is going a long way* " (=and). " I
walked for another three hours, even though [*quand même*]
that is a lot " (correct or juxtaposition). " I ate another
roll, even though [*quand même*] *that's not dear* " (=and
or because). " I slapped Paul's face, even though [*quand
même*] *he is crying* "(=and).
Shortly after this we repeated the same sentences to
Ral, who completed them in the following manner :
" Emile is playing in the street, even though [*quand même*]
it is fine " (=and). " It is warm to-day, even though
[*quand même*] *the weather is fine* " (=and or because).
" I ate another roll, even though [*quand même*] *it is nice* "
(=and or because), etc.
Don (age 6) : " I walked for another hour, even though

[quand même] I like walking " (=because). " She boxed my
ears, even though *[quand même] she was horrid "* (=be-
cause). " I have been given a tricycle, even though *[quand
même] I like them very much "* (=because).

Kiss (age 5½) : " He was given a piece of cake, even
though *[quand même] he had been a good boy "* (=because).
" He tore his pinafore, even though *[quand même] he
caught himself on a hook "* (=because).

Maz (age 8) : That man fell out of the cart, even though
[malgré] the horse slipped " (=because). " It is hot to-day,
even though *[malgré que] it is raining "* (correct). " That
man fell off his bicycle, even though *[malgré que] he
pedalled too hard "* (=because). " He got angry with me,
although *[quoique] I would not talk to him "* (=because).

Tac (age 9) : " He must be taken care of, even though
[malgré que] he has hurt himself " (=because). Tac also
uses *" malgré que "* in the sense of ' and ' of ' but,' and of
' although.'

Gug (age 9) : " I did not get wet although *[quoique]
I had an umbrella "* (=because).

Examples might be multiplied indefinitely, and of each
one of the four conjunctions we have examined. It does
not therefore seem altogether reckless to make the statement that at the age of the children we were studying,
explicit discordance, *i.e.* that which is indicated by a
conjunction of subordination is not yet understood. This
does not mean, however, that the same applies to implicit
discordance such as is indicated by a conjunction of
co-ordination like ' but ' or by an adverb serving the same
function.

Our technique of course is open to criticism. It is one
thing to feel the difference between a causal relation,
a relation of juxtaposition, and a relation of discordance
when one hears someone else talking (as when a child hears
an adult talking), and quite another to be able to handle
those relations oneself to the extent of being capable
of completing a sentence in which one of them is implied.
We quite agree. But equally legitimate is the claim that
all real understanding involves at least the beginnings of
right use, just as elementary arithmetic is only understood

from the day that it can be applied. Furthermore, between understanding a word and using it aright the difference is not of kind but of degree ; in actual fact the interval between them is only of a few months.

Having disposed of this objection and making due allowance for the difference between language that is understood and language that is spoken, we may now ask to what factors is due this failure to understand discordance. For this purpose it will be necessary once more to distinguish between implicit and explicit discordance.

Explicit discordance, or in other words, discordance indicated by the conjunctions of subordination (*quoique, bien que, malgré que, quand même*) would seem most probably not to be understood until about the age of 11–12, and at any rate not before the age of 10. Why this date ? The reason would seem to lie in the logical nature of the relation of discordance. For this relation, unlike those of causality or any others indicated by the word ' because,' necessarily presupposes a knowledge of general propositions ; or at any rate it presupposes the awareness of propositions of a greater degree of generality than is the case in causal relations. Compare for instance, the two following propositions : " This piece of wood floats because it is light," and " This pebble has sunk to the bottom of the water although it is light." For the first affirmation it is in no way necessary for the child to know the general law that ' all light bodies float.' The statement points to such a law but does not imply it. For two things have come to our knowledge through the experiments which we made in this connexion (see Chap. IV). 1°. The same child who has just said that a certain piece of wood floats because it is light, within a few minutes later says of another piece that it floats because it is big, that a big boat floats because it is heavy and is being rowed along and has strength, and so on. 2°. On the other hand, this same child knows perfectly well that a little nail or a little pebble that immediately sink to the bottom

are ' lighter ' than the piece of wood of which he said
that it floated because it was light.   In a word, if we take
the proposition : " This piece of wood floats because it
is light " from any one of these aspects, it does not necessitate the knowledge of a law ; it is merely one particular
explanation amongst others given by the child.   The
view that children deal with ideas and propositions
that are more general than those of the adult mind has
been widely held.   Ribot [1] and others, however, have
shown that this is a delusion.   The child simply applies
as often as he can, through sheer economy of thought, an
explanation which he has found in some particular case.
But this does not prove that he is *trying to find* explanations or general laws.   On the contrary, our experiments
have shown us that a large number of different and even
contradictory explanations can co-exist in one child's
mind (see Chap. IV).   Our treatment of ' because ' and
' then ' has, moreover, prepared us for the fact that
the faculties of generalization and deduction are still
at an extremely primitive stage of development in the
child.

Now let us consider the proposition : " This pebble has
sunk although it is light."   Such a statement as this
necessarily presupposes the knowledge of an exception
and (since there are no exceptions without laws) the
knowledge of some more or less general law such as
precisely " All light bodies float," or " Most light bodies
float," etc.   True, we must not exaggerate the need for
the conscious possession of such general propositions in
order to make use of the term ' although ' (*quoique*).
For example, the proposition, " I have not got wet,
although it has been raining " does not call for a much
greater power of generalization than the proposition :
" I got wet because it was raining."   Nevertheless, it seems
to us indisputable that the mental habits involved in
the use of discordance require to an appreciably greater

1 Ribot, *L'évolution des idées générales*, Paris, 1915, 4th ed.,
p. 38.

extent than do those indicated by the use of ' because ' that the subject should be able to make use of general propositions and of necessary deduction.

We are now in a position to see why explicit discordance comes to be understood round about the age of 11–12. Our previous enquiries have shown, and the next chapter will show anew, that the age of 11–12 marks the moment when the child becomes capable of formal thought, *i.e.* of strict or necessary deduction. Now formal deduction is that which appeals to general propositions which are assumed for the purpose of regulating the course of an argument. It is therefore probably no coincidence that the capacity for discordance should make its appearance at the same moment as that for formal deduction. For both these phenomena are the result of an advance in the child's capacity for generalization.

As to implicit discordance, the reasons will soon be forthcoming for dating its advent between the years of 6 and 8. In the meantime we must examine what are the relations which unite the term ' although ' and the term ' but.'

§ 8. DISCORDANCE, AND THE EXPRESSION ' BUT.'—We may regard it as established that for a long time the conjunctions expressing discordance are not understood and are even confused with the conjunctions of causality. It is now time for us to ask what meaning is assigned to these conjunctions when the subject begins to understand them. It is, as will easily be seen, the meaning of ' but.' Here are some examples.

Léo (age 8) and Kle (age 8 ; 1) : " I ate another roll, even though [*malgré que*] I am still hungry " (=but or because ?).

Mar (8 ; 10) : " I have some big friends, even though [*malgré que*] I have some little ones as well." (The word ' as well ' is significant in connexion with the meaning of *malgre que*.) " I have some big friends, even though [*malgré*] they are not horrid." Tac (age 9) : ". . . although [*quoique*] they are not horrid." Roch (age 8 ; 4) : ". . . even though [*malgré que*] they are very nice." Leo (age 8) :

" I walked another three hours, although [*quoique*] *I am not tired* " (Kle, age 8 ; 1).

Finally, this example of a ten-year old child, Grand (age 10 ; 4) : " We are pupils, although [*quoique*] *we are not too old*—What does ' although ' mean ? *It means that we are not too old*—Say another word instead of ' although.' Would ' because ' do : We are pupils *because* we are not too old ?—*No, because there are some pupils that are quite old*—Would ' even though ' [*malgré que*] do ?—*Yes*—What does it mean ?—*We are pupils but* (!) *we are not too old.*"

These few examples show very clearly that the conjunctions ' although,' etc., when they first come to be understood as indicating discordance, are interpreted simply as meaning ' but.' Now we have seen that this deformation of meaning is not without analogy with the substitution of ' and ' for ' because.' Indeed, the term ' but ' stands in the same relation to ' although ' as does the term ' and ' to ' because.' Just as the sentence " The glass was broken *because* it fell " can be changed into " The glass fell down *and* was broken," so likewise we can change ' although,' " The glass was not broken, *although* it fell down " into ' but,' " The glass fell down, *but* was not broken." The question may therefore be asked why the child has this tendency to substitute ' but ' for ' although.' There is a psychological and a logical reason for this linguistic phenomenon.

It should be noted in the first place that language [1] itself tends this way, for *quand même* is taken both in the sense of ' although ' (" Le verre ne s'est pas cassé *quand même* il est tombé ") and in that of ' but ' (Le verre est tombé ; il ne s'est *quand même* pas cassé). It is clearly to this circumstance that we must attribute the fact that according to our statistics, *quand même* was the best understood of the words denoting discordance.

But this does not suffice to explain the tendency shown by our children to replace ' although ' by the word ' but.' In order to understand this we shall have to introduce

[1] The French language. See foot-note on p. 37 [Translator's note].

factors which are relevant to the psychology of thought itself.

The comparison we have just drawn between ' but ' and ' and ' should put us on the right track. The term ' but ' expresses only a ' feeling of discordance ' instead of making the actual discordance explicit, and similarly the term ' and ' only indicates a ' feeling of togetherness ' instead of making explicit the actual relation of causality or implication. Indeed the word ' but ' indicates a sort of juxtaposition between two discordant judgments, yet does not call for any knowledge of general propositions. Thus, when we say " This is hard, but not that " (see below, the sentence of Dan) instead of " This is hard, although that is not," the two statements may be identical from the point of view of logical analysis, but from the psychological point of view there is between them the whole difference that separates the implicit from the explicit. The first of the two sentences marks a simple surprise and a simple opposition. There is certainly a feeling of discordance, but it is not made sufficiently explicit to involve awareness of an exception to a general rule. The second sentence brings out far more clearly a feeling of exception : " This is hard, although that is not " really means " These two objects ought to be either both hard or both soft," or " According to the rule there is no reason why one should be hard and the other not." There is therefore between those two sentences the same difference as between ' and ' and ' because.' " It is granite and it is hard " is not so strong as " It is hard because it is granite." True, these are only fine shades of meaning, but fine shades or of the very essence of thought. . . . All we ask the reader to concede is that ' although,' i.e. quoique, quand même (taken as a conjunction), bien que, etc., indicate discordance or the exception to a general rule more explicitly than do ' but ' or quand même (taken adverbially). Let us now try to establish the fact that implicit discordance does not make its appearance before the age of 7–8 (actually from the age of 6), and to determine a reason for this date.

It is obvious that since implicit discordance can be denoted by a simple ' but,' the question will be raised whether every ' but ' does not denote a discordance which could be expressed by ' although.' Now the word ' but ' [*mais*] appears very early, almost as early as the word ' and.' Is there any point then in making implicit discordance begin at the age of 7-8, and should this relation not be allowed to have existed from the very beginnings of intellectual life in the child ?

If the use of the word ' but ' be examined in the language of children between 3 and 7 it will be seen to be of a singularly primitive character. Here are a few of the senses of the word, taken at random and without any attempt to submit them to an exhaustive or systematic classification.

In the first place, and especially with very small children, the term ' but ' very often denotes simply a surprise relatively to what the child was expecting or relatively to the momentary direction of his thoughts.

Dan (age 3½) : " *But why is your's broken* [your pencil] ? " " *But why are they* [his friends] *going up there* [to the second floor] ? " " [Trying to hang up his overall]. *But how do you hang this up ?* " " *But those ones* [those boats] *don't go well*," etc.

In such cases as these—and they are the most numerous — there is no question of discordance. By turning round the ' but ' we should not get an ' although,' for the simple reason that there is no causal or logical relation there to be at fault. The word ' but ' here does not even indicate opposition between two objective characters ; there is only surprise or opposition relatively to what was expected.

A slightly more advanced form is found when the term ' but ' marks an opposition but one that does not yet constitute an exception to causal or logical relations. Thus ' but ' here is strictly equivalent to ' and not.'

Dan (age 3½) : " He does gymnastics—*But not Rhyth-mics.*" "It is not hard now—*But that is hard.*"

These two meanings are, moreover, so little differen-tiated from juxtaposition that the child occasionally uses the two words ' and ' and ' but ' together.

Del (age 6): " *Why does it rain at Geneva but and not [et mais pas] at Nyon ?* "

A more precise use of ' but ' is that which occurs in objection, as when the word serves to introduce either an intellectual objection or one arising out of the action in which the subject is engaged. But in these new cases, as in the earlier ones, the word ' but ' still falls short of complete equivalence with an ' although ' or a *quand même :*

Non-intellectual objections : " Well then, put the spoon into another drawer—*But there's one there already.*" "[After having been told to sing] *But I've never learnt. Mother never taught me to.*"
Intellectual objections : " *Why are there two threads there ?*—To make it hold properly—*But why are there two threads there ?* "

In short, the only cases in which the term ' but ' really denotes an implicit discordance are those in which the word occurs, not at the beginning, but in the middle of a sentence, and of a sentence containing a causal relation whether logical or psychological. Now such sentences were not to be found before the age of 6, and the two examples we have between 6 and 7 are anything but unequivocal.

Lev (age 6½) : " [Suns] *are round, but they have no eyes and mouth.*" " *It is more than that, but that's right.*"

In both these cases ' but ' can be replaced by ' although ' (That is right, although it comes to more than that), but the discordance in such examples is obviously still very implicit. Besides, we only found two at the age of 6 and none below this age. It is therefore better to date the appearance of discordance from the moment when *quand même* first begins to be used (adverbially) and is understood. The word, as we saw, occurred with Lev at the age of 6 (never with Pie) but is generally not understood until the age of 7.

In our enquiries bearing upon causality, moreover, we often noticed the difficulty which children seem to experience in discovering even the most elementary discordances and the persistent tendency they have to put ' and ' or ' and then ' in place of ' but.'

For example Leo (age 7) is talking about the shadows we cast as we walk along : " Do we make them at night too ?—*We make them and then* (=but) *we don't see them, because it is dark.*"

It is therefore only round about the age of 7 that discordance comes to be understood and properly handled, not in its explicit form as indicated by ' although,' but in its implicit form as indicated by *quand même* taken adverbially or by certain uses of ' but,' as in the example we gave above, in which both words are united : " Every one has come in, but Mlle L. will go out all the same [*quand même*]." What factors can we look to in explanation of this age of 7 ? For the moment we are ignorant. A hypothesis nevertheless suggests itself. Discordance or at any rate explicit discordance arose, as we saw, from a feeling of exception to a general rule. But what are the mental operations by which rules are postulated, and above all by which exceptions are felt ? They are what logicians call logical addition and multiplication.[1] Let us take the expression, "The wind is not alive, but it moves all the same [*quand même*]." In order to express himself in this way, the child must have come to think that all living things move, but that all moving things are not necessarily alive. He must therefore conceive life as the result of logical multiplication or of the ' inter-

---

[1] For definition of these terms see Chap. IV, § 2.

E

ference ' of movement by other characteristics, such as
the capacity for taking nourishment, etc. In other words,
a thing, to be alive, must *both* move *and* take nourishment,
etc. Such must be the thought of the child.

Now, as we have already shown and as we hope to do
again (Chap. IV, § 2), the child is incapable before the
age of 10–11 of handling logical multiplication with any
method, in other words, he is unable to understand
alternation, opposition, disjunction, etc., at any rate on
the plane of verbal thought. (As, for example, in the
following test : " If this animal has long ears, it is either
a donkey or a mule. If it has a thick tail, it is either a mule
or a horse. Now it has long ears and a thick tail. What
is it ? ") This, therefore, is the reason why general propositions are not used by children before this age (since such
propositions are the result of logical additions and multiplications), and also why explicit discordance does not
appear before this date (since discordance is an exception
to rules or, if our new terminology be preferred, a logical
multiplication or interference of one rule by another).
Most of the cases of inability to perform logical multiplication which we shall give in Chapter IV in connexion with
children's definitions are prior to this stage of development.
It is between the ages of 7 and 8 that the child begins to
avoid self-contradiction.   From this moment, *i.e.* from
the moment when the first logical multiplications make
their appearance on a concrete and not on the verbal
plane, implicit discordance is possible.   This, at least, is
the only idea we can form of that synchronism which it
was our aim to establish.   As to the psychological factors
which explain the advent of logical multiplication, these
will form the subject of a later enquiry.

III. Conclusions

The time has now come for us to draw a few conclusions
from this somewhat lengthy analysis. We shall do no
more, however, than set down certain landmarks which

will serve as headings for our fourth chapter (How the Child Reasons).

Let us suppose that future research is undertaken dealing with a far larger number of children's sentences, and involving a far more thorough examination both personal and collective than that to which we had to limit ourselves. Let us further suppose that these researches eventually demolish the age-limits which we have given, eventually show that difficulties experienced by children with regard to ' because ' are on the average more or less lasting than we had thought. We believe that in spite of such changes our qualitative analyses would remain of value on a large scale. We would still claim that the child's difficulty in the use of the empirical or logical ' because,' in the use of ' therefore ' and ' then,' or in the use of the terms of discordance are bound up with logical difficulties which in their turn we would still claim to be traceable to social factors such as argument, collaboration between children, and so on.

What further conclusions are to be drawn from this study of reasoning in the child ? In the first place we must emphasize the fact that the above enquiries do not bear directly upon reasoning nor, above all, on causality in the child. They bear simply upon his aptitude for inventing sentences, in a word, upon his aptitude for narrative and argument. Now these aptitudes should be neither exaggerated nor underestimated in their importance. The practice of narrative and argument does not lead to invention, but it compels a certain coherence of thought. A mind incapable of argument and guilty of the verbal confusions which we have been examining in children may be creative, but it is certainly not logical. From this point of view the grammatical study which we have been making leads to certain conclusions, and in particular, to the two that follow. Firstly, that the child, unconscious as he is of his own thought-process, can only reason about isolated or about more or less special cases. Secondly, and this is the most important—that his judgments, being juxtaposed, are lacking in logical necessity.

The study of logical justification showed that if the child is unable to give a logical reason for his judgment, even when this judgment is true in itself and correctly introduced in the context, this is because he is not conscious of the motives that have guided his choice. Things happen then more or less as follows. In the presence of certain objects of thought or of certain affirmations the child, in virtue of previous experiences, adopts a certain way of reacting and thinking which is always the same, and which might be called a schema of reasoning. Such schemas are the functional equivalents of general propositions, but since the child is not conscious of these schemas before discussion and a desire for proof have laid them bare and at the same time changed their character, they cannot be said to constitute implicit general propositions. They simply constitute certain unconscious tendencies which live their own life but are submitted to no general systematization and consequently lead to no logical exactitude. To put it in another way, they form a logic of action but not yet a logic of thought.

This absence of conscious realization explains why the child only reasons about particular cases.[1] Since the schema is the only general element in childish ratiocination, and since the schema remains unconscious, the child will become aware only of the discrete objects which occupy his mind. Thus the study of ' because ' in logical justification showed that even when the child tries to prove his statements, he appeals neither to laws nor to general rules, but to singular and specific reasons : " The little cat ate the big dog," " The little cat is little and the big dog is big," " On the way there the road goes up," etc. Furthermore, this was confirmed by an examination of the deduc-

---

[1] According to current logical terminology the opposition usually made is between *general* judgments and *singular* or *individual* judgments. The terms *universal* and *particular* are concerned only with the quantity of the attribute in relation to the subject, and with the extension of the subject.

tions introduced by the word 'then.' The deduction moves from one individual case to another : " Then I shall be alone," " Then it is inside out," etc. Finally, our study of discordance indirectly confirms the same law. If children never make use of explicit discordance and do not understand implicit discordance until after the age of 7–8 this is obviously because the notion of an exception to a rule which is presupposed in the notion of discordance between cause and effect is not a primitive notion, and is not one that is familiar to them. For there to be exceptions, there must obviously have been rules, and if the child fails to understand the fact that there are exceptions, it must be because he has never formulated any rules.

The consequence of this fact that the child's formulated thought only takes place in connexion with particular or specific cases is that we cannot speak about deductive thought as such before a very advanced stage of development. For deduction presupposes general propositions, whether these serve to characterize the individual objects with which the reasoning process is concerned, or whether they constitute the aim which the process of deduction has set out to reach. Now the motor schemas of which we were speaking just now cannot do the work of general propositions, and what prevents them is the fact that they do not confront one another in the subject's consciousness and thus give rise to syntheses and oppositions which alone would favour the appearance of logical addition and multiplication.

Provisionally, therefore, we have established three points : absence of conscious realization (*prise de conscience*), absence of general propositions, and absence of deduction. We shall discuss these later on as they deserve and with fresh methods which will be introduced in Chapter IV. In the meantime let us confine ourselves to the analysis of the phenomenon which explains them all —' juxtaposition.'

In studying the conjunctions of causality we saw that

the child tended simply to juxtapose his statements instead of making their causal relation explicit. When the child is given sentences to complete which contain such relations, he shows signs of hesitation or even of confusion between the different possible relations—causality, consequence, etc. Furthermore, our study of logical implication showed that the desire for justification and proof remained at a very rudimentary stage of development till about 7–8, and that again in this connexion the childish tendency was to juxtapose his statements instead of making them imply one another in such a way as to make deduction possible. Finally, our examination of the conjunctions of discordance revealed a third variety of juxtaposition. The child, unable to handle explicit discordance such as is expressed by ' although ' and other conjunctions of subordination, replaces these conjunctions by the word ' but ' which has precisely the effect of juxtaposing the discordant propositions instead of indicating their exact relations.

The child's style and even his thought are therefore comparable to his drawing. A number of details are correctly indicated : The drawing of a bicycle by a child of 6, for example, will show, in addition to the frame and the two wheels, the pedals, a chain, a cog-wheel, a gear. But these details are juxtaposed without any order; the chain is drawn alongside of the cog-wheel instead of being correctly inserted, and the pedals are suspended in mid-air instead of being fixed. Thus everything happens as though the child really felt the relations in question, knew that the chain, the pedals and the cog-wheel were necessary to set the machine in motion and that these different pieces " went together." But this is as far as his consciousness of the relations goes ; it does not extend to a precise knowledge of the details of insertion and contact. The drawing is therefore comparable to the thought, and the thought to the drawing. Both juxtapose instead of synthesizing.

We have now reached the point when we can ask what

relation this phenomenon of juxtaposition bears to that of syncretism (*cf.* L.T., Chap. IV), which seems to be its exact opposite. In visual perception, juxtaposition is the absence of relations between details ; syncretism is a vision of the whole which creates a vague but all-inclusive schema, supplanting the details. In verbal intelligence juxtaposition is the absence of relations between the various terms of a sentence ; syncretism is the all-round understanding which makes the sentence into a whole. In logic juxtaposition leads to an absence of implication and reciprocal justification between the successive judgments ; syncretism creates a tendency to bind everything together and to justify by means of the most ingenious or the most facetious devices. In short, in every sphere, juxtaposition and syncretism are in antithesis, syncretism being the predominance of the whole over the details, juxtaposition that of the details over the whole. How are we to account for this paradox ?

In reality these two features are complementary. As soon as perception, even in the adult, fails to analyse an object, whether on account of its novelty or its complexity, we see the two phenomena reappear. On the one hand, because of its insufficient discrimination of detail, perception creates a vague and indistinct general schema, and this constitutes syncretism. On the other hand, through having failed again to discern a sufficient amount of detail, perception cannot make the insertions and relations sufficiently precise, and this constitutes juxta-position. The predominance of the whole over the parts or that of the parts over the whole is in both cases the result of the same lack of synthesis, synthesis being in a manner the principle of equilibrium between the for-matory tendency of the schemas and the analytical tendency.

Or rather—for the mind is not static, but in a state of perpetual movement—syncretism and juxtaposition con-stitute two phases alternating over indefinite periods in the mind of the child, if it be granted (as everything seems to prove) that the latter is less synthetic than ours. Sometimes the child builds up new general schemas, tries to connect everything, and tries to incorporate the new and unexpected elements into the old accustomed framework. At other times the discovery or the sudden emergence of unclassifiable and incomprehensible phenomena will burst these frameworks and dissolve the schemas until new systems are formed, only to be destroyed in their turn.

The position is particularly clear with regard to causal explanation and logical justification. We examined (L.T., Chap. V) the child's tendency to explain everything, and consequently to have recourse to pre-causal reasons born of a kind of confusion between the physical or causal order of things and the psychical or logical order. It is therefore perfectly natural that such a tendency should be accompanied by a certain clumsiness in the handling of genuinely causal relations, as our examination of causal conjunctions has just shown to be the case. It is the same lack of adaptation to the actual way in which phenomena fit into one another that gives rise both to such premature syntheses and to such defective analyses. It is very natural too, and in no way surprising that this tendency to immediate justification of phenomena and events should be pre-logical as well as pre-causal (since it is born of a failure to discriminate between logical and causal sequence), and that it should consequently be accompanied by a really defective and awkward use of logical implication. For to be unadapted to the way in which phenomena effectively fit into one another goes hand in hand with being unadapted to the relations between judgments. These are only two special cases of the general law according to which defective synthesis involves both syncretism and juxtaposition.

Moreover, this kinship between syncretism and juxtaposition points clearly to the interpretation which it befits us to give to the latter phenomenon. For juxtaposition is after all the sign of the complete absence of necessity from the thought of the child. The child knows nothing either of physical necessity (the fact that nature obeys laws) nor of logical necessity (the fact that such a proposition necessarily involves such another). For him everything is connected with everything else, which comes to exactly the same thing as that nothing is connected with anything else.[1]

[1] The reader must bear in mind that the hypotheses and statistical results drawn from the material in this chapter are valid *only* for the use of the French words, *parce que, puisque, donc, alors, quoique*, etc. Analogous experiments would have to be carried out on English children before any objective results could be obtained as to the use of ' because,' ' since,' ' therefore,' ' then,' ' although,' etc. The same consideration holds for similar material in subsequent chapters. [Translator's note.]

CHAPTER II

FORMAL THOUGHT AND RELATIONAL JUDGMENTS[1]

THE LOGICAL SIGNIFICANCE OF THE BINET-SIMON TEST BY ABSURD PHRASES.[2]

IT is not our intention to devote this chapter to all the questions connected with formal thought and relational judgments in the child. Our aim is solely to indicate the bond which unites these two problems to that of childish ego-centrism and to the correlated questions which we have studied in connexion with the ego-centrism thought in general. The nature of this bond can be most clearly brought out by the study of certain mental tests which bring in the incriminated factors, and it is for this purpose that we have chosen one of the Binet-Simon tests of intelligence.

The five absurd phrases of the well-known Binet-Simon test call for fairly subtle powers of reasoning on the part of the child, powers whose analysis it would be interesting to undertake. The question arises why some of these apparently glaring absurdities are not discovered by the child until he reaches the age of 10 (or even 11, as some have claimed). There is as yet so little material on child logic that it is well to take what one can find ; while from another point of view, tests of all-round intelligence or of age level like those of Binet and Simon will gain in interest when it is known, in connexion with each test, which of

---

[1] With the collaboration of Mlle Emmy Cartalis.

[2] Binet, A., et Simon, Th., *La mesure du developpement de l'intelligence chez les jeunes enfants*, Paris, 1917, pp. 56–58.

the factors that go to make up intelligence is being measured. At first sight such an analysis seems very remote from the questions examined in our first chapter. But in reality this is not so. In the first place, the use of the logical ' because ' and of the conjunctions of discordance seems, as we saw, to presuppose the capacity for observing rules in reasoning and consequently the power to make use of formal deduction. It will be our business to discover what are the conditions to which this formal thought is subjected. In the second place, having studied the nature of syncretism and juxtaposition —both of them consequences of ego-centrism on the structure of thought—it will be necessary to examine the difficulty which children experience in handling relational judgments properly so called, a difficulty which is connected with the phenomenon of juxtaposition and is likewise the outcome of childish ego-centrism. Seen from this double point of view, an analysis of the Binet-Simon test will constitute a natural sequel to our enquiry.

To this end, we set out to interpret the answers of some 40 schoolboys of Geneva between the ages of 9 and 11–12 in the following manner. The child is first of all examined by means of the Binet-Simon [1] technique, then, having obtained an answer, we make the child repeat the absurd phrase by heart. The phrase is generally deformed by the child in a significant manner. We then read him the exact text so as to eliminate all factors due to inattention or forgetfulness. Finally, we ask the child to arrange the sentence himself in such a way that " there should no

---

[1] Our readers will remember the five absurd sentences of the Binet-Simon test :—

1° A poor cyclist had his head smashed and died on the spot ; he was taken to hospital and it is feared that he will not recover.

2° I have three brothers : Paul, Ernest, and myself.

3° The body of a poor young girl was found yesterday, cut into 18 pieces. It is thought that she must have killed herself.

4° There was a railway accident yesterday, but it was not very serious. The number of deaths was only 48.

5° Someone said : If ever I kill myself from despair I won't choose a Friday, because Friday is a bad day and would bring me ill luck.

longer be anything silly in it." It is also advisable, in the
question of the three brothers for example, to take illus-
trations from the child's own life. In this way one finally
comes to understand more or less what he is saying.

§ I. FORMAL REASONING.—According to our results
the order of difficulty of the tests was as follows : the
questions of the *three brothers* and of *Friday* were the most
difficult, the questions of *accident* by far the easiest.[1]
Out of 44 children between 9 and 12 (and 3 of 14), 33 solved
the question of the young girl cut into 18 pieces, and
35 that of the railway accident, as against only 13 who
understood that of the 3 brothers and 10 that of Friday.
As to the test of the cyclist who died on the spot, 24
children passed it, but it contains two purely verbal
difficulties which have nothing to do with logic, the word
réchapper (Engl. recover) is often taken to mean *s'échapper*
(to escape), and *mort sur le coup* (dead on the spot) is
interpreted as *mort sur le cou* (dead on the neck). This
being so, the test is not very conclusive.

Why is it that the accident tests are easier than the
others ? It is because they appeal directly to the child's
sense of reality without any presuppositions about the
data. Whereas to avoid killing oneself on Friday is
absurd only to anyone who believes in the unlucky character of Friday. In order to discover this absurdity the
child has therefore to place himself at the point of view
of the person who lays down the premises. The reasoning takes place relatively to a given point of view, which
is a psychological operation of far greater difficulty.
Similarly, in the question about the brothers, the child is
obliged to place himself at a point of view which is not
his : the family he is told about consists of three brothers,
and he is expected to place himself at the point of view of
one of them so as to count the latter's brothers. Here
again, there is a relativity of view-point which involves

---

[1] The result tallies with what has been generally found by writers who
have verified the Binet-Simon tests.

a very delicate mental operation. On the other hand, to judge that a woman cut into 18 pieces has not killed herself or that a dead cyclist cannot be resuscitated is a direct judgment of observation. It does not presuppose any preliminary change of point of view, but simply a certain sense of reality or, as M. Claparède has called it, a *sens des contingences*. Finally, to describe as ' serious ' an accident in which there are 48 deaths might seem to involve a formal kind of reasoning if one started from a given definition of the word ' serious.' But this question does not occur to the child ; here again his judgment is immediate and absolute, very different therefore from that involved by the tests of Friday and the three brothers.

In conclusion, the last two tests are difficult because they necessitate reasoning of a relative and formal kind, the others are easy because they involve only immediate judgments made from one's own point of view.

Let us try, quite shortly, to justify these statements with regard to the Friday test. The wrong answers given to this test give us the clue to the child's difficulty. Most of them show an inability to accept the premisses as such and to reason from these premisses in a purely deductive manner.

" *People can kill themselves every day,* says Bai (age 9 ; 6), *they don't need to kill themselves on a Friday.*" " *Friday is not unlucky,*" says Van (age 9 ; 10). " *He doesn't know if it will bring him ill luck* " (Berg, 11 ; 2). " *Perhaps Friday will bring him good luck* " (Arn, 10 ; 7), etc.

The children all refuse to admit the premisses and do not see that that is not the point. What is required is to accept the premisses, then to reason correctly, *i.e.* to avoid the contradictions of the test.

But the subjects do not see the contradiction because they do not attempt to reason from the point of view of the person who is speaking. They do not get out of their own point of view, and consequently stick at the premisses, which they refuse to admit even in the capacity of data.

Campa (10 ; 3) and Ped (9 ; 6) are in exactly the same predicament, but they try to justify the premisses : " *It is a day when you must never eat meat.*" There is therefore nothing absurd to them in the test, but again this is because they do not reason from the data but judge the latter from their own point of view.

But from the moment that the child admits the premisses as given, without justifying or invalidating them, he is ready to resolve the test correctly. Some of them are of opinion that " *he would do better to kill himself on Friday, since it is an unlucky day,*" and then the correct answer comes : " *Since he would be dead it couldn't bring him ill luck* " (Blei, 10 ; 10).

Thus the difficulty of reasoning formally (*i.e.* of admitting a datum as such and deducing what follows from it) is the real difficulty of the test. That is why this test is, in our opinion, better suited to the age of 11 or even 12 than to that of 10. Indeed, there was an interval of at least a year between the success of this test and that of the accident tests.

We are now in a position to understand what formal reasoning really consists in, and how its structure may be influenced by social factors such as ego-centrism and the socialization of thought.

The first deductive operation of which the mind is capable consists either in foreseeing what will happen when such and such conditions are given, or in reconstructing what has happened when such and such results are given. This is a step forward in intellectual growth which the child is able to take very early. In the spontaneous questions of children before the age of 7–8 (L.T., Chap. V, § 9) we found a large number of ' ifs ' which point to this primitive form of deduction. " *If I put a dragon and a bear, which would win ?* " But before the age of 7–8 we have only a kind of pseudo-deduction in the course of which the child deems it possible to foresee everything, because he cannot conform to those habits of control and verification which set a limit to the scope of hypotheses.

After the age of 7–8, on the contrary, the child becomes more exacting in the matter of control and therefore knows better how to distinguish hypothesis from reality. To this stage correspond the development of the logical ' because ' and the beginnings of correct deductive reasoning. But all reasoning at this stage is still limited by one essential qualification : deduction bears only upon the beliefs which the child has adopted himself, in other words, it deals only with his personal conception of reality. The child will be able to say : " Half 9 is not 4, because 4 and 4 make 8," or [when he has failed to find an object in one box and is pointing to the next one] " *Then it must be in that box, anyhow !* " etc., because in these cases deduction deals with propositions which he admits personally, or rejects personally. But if we say to a child : " Let us admit, for example, that dogs have six heads. How many heads will there be in a yard where there are 15 dogs ? " the child will refuse to give an answer, because he will not ' assume ' the hypothesis. We, on the contrary, even though we admit that the premisses are absurd, will be perfectly able to reason from them and conclude that there will be 90 heads in that yard. This is because we distinguish between real or empirical necessity (dogs cannot have six heads) and formal or logical necessity (if dogs had six heads there would necessarily be 90 heads, etc.) Even without using absurd premisses, the experiment can be made, simply with arbitrary premisses. We endeavoured to do in this as follows : [1]

Let us take the test which we owe to Burt : " If I have more than one franc, I shall go by taxi or by train. If it rains, I shall go by train or by motor. Now it is raining and I have half a louis (10 francs). How do you think I shall go ? " The test cannot be said to be absurd, it is simply arbitrary. The gentleman in question had his own reasons for not taking a taxi if it rained, etc. It is

---

[1] See J. Piaget, " Essai sur la multiplication logique et les débuts de la pensée formelle chez l'enfant," *Journ. Psych.*, vol. 19, pp. 245 sq.

just as arbitrary to say to children, as is constantly done in problems of arithmetic : " It takes two hours to fill a cistern with a tap giving three litres a minute," etc. The whole point is to know whether the child will be able to adopt or ' assume ' these arbitrary premisses and reason from them as though he believed them.

Experiment showed that in Paris this test, together with others requiring the same aptitudes, did not succeed till the age of 11. The reason was that as in the case of the Friday test the children below this age refused to assume the data without questioning them, and want either to justify or to supplement them. Between the ages of 7 and 10 we had answers like : he will go in the train " *because it is quicker,*" in the bus " *because it is nicer in the bus,*" in a taxi " *because it isn't dear,* 10 *francs is enough,*" etc.

Of course this test is complicated by two alternatives, and necessitates very difficult logical operations. It was therefore expedient to check its results by others. The Friday test was a useful index in this connexion since it too did not succeed until the age of 11, although it contained no special difficulty except that belonging ·to all formal reasoning.

Moreover, we are here in presence of a fact which anyone can observe for himself by questioning a child. Up to a certain age it is almost impossible to make a child assume a suggested hypothesis unless one forces him to believe it and thus changes it into an affirmation. In the experiments on air which we shall publish shortly we find children from 8 to 10 who know that there is air everywhere, particularly in this room. We say to them : " If there were no air would this [an object suspended by a string which we swing round rapidly] make a draught ?— *Yes.*—Why ?—*Because there is always air in the room.*— But in a room where all the air had been taken away would it make any ?—*Yes, it would.*—Why ?—*Because there would be some air left,*" etc. Or with younger children in an enquiry into animism : " If you could touch the sun, would he feel it ?—*You can't touch him.*—Yes, but if you could manage to, would he feel it ?—*He is too high up.*—Yes, but if. . . .," etc.

This shows us what formal deduction really is ; it consists in drawing conclusions, not from a fact given in immediate observation, nor from a judgment which one holds to be true without any qualifications (and thus incorporates into reality such as one conceives it), but in a judgment which one simply assumes, *i.e.* which one admits without believing it, just to see what it will lead to. This is the form of deduction which we have placed round about the age of 11–12 as opposed to the simpler forms of inference which appear first.

These tests of ours will perhaps give the impression that formal deduction is a very special form of thought and of very little use to children. But this is far from being the case. In the first place all mathematical reasoning is formal or, as the logicians put it, hypothetico-deductive. Whenever we say to a child : " Let this be a triangle," or " A piece of cloth costs 12 francs," we are forcing him to reason *in conformity with premisses that are simply given*, which means disregarding reality and even suppressing any memories or real observations which might block the way to the process of reasoning. Reasoning of this kind is done from pure hypotheses. Even if the subject-matter be of a concrete nature and the problems given to the child contain measurements and actual observations, the sort of reasoning required is none the less formal in the sense that the child will have to remember a number of rules and definitions which are independent of his own observation. Either a mathematical problem is presented to a child as a purely empirical problem, in which case he will be kept in ignorance of the deductive power of even elementary arithmetic ; or he will be compelled to reason strictly, but then this process, in so far as it appeals to fixed rules and to previously admitted propositions, will be a process of formal reasoning.

Nay, more ; all deduction, even when it deals with

F

reality given in direct observation, is formal to the extent that it claims to be strict. For deduction that is concerned with objects such as they appear to us in direct observation can obviously not be strict, but only probable, or based on analogy. From the fact that water boils at different temperatures according to pressure, nothing precise can be deduced. In order to deduce strictly one must 1° bring about certain ideal conditions such as could not be realized in immediate experience, and in this way reach the knowledge of laws which will perhaps never be verified but will remain mere constructions of the mind ; 2° one must deal with ideal objects, *i.e.* objects defined clearly and in such a manner as to prevent their being confused with the variable objects presented in observation. (The chemical definition of water, H_2O or H_2O_2 stands for a body that is never found pure in nature). So that the form of deduction which is a necessary condition for arriving at general laws or mathematical relations is such that the stricter it is, the more formal it becomes ; that is to say it will have to presuppose ideal definitions and hypotheses which cannot be directly verified.

Now theoretical as these conditions may appear, they are none the less indispensable to the psychology of the child's mind. When boys of 9–10 years old spontaneously give weight as an explanation of why bodies float, one often feels that they have some intuition of density. They will say, for instance, that given equal volumes (*i.e.* when they are shown two equal volumes, one of wood, the other of water) wood is lighter than water. Before the age of 9, on the contrary, children who have just declared that wood is light, think that it is heavier than water. What is this very marked progress shown at the age of 9 but an attempt—implicit as yet—to replace immediate reality (absolute weight without any reference to volume) by a ratio (weight/volume), *i.e.* to replace the real object by a slightly more ideal object. By following this mental orientation the child will inevitably come to apply formal deduction to nature herself, and he will do so to the extent that he substitutes ratios, laws and fixed (*i.e.* ideal) definitions for simple empirical observation. We have expatiated at some length upon this subject in order to show that formal deduction, *i.e.* reasoning from premisses that are merely assumed and not supplied by immediate belief is of fundamental importance, not only in mathematics, but in every kind of reflection about nature. Let us now return to the origins of formal thinking. The above analysis has shown that two factors were particularly necessary for the right functioning of any formal reasoning : 1° a sort of detachment from one's own point of view or from the point of view of the moment, enabling one to place oneself at that of others and to reason first from premisses admitted by them, then more generally from every kind of purely hypothetical proposition ; 2° owing to the mere fact of having placed oneself inside the beliefs of others, or more generally inside a hypothesis, one must, in order to reason formally, be able to remain on the plane of mere assumption without surreptitiously returning to one's private point of view or to that of the reality of the moment. To be formal, deduction must detach itself from reality and take up its stand upon the plane of the purely possible, which is by definition the domain of hypothesis. In a word, formal thought presupposes two factors, one social (the possibility of placing oneself at every point of view and of abandoning one's own), the other, which is connected with the psychology of belief (the possibility of assuming alongside of empirical reality a purely possible world which shall be the province of logical deduction).

What is the relation of these two factors to one another ? Does the logical factor, *i.e.* the construction of a hypo-thetico-deductive world give birth to the social factor, *i.e.* to the possibility of entering into the point of view of others, or is the reverse the case ? What we have seen of the part played by social factors in the development of the child's mind can leave us in doubt upon the matter. It is only from the moment that a child can detach himself from his personal beliefs and enter into any foreign point of view that he really will know what is meant by a hypothesis. Before this, of course, he will make use of the word ' if,' but he will not have given up his realistic habits of thought, he will not have been doing more than imagining a world different from the real world, but in which he nevertheless believes to a certain extent. It is only from the day that the child has said : " I understand. Let us admit your point of view. Then if it were true . . . this is what would happen . . . because . . .," that a genuine hypothesis or a genuine assumption (*i.e.* one which is not believed in at all, but nevertheless analysed for its own sake) has really dawned in his mind. Here again it is social intercourse, but of a far more delicate order than that which we have spoken of previously, that modifies the structure of thought. In this connexion the Friday tests or others analogous to it are of the greatest interest. They show at what age the child is capable of making the simplest assumptions, those which independently of any mathematics or any reflection upon nature betray a capacity for reasoning from premises which one does not believe in before verification.

Now on the strength of the Friday test and certain others which were studied on a previous occasion the age to which we have assigned the possibility of formal reasoning is 11–12. Why this date ? It is always dangerous to give reasons for the synchronisms shown in mental development, but if formal thought is really dependent upon social factors, then it is not impossible that this age should be related to the second critical phase of social life in the child. Every one knows that at the age of 11–12 children have a marked impulse to form themselves into groups, and that the respect paid to the rules and regulations of their play constitutes an important feature of this social life. It is therefore at this age that arguments between boys will become not only more closely knit than

before, but more definitely directed by the desire for
agreement and co-ordination.

Here is a typical example of the social behaviour of
children of 11. Eight boys between 10–11 are preparing
for a snow-fight in a Geneva street where we are observing
them. They begin, oddly enough, by electing a captain.
" *Who votes for T ?* " says the ringleader (three boys
raise their hands).—" *Who votes for S ?*" (four boys raise
their hands, amongst them one who had already voted
for T).—" *You can't vote for both, because you can never
vote for two people !* " [Note the application of an assumed
rule.] Then the little band chooses a name. " *Let's say
that we are the . . . Company* [the name escapes us] *of the
rue de la Dôle.*" The two camps then take up their
positions at equal distances from the umpire, who is the
ringleader previously mentioned. One of the boys moves
too far forward. The leader says : " *Then we'll say* [if
anyone moves too far forward], *he is in Coventry !*"
[Note the assumed rule.]

This example shows very clearly the type of argument
current at this age (and unknown in this explicit form at
any earlier age) : 1° Assumption of new rules as the need
for them arises ; and 2° application of these rules by
means of formal deduction. Small wonder if such social
habits develop reciprocal understanding and lead to new
habits of thought. Indeed, it is to this very conclusion
that M. Cousinet has been quite naturally led by experiments he has been carrying out on collective work in
school life.[1]

---

[1] M. Cousinet, it will be remembered, tried to introduce into primary
education the spontaneous life which children exhibit in their play.
According to him, games are at first imitation and auto-illusion (the
thief and the policeman are really acted) and later on simply become
well-organized competitions (the game of the thief and the policeman
becomes a game of pursuit with increasingly complicated rules). Now
this socialization of play, this interest in rules reaches its height at
about the age of 11–12 ; and this is the age when collective school work
with spontaneous organization of the task in hand proves to be the most
profitable. *Cf.* a work which M. Cousinet will shortly publish on the
child's social life.

There would seem then to be two critical periods in the social and intellectual life of the child : the age of 7–8 accompanied by the decline of ego-centrism, the earliest motivated (or 'genuine,' see L.T., Chap. II) arguments; and the first appearance of the desire for verification or for logical justification ; and the age of 11–12 which is the age of societies governed by rules, and that in which formal thought first comes into being.

§ 2. THE THREE BROTHERS TEST.—The three brothers test requires that the child should find a contradiction between the existence of three brothers in one family (Paul, Ernest, and myself) [1] and the proposed judgment, " I have three brothers (Paul, Ernest, and myself)." In order to find this contradiction, the child must be able to distinguish between the point of view of the total number of the brothers and the point of view of the relation between these brothers. The first we shall call the point of view of membership, *i.e.* of the relation between an individual and the whole group of brothers *of which he forms a part;* the second, *i.e.* that which stresses the connexions between *individual members of the same whole* we shall call the point of view of *relation.* The first point of view is generally marked by the verb *to be* and the predicative judgment (we *are* three brothers, I *am* a brother), the second by the verb *to have* (I *have* three brothers), by the possessive adjective (*my* brothers), or by the preposition *of* (I am the brother of Paul). [2] It soon became evident that these points of view remain undifferentiated in the possessive expressions as they are used in children's language (I *have, my, of,* etc.), which expressions can easily be misinterpreted as having the same meaning as when they are used in adult talk.

This lack of differentiation will be the object of our study. We shall try to prove that the different types of childish reasoning called forth by the three brothers test can all be

---

[1] Three *sisters* if the experimenter is a woman (Pauline, Jeanne, and me).
[2] " Myself " seemed, in the context, less clumsy than " me " as a translation of *moi.* Cf. footnote on p. 61 [Tr.].

explained by an inability to distinguish the point of view of relation (the relation of brother to brother) from the point of view of membership. Let us begin by simply describing the phenomenon and confining ourselves to logical analysis. The psychological explanation will be attempted later on.

The different forms of reasoning which we met with can be reduced to five types. These do not appear in any regular order, and the same child may alternate between one and the other to an indefinite extent.

First type.—This type of child does not reckon *myself* as a brother ; not because he has understood the test, but because he forgets or does not know that *myself* I am a brother for my own brothers. Thus the child seems to be placing himself at the point of view of relation (I have two brothers), but he argues from this proposition to the existence of two brothers altogether in the family : I have two brothers [therefore] we are two brothers.

Examples.—(Di, age 9 ; 4) : " *She has two sisters, she has, she's not a sister.*" Does this mean that the child has understood the test ? " *Why is she not a sister ?— Because she is a little older than the others.*—How many sisters are there in the family ?— *Two.*" This piece of reasoning seems simply to be suggested by the test and the experimenter. We made a point of verifying this. Two months later Di had forgotten the present test (having undergone several others on the day that he was questioned about the three brothers), and he gave us, concerning his own brother, exactly analogous answers, which the reader will find presently along with other examples of spontaneous reasoning on the part of children.

Matt (age 9 ; 1) also thinks that there are only 2 sisters in the family. Blei (age 10 ; 10) asserts : " *There are 2 sisters, Pauline and Jeanne,*" and again : " *You say you have 3 sisters, but you are* [sic] *only 2 sisters. You don't count.*" And Ped (age 9 ; 6) : " *You, you're not a brother.*" All these subjects reckon like Matt that there are 2 brothers in all in the family.

According to ordinary evaluations these answers would be considered correct. Binet and Simon do not discuss this point, but evaluations published by Mlle Descœudres [1] yield 22 + as against 2 — to the answer : " You are not a sister." This answer strikes us as essentially ambiguous. If the child means : " You are not *your* sister," then of course it is right. But very often, as in the case of the subjects quoted above, the child means : " You are not a sister either for yourself or for the others. You have two sisters, but each one of them has one sister only, etc." The family, as Di, Matt, and the others explain, consists of two sisters and " myself." These judgments may seem rather improbable, but we shall show later on that they are commonly met with when children are questioned about brothers of their own, without ever having undergone the Binet test. The child has simply not yet noticed that the word ' brother ' denotes a reciprocal relation : if I have a brother, I am myself a brother. In other words, the child uses the word ' brother ' like the word ' father ' : " I have a father, but I am not a father myself."

In conclusion :

1° Children belonging to this first type seem to place themselves at the point of view of the relation of brother to brother : " I have two brothers." But this relation has not yet become symmetrical and does not lead to the conclusion " I am therefore their brother," nor to the more important one of " We are therefore three brothers " ; it is therefore not a relation in the sense in which we have chosen to use the term.

2° The use of the possessive expressions therefore raises an interesting problem. How can the child use such forms of speech as " *I have* two brothers " or " *my* . . .," without realizing that the possession is reciprocal ?

3° This stage does not admit of the possibility of passing from the judgment of membership to a judgment of relation, since the two points of view are as yet undifferentiated. " I have two brothers " and " We are two brothers " are verbal forms between which the child has not yet learned to distinguish.

[1] *Arch. de Psych.*, vol. 16 (1917), p. 333.

Second type.—The child belonging to this type realizes that if I have two brothers, I must be a brother for them, and that therefore there are three brothers in the family. But the Binet-Simon test has ceased to be absurd. The child is quite willing to look for what is ' silly ' in it, since he has been asked to do so, but he sets about the task without conviction :

Pern (age 9 ; 6), Tiec (age 10), etc., declare in spite of several readings that there is nothing ' silly.' Bar (9 ; 4) explains why this is so. He repeats the test correctly and can see nothing absurd in it. He announces in answer to our question that there are three sisters in the family : " *There is Jeanne and Pauline, that makes 2, so there is one missing.*" Thus he has taken the expression " I have 3 sisters " to mean " We are 3 sisters," since he feels obliged when he enumerates " my " 2 sisters to make it clear that one is missing. This missing sister is not, as some of the other subjects suppose, a fourth sister, it is ' myself.'

Bonv (age 9), likewise answers after the second reading : " What is there silly ?—*Because you could have said : Paul, Ernest, and myself are my 3 brothers.*" Thus the Binet-Simon test contains nothing absurd for him.

CONCLUSION : 1° In complete contrast to the last type, the child remembers that ' myself ' is also a brother. But he fails to distinguish verbally between the point of view of membership and that of relation, so he says : " We are three brothers, and I have two brothers." He confuses the two for lack of the necessary means of expression in a formula copied from that of Binet and Simon.

2° This is not merely the outcome of suggestion due to the test. Later on it will be seen that the child often uses the same expressions spontaneously.

Is the confusion then purely verbal ? But verbal confusion, when it is concerned, as in this case, with a relation and not simply with an unknown word is always the sign of logical confusion. In this particular case, the child juxtaposes in one expression two attitudes which it has never interested him to separate.

3° The point of view of membership and that of relation are not yet distinct, *i.e.* the expression " I have " does not always indicate a relation between individual members of one whole, but a relation between the individual and the whole to which he belongs : " I have three brothers, to whom I belong." In the last type which we examined the individual did not form a part of this whole group of brothers of which he says " I have . . ." ; in the present type he does form such a part. This is the only difference, but there is as yet no genuine judgment of relation.

4° Types I and II often succeed one another in inverse order to that which we have described. Occasionally too, type II does not constitute a stage, but the child passes straight from I to III. The matter must be settled in each particular case.

Third type.—In this third stage the child tries to distinguish between the point of view of membership and that of relation, and in order to do so he tries to place himself at the former only. He therefore puts ' myself ' on an equality with the other two brothers and concludes that the absurdity lies in the absence of any name. The names of all three brothers ought, so he thinks, to be given, but this does not mean that ' myself ' does not possess— as in the preceding stage—three brothers, including ' myself.'

Here is an example which will serve as a transitional case between the last stage and this one : Mai (9 ; 6) begins by saying : " *I ought to have another brother, because I count as one,*" knowing all the time that the family consists of 3 brothers. In other words, " We are 3 brothers " and " I have 3 brothers " are still synonymous. But Mai is shocked by the expression " I have 3 brothers, Paul, Ernest, and myself," because Paul and Ernest form a separate group. Thus Mai makes an implicit distinction between the point of view of relation and that of membership, but does not realize that from the first of these two view-points, ' myself ' has only 2 brothers. Exactly as in the case of Bar, Mai holds that " *there is a brother missing,"* which means that as in the last stage he reckons himself among his own brothers. He guesses at the solution in a form which constitutes the third type ; what is missing is the name of ' myself ' : *" There is a name missing."*

It should be noted that this act of wanting a name only repeats the confusion of the second type in a new form. What the child demands in order to remove the absurdity, is simply that one might be able to pass from the point of view of relation " I have three brothers " to the point of view of membership " We are three brothers," without changing the sense of the word brother. The act of giving ' myself ' a name seems to him sufficient for this purpose.

Gavai (9 ; 11) says : *" The name of the girl is missing . . . of the girl who gives the names, the names of the others.* —How many sisters are there in the family ?—*Three, Pauline, Jeanne, and myself.*—How many sisters has Pauline ?—*None.*—How many has Jeanne ? *None.*— And how many sisters have I ' myself ' got ?—*One, the one where there is no name given."* This case is very clear as regards the meaning of the ' missing name.' As to the answer that neither Jeanne nor Pauline have any sisters, this is a type of statement frequently met with, and can be traced to the phenomena of the first stage : " I have 2 sisters but I am not their sister."

Schm (10 ; 6) is equally clear. The phrase is absurd, " *because the last one didn't give his name."* And when he tries to put the sentence " so that it should not be silly," Schm gives : *" I have three brothers, Paul, Ernest, and William,"* meaning that there are 3 in the family and that William is ' myself.' He had never thought there were 4, and when he is asked to put himself in the place of Paul, Schm assigns to him 2 brothers, as he does to each of the two (showing at this moment that he has realized the point of view of relation) which makes a total of 3. From this Schm concludes once again : *" I have 3 brothers, Paul, Ernest, and William."*

It is in the same way too that Chan (age 9) says : *" What is silly is that you don't say your name,"* but he adds after having correctly repeated the general gist of the test : *" I don't think it is silly, but only that there is nothing else in the riddle."* In other words, there is nothing absurd in concluding from " I have 3 brothers " the fact that " We are 3 brothers," but it would have made things clearer to have given his name.—Salv (12 ; 5) and Cler (10 ; 9) are in the same position.

This again will show that the exact appreciation of an answer like " you mustn't say ' myself,' you must say a name " is an extremely delicate task, and this is confirmed by the judgments collected by Mlle Descœudres (12 + as against 12 −).[1] Analysis is always required in order to understand what the child meant to say.

Thus we may say :

1° This type of reasoning has the same structure as the last, but the child tries to distinguish the point of view of the group of brothers from the point of view of the brother who says ' myself.' As he cannot succeed in doing this, *i.e.* in finding the requisite logico-verbal expressions, the child simply sacrifices the first point of view and replaces the term ' myself ' by an equivalent name, hoping in this way to put all the brothers on an equal footing.

2° But the child still sticks to the formula " *I have* . . . etc.," whence the verbal form " I have 3 brothers, Paul, Ernest, and (a name)." The two points of view of membership and relation have therefore not yet been distinguished from one another.

3° With regard to the order of appearance it sometimes happens that this type does not constitute a special stage. Some children never go through it at all. Others reach it by different paths, starting, for example, from the next type. Others again come to it directly by starting from type I.

Fourth type.—The starting-point of this type is the same as that of the last, but the method of procedure is reversed. The child no longer tries to eliminate ' myself ' and the point of view of the relation between the brothers, but tries, on the contrary, to find out how many

---

[1] Descœudres, *Arch. de Psych.*, vol. 16 (1917), p. 334.

brothers each separate brother has himself, and reaches in this way a total of four. The curious thing is that the child's reason for finding four brothers in the family is not that the test says: " I have three brothers," but that the two brothers who are named in the test have not got the same brother as has 'myself.' This curious calculation is again due to the lack of a definitely relative point of view : each of my brothers has his own brothers which are not mine. I ' myself ' have one of my own as well, which makes 4 altogether.

Ducho (age 9), for example, says at the first reading : " *You can't tell what the third one is called,*" which is a third type answer, since the child believes for the moment in a total of three brothers. Then he reads the test again and concludes : " *Well, Paul has two brothers, Ernest two, and 'myself' has two friends as well, and we don't know what the last one is called.*" Ducho then comes to the conclusion that " *there are four in the family.*"

The answer is remarkable, and gives a very clear picture of the mechanism of reasoning at this stage, in which the points of view of the several brothers are juxtaposed and added together, because the subject is unable to pass from one to the other by means of a judgment of relation. For by ' the last one ' Ducho means a brother who is the peculiar possession of ' myself ' without belonging either to Paul or to Ernest.

Paraz (10 ; 6) says in the course of three successive readings, " *There are three brothers, Paul, Ernest, and myself,*" which seems right enough ; but this makes four brothers altogether " *because there are three brothers and then myself as well.*" Riv (9 ; 8) presents an analogous case. Schnei (11 ; 3) throws more light on this quaint form of reasoning. He begins by declaring that there is a name missing (3rd type). Then he concludes that there are four sisters, but as an afterthought and in the following manner. Pauline has two sisters (Jeanne and myself), Jeanne has a sister (Pauline), and ' myself ' has yet another sister (the 4th). ' Myself ' is not a sister to Pauline and Jeanne—precisely as in the 1st stage—and it is in virtue of this lack of symmetry that ' myself ' has a fourth sister. Campa (10 ; 4) after having assigned two sisters to Pauline, two to ' myself,' which is so far correct, declares that the absurdity is as follows : " *They each have two sisters. It is silly that they should not all have the same sister.*" The reader will recall that Gavai, at the 3rd stage produced calculations of this kind.

CONCLUSION : 1° This type of child has not yet realized the reciprocal character of the brother relationship. It should be noted, moreover, that at none of the preceding stages is this character recognized as such, as was shown by several children of types II and III.

2° In trying to pass from the relation between brothers to the total group of brothers, the child reasons as follows : He assigns, for example, two brothers to each of the brothers indicated in the test, but as he fails to establish reciprocal relations between them, each one has brothers of his own, thus bringing up the total to 4 and sometimes 5.

3° The usual number 4 is clearly related to the statement of the test, " I have 3 brothers " ; but the child does not jump immediately from this statement to the number 4 by saying " 3 brothers and myself, that makes 4." The path he follows is less direct. When the test is read, the child wonders whether the brothers number 3 or 4, and then embarks upon various attempts at non-reciprocal relations which we shall examine presently.

Children of this type must therefore be clearly distinguished from those who, as in the next stage, assume the existence of four brothers from the first.

4° As to order of succession, the present type may follow immediately upon the first, or the second. The child may also pass from this type to the first or the third, and not to the fifth. Finally, a certain number avoid it altogether.

Fifth type.—At this last stage we come to the right solution of the test. The child either insists upon a fourth brother in virtue of the statement " I have three brothers," or else reduces to 2 the number of brothers which " I have." The following answers may be admitted as correct :

Celler (9 ; 5) : It is silly " *Because there are not three sisters if there is him* (she) *as well.*" Batta (9 ; 0) " *Because*

she only has two brothers and *counts herself as a brother.*"
Stuck (9 ; 0) " *Because the third is missing. They have
forgotten to put him in.*"

The point of view of relation and the point of view of
membership have at last been distinguished one from
another.

§ 3. COUNTER-TEST : CONVERSATION WITH THE CHILD.
—It is important before going any further, to lay stress
on a question of method. The result of experiment and
analyses carried out by means of a test is valid only if it
is confirmed by questions asked in conversation and by
current observation. In experiment one always runs
the risk of creating an artificial atmosphere in which the
child acts in obedience to a mechanical kind of logic. This
may certainly be an index of what is going on in portions
of the child's life which present the same features of
verbalism and constraint, but it gives no information
about his spontaneous thought. We must now therefore
endeavour to verify the results of the preceding
experiments by means of ordinary observation.

One more precaution : a careful distinction should be
made in studying the child mind between implicit understanding, which cannot be formulated, and explicit understanding, which finds expression in words. The phenomena
which we have been studying and most of those which we
shall presently deal with are misunderstandings only from
the second point of view. The objection may therefore
be raised that these phenomena do not belong to the child's
actual intelligence but to his language. But language
does not constitute a mere system of notation for the child.
It creates in his mind a new reality—verbal reality which
does not merely reflect the reality given in sensation, but
is superimposed upon it. The child will admit on the
verbal plane certain illogicalities which he would deny to
concrete reality. Our fundamental working hypothesis is
therefore that these are the very same illogicalities which
at an earlier stage the child exhibited in the sphere of

practical observation. There has simply been a process of shifting from one type of mental operation to the other. The child who gets muddled by the Binet-Simon test would reason correctly if the test were treated as a game, and this he would not have succeeded in doing a few years back. The difficulties which he would have met with in the real world (and which we shall presently reveal by showing what children say about their own families) are simply carried over on to the plane of language. When he is faced with the fictitious beings created by words, the child goes through the same process of reasoning as formerly, when he was confronted with the real beings given in direct observation.

The question we have to settle is therefore whether the phenomena described in the preceding analyses are to be found in the conversations which one can have with children, independently of any preconceived experiment and of the Binet-Simon test in particular. Now it will be shown that the forms of reasoning of the 1st, 2nd, and 4th types are reproduced word for word by the children who are questioned in this way. We shall not, for the moment, concern ourselves with this circumstance, for it raises the wider problem (which will occupy us later on) of the actual development of the notion of brother (or of cousin or of family) from the point of view of child logic. We shall simply summarize a certain number of the answers—the minimum necessary for the confirmation of our results.

Here are two children, Raoul and Gerald (4 ; 6 and 7 ; 2) : " Raoul, have you any brothers ?—*Gerald.*—And has Gerald a brother ?—*No, only me has a brother.*—Oh, come ! Hasn't Gerald got a brother ?—*Raoul ? . . . No, he hasn't got one.*" Gerald, after giving the same answers in respect to Raoul, hits upon the right solution.

Jacq (7 ; 6) : " Have you any brothers ?—*Two* [Paul and Albert].—Has Paul any brothers ?—*No.*—You are his brother ?—*Yes.*—Then Paul has some brothers ?— *No,*" etc. He is then told the solution and seems to understand it. " And has your sister any brothers ?—

Two, one brother Paul and one brother Albert [he leaves himself out again]. An hour later : " Has Albert any brothers ?—*One* [Paul].—And Paul ?—*One* [Albert].— And your sister ?—*Two.*"

Labert (8 ; 6) : " Have you any brothers ?—*Arthur.*— Has he got a brother ?—*No.*—How many brothers are there in the family ?—*Two.*—Have you got any ?—*One.* —Has he got any ?—*None at all.*—You are his brother ?— *Yes.*—Then he has got a brother ?—*No.*"

Di (9 ; 6) one of our 1st type subjects examined three months after the Binet-Simon test : " Have you any brothers ?—*One.*—Has he got a brother ?—*No.* You are his brother, aren't you ?—*Yes.*—Then he has a brother ? —*No.*"

In a word, the answers of type I, " You are not a brother, etc.," seem to admit of being brought into connexion with this manifest delusion on the part of children, viz. that they cannot succeed in placing themselves at their brother's point of view and yet still reckon themselves as brothers. They certainly use the term ' brothers ' to denote the group of brothers in a family, but they never form a clear idea of how many brothers each one of their brothers possesses himself.

As to the second type, here are two spontaneous expressions uttered by children of 4 and 12, which show very clearly that ' howlers ' are not simply created by our experiments :

Mag (4 ; ½) : " Have you got a sister ?—*Yes.*—And has she got a sister ?—*No, she hasn't got a sister. I am my sister.*" Simo (11 ; 9) says that " *there are three children in my family,*" and adds, without having been asked for any details : " *I have two brothers and a sister.*—And you ? —*I am one of the children too.*—What are your brothers called ?—*Albert, and I am called Henry.*" Thus, like Bonv and the others he says : " I have two brothers," and reckons himself as one of them even though he has never passed the Binet-Simon test. Fal (7 ; ½) : " *I have only one sister and one brother* [counting himself]." Kan (7 ; ½) presents the same case.

Verbal forms such as these are easy to understand. As soon as the child has discovered that he is himself a

brother, he says ' my brothers ' and counts himself as one
of them.   More remarkable is the fourth type of reasoning
which we find in its spontaneous form in the way in which
Jacq and others assign different numbers of brothers to the
various brothers of the same family.   For instance, Jacq
has two brothers, his brother Paul has only one, as
also his brother Auguste.   But here is another complete
example :

Gys (8 ; o) : " Have you got a brother ?—Yes.—
And your brother, has he got a brother ?—No.—Are you
sure ?—Yes.—And has your sister got a brother ?—No.
—You have a sister ?—Yes.—And she has a brother.—
Yes.—How many ?—No, she hasn't got any.—Is your
brother also your sister's brother ?—No.—And has your
brother got a sister ?—No.—How many brothers are
there in your family ?—One.—Then you are not a brother ?
(He laughs.)—Yes.—Then your brother has got a brother ?
—Yes.—How many ?—One.—Who is it ?—Me."

This example combines types I and IV : Gys will not
allow to his brother and sister the reciprocity of relationship which he assigns to himself.

These few facts give us the right to conclude that
the forms of reasoning observed in connexion with the
Binet-Simon test are to be found in a spontaneous state
in the simple conversations which may be held with
children.

It would be interesting to arrange these logical phenomena in accordance with different fixed ages.   This problem will occupy us in the course of the next chapter.

§ 4. PSYCHOLOGICAL INTERPRETATION OF THE JUDG-
MENT OF RELATION.—The conclusion to be drawn from
the above analyses is that the difficulty experienced by the
child in understanding either the three brothers test or
the simple questions concerning his own brothers and
sisters is really a difficulty in handling the judgment of
relation.   The child can quite easily succeed (from about
the age of 6 as we shall show) in forming judgments about
the whole group of his brothers and sisters, but the
relation between them escapes him, because he does not

give to the term ' brother ' or ' sister ' the relative, *i.e.* in this particular case the reciprocal, or (in logical parlance) the symmetrical sense which we assign to it. In other words, " Paul is my brother " does not yet imply " I am Paul's brother." The different types we have distinguished exhibit just those fluctuations in the course of which the relative sense of the word ' brother ' comes to be distinguished from the sense conferred upon it by the point of view of the judgment of membership only.

How are we to account for this curious difficulty ? In the first place we must remember that this difficulty in grasping the relativity of ideas is universal in childhood. We shall meet with an example in the next chapter in connexion with the notion of right and left. But the points of the compass, terms of measurement, and even comparative expressions are all the occasion for a process of laborious groping, analogous in its origin to that which we have just been examining. This is why we submitted to lengthy analysis the difficulties raised by a test of Burt's or by the simpler test which follows : " Edith is fairer (or has fairer hair) than Suzanne ; Edith is darker than Lili. Which is the darkest, Edith, Suzanne, or Lili ? " This is what we found :

Instead of tackling the matter by means of judgments of relation, *i.e.* by making use of such expressions as ' fairer than ' etc., the child deals simply in judgments of membership, and tries to find out with regard to the three girls whether they are fair or dark (speaking absolutely). It is exactly as though he reasoned as follows : Edith is fairer than Suzanne, so they are both fair ; Edith is darker than Lili, so they are both dark : therefore Lili is dark, Suzanne is fair, and Edith is between the two. In other words, owing to the interplay of the relations included in the test, the child, by substituting the judgment of membership (Edith and Suzanne are ' fair,' etc.) for the judgment of relation (Edith is ' fairer than ' Suzanne),

---

[1] See J. Piaget, " Une forme verbale de la comparaison chez l'enfant," *Arch. de Psych.*, vol. 18, pp. 141–172.

comes to a conclusion which is exactly the opposite of ours. Let us recall a few examples.

Gw (13 ; 9) tells us : " *Edith would be far the darkest of the three since she is darker than Lili, but then, on the other hand, she is fairer.*" Therefore she " *is middling. Suzanne is fair. . . . Lili is dark. . . . Lili is the darkest and Suzanne the fairest* " (p. 146).

Other subjects see a contradiction in the test. Fo (9 ; 4) : " *You can't tell, because it says that Edith is the fairest and the darkest* " (p. 165). Hec (10 ; 2) : " *You can't tell : Edith is fairer than Suzanne and darker than Lili !* " (p. 165).

Others make an attempt at the judgment of relation, but immediately divide the found relations into three classes. Mai (11 ; 8) : " *Suzanne is like Edith* [and both are darker than Lili], *and there is none in the middle. Since they are both ' darker ' they are the two dark ones* (p. 160)."

Gw (13 ; 9) at the fifth reading of the test : " *Once Suzanne is the darkest and once Edith is,* [therefore] *Suzanne is the same as Edith, and Lili is the fairest* " (p. 146).

These answers clearly betray their kinship with those obtained by means of the three brothers test. In both cases judgments of relation are constantly being transformed into judgments of inherence (inclusion or membership).

What is the origin of this difficulty in handling relations and of this tendency to replace the logic of relations by the simpler logic of membership and inclusion ? Our study of the different stages through which the child must pass before coming to the correct solution of Burt's test [1] led us to the following conclusions. There is first a stage at which the child cannot retain the two premises of the test in his memory and therefore fails to keep before his mind the relations in question. He retains only fragmentary images : Edith and Suzanne =fair, Edith and Lili =dark, etc. Then there is a second stage in which the child achieves a single grasp of the various data, but

[1] See p. 89.

reasons in the manner which we have described. Finally, there is a third stage in which he succeeds in reasoning correctly, but any distraction or momentary deficiency in the synthesis will throw him back on to mistakes comparable to those which belong to the earlier stages. All this looks as though a very important part were played by attention or rather by apperception or the form of synthesis. In so far as the field of consciousness is restricted, relations pass unnoticed, and only individuals are taken in with their particular characteristics independently of comparison. Hence the possibility of judgments of membership, since these call only for the perception of individuals taken singly, or taken as a whole but without comparison. But in so far as the field of consciousness expands, individuals are no longer given singly or ' en bloc,' they are compared in groups of two or more. At this point judgments of relation or comparison become possible.

But this description which is adequate for the Burt test is still very static. The problem remains as to why the child's field of consciousness should be so narrow and why individuals should be perceived singly without any relations to each other nor to the child himself. Now, if the child makes no attempt to find the connexions which unite individuals severally, if he regards them as something absolute, without taking account of the relativity of their characters and of their points of view, might it not be because he has never compared himself to these individuals ? In other words, if he fails to understand why a friend of his can be both fairer than another friend and darker than a third, might this not be because the child has never suspected that such and such a person whom he has always considered fair may be looked upon as having chestnut-coloured hair by children who are themselves very fair, and so on ? In short, is it not because he has always taken his own point of view as something absolute that the child remains ignorant of the habits of relativity and comparison, and that his field of consciousness is still restricted ? Thus the difficulty in handling the logic of relations would seem to be a new consequence of childish ego-centrism ; ego-centrism leads to naïve realism, and this realism, which is by definition the ignorance of all relations, leads to logical difficulties every time there is a question of substituting the logic of relations for that of membership or inclusion.

These psychological factors show up very clearly in the case of the brother and sister relationship. One must be very careful, in examining children in the manner we have described, not to interpret their mistakes as actual fallacies, *i.e.* as mistakes in reason. The child's attitude betrays only a deficiency of attention or, strictly speaking, a faulty point of view, due to the fact that he has not yet asked himself the question as we ask it. He has always considered his brothers and sisters from his own point of view, calling them brothers and sisters, counting them up without including himself, or counting the family only as a whole. But the thought of their individual viewpoints has never crossed his mind ; he has never asked himself what he was to them, nor whether he counted as one in their collection of brothers and sisters. When, therefore, he is questioned on this point, he does not give the result of any previous reasoning nor even of any explicit reasoning at the moment, but instead, he brings to our notice what may be called an optical illusion of the intellect. This pseudo reasoning consists in a series of immediate judgments following one another in freedom from all logic. We have here what might be called ' innocence ' of judgment, in comparison to what Ruskin has called in the sphere of perceptions ' innocence of the eye,' by which he means ignorance of perspective.

If then—and this applies to our previous enquiries as well—we have expressed child thought in the terms of adult logic, the reader must be careful not to see in these terms anything more than a mere system of notation, or, as we have said elsewhere,[1] a " label attached to the

[1] J. Piaget, *loc. cit., Arch. de Psych.*, p. 143.

facts." As a psychological process the child's reasoning remains independent of these notations. It consists in a series of attitudes which bring each other into play according to psychological laws which should be specified in each particular case (as we are trying to do now in the case of the three brothers) and not in a string of concepts which imply one another logically. The task of carrying out this psychological analysis is still in its early stages, and nothing could be farther from our intention than to reconstruct the thought of the child on the pattern of adult mentality. On the contrary, it will perhaps one day be the task of child logic to explain that of adults, if as the historicocritical method maintains, it is to history that we must look for further light upon the nature of thought. There may therefore be a certain advantage in sticking to a logical terminology, precisely because of this eventual explanation of adult reasoning which we hope to draw from the formation of reasoning in the child.

But to return to the ego-centric illusion of our children's judgments. In virtue of the ' innocence ' of his judgment, the child reasons as though he were the only thinker in question ; his point of view about his family seems to him the only one possible and excludes all others. For him therefore it is not a subjective point of view, but that of absolute reality. Consequently, as he is not conscious of his own subjectivity, or more simply of himself, he places himself on a completely different plane from his brothers, and this is what prevents him from seeing that he is a brother to his brothers on precisely the same grounds as they are brothers to him.

Thus when all is said and done, it is once more to the ego-centrism of thought that we must appeal in order to explain the incapacity for even the most elementary relativism of thought. To understand a relation—that, for instance, of brother to brother—means thinking of at least two points of view at the same time, those of each of the brothers. Absolute notions like those of ' boy,' etc. presuppose only one point of view. The judgment " Paul is a boy " remains the same whatever may be the perspective adopted.

The full importance of the ego-centric illusion will now be manifest. The explanation just given with regard to the notion of brother holds for all relative notions. If for the child things are absolutely to the right or to the left, or as we have just seen, absolutely dark or fair, and so on, it is because up to a certain age the child fails to realize this very simple fact that one of his companions whom he holds to be big, or dark, or horrid may perfectly well be regarded by a third party as small, or fair, or nice, without the third party being necessarily either a fool or a knave.

We have two more remarks to make. The first is concerned with the distinction between the verbal and the concrete plane of reality. The difficulties we have been describing are independent of language, and even take place in ordinary life. They may therefore be said to disappear sooner than verbal difficulties. After the age of 7–8, as we shall see in the next chapter, *i.e.* at the very moment when primitive ego-centrism is on the wane, a certain proportion of the children succeed in saying how many brothers and sisters their own brothers and sisters possess (the test is successfully passed at the age of 10). The mistakes which go on after this age are therefore due to a shifting of these difficulties on to a new plane—that of reality imagined verbally. This is why the Binet-Simon test of the three brothers is not successful till the age of 11, the age of formal thought. If the test were played instead of being spoken, if the characters were given concrete form, the children would make no mistakes. But as soon as they are talked to, they become confused.

How do these difficulties come to be shifted from the plane of action to the verbal plane ? In other words, why does the mere fact of speaking a relation cause those difficulties to reappear which had been disposed of on the plane of action ? We do not think that the difficulty is only one of visualizing or imagining situations which in action the subject was able to perceive as such. There is more in it than that. The difficulty is one of conscious realization. For the child to be able to distinguish the adult verbal expressions which definitely characterize membership (we are three brothers) from those which denote relation (I have two brothers), something more is needed than simply to be able to imagine the different points of view ; the subject must have quite definitely and consciously become aware of a distinction which, though it may play a part in his actions, can do so without necessarily obtruding itself upon his notice. This is why language is so important. It is the index of what has become conscious, and too much care cannot be taken in the study of the verbal forms used by the child. In themselves they mean nothing, and one must beware of taking them literally. Thus, when a boy of 10, for example, tells us : " *You are not a brother*," or a girl of 4 : " *I am my sister*," it would be idle to find more in such statements than simple confusion. But in their current use such verbal forms are significant. If we look at them in a negative light, as it were, and not in regard to their positive contents, they point to logical difficulties ; they show that the child has not yet consciously realized the difference existing between operations which on the practical plane he perhaps finds it quite easy to keep separate.

And this is why, even if the difficulties relating to immediate judgments such as " I have *x* brothers " and " My brother Paul has *x* brothers " tend to disappear towards the age of 7-8, and have vanished at the age of 10, these same difficulties may very easily reappear on the verbal plane and prevent the Binet-Simon test of the three brothers from being passed before the age of 11, *i.e.* before the age of formal and discursive thought.

In this connexion—and this is our second remark—it might be interesting to enquire for what purpose the child uses such expressions as ' have ' (I *have* two brothers) or ' my ' (*my* brothers) or ' of ' (the brother *of*)—all of them forms which denote relations in adult speech, and which must consequently have a peculiar meaning for the child.

Now it is obvious that our enquiries confirm the results which we obtained on another occasion : [1] the child still confuses the three different meanings of the term ' of '— the possessive, the attributive, and the partitive.

When a child between 7 and 9 is asked what is meant by the expression " Part of my posy is yellow " or " Some of my flowers are yellow," he will generally answer, even though he knows that a part is a fraction, that the posy is entirely yellow and that it is made of a part which is yellow. " The part that is with the posy " is a childish expression which we meet with occasionally, and which expresses just this peculiarity that the posy and the part are one and the same thing (the part being thought of simply as an object which is incomplete or isolated from the whole).

If we analyse these phenomena we discover further that the three meanings of the genitive ' of ' are still further confused in the following manner : 1° the partitive sense (half *of* the cake) ; 2° the possessive sense (the hat *of* the gentleman) ; and the attributive sense (the nature *of* God). Thus the child understands ' Some of my flowers ' in the way in which one says ' the shape *of* the posy,' the shape belonging to the posy though it is inseparable from it. This undifferentiated childish relation we have named the relation of *property*.

Now this phenomenon, apparent in the preposition ' of ' can be recognized in the use of the relation ' to have '. For in the use of language the two relations ' of ' and ' to have ' are equivalent. One can say " The nature *of* the man " or " The man *has* a nature . . .," etc. The verb ' to have ' also denotes sometimes a possessive (I *have* a hat), sometimes an attributive relation (That line *has* a length of 3 m.), sometimes a partitive relation (this cake *has* six pieces) ; or it can mark the

[1] J. Piaget, *Journ. de Psych.*, 1921, vol. 18, p. 470 sq.

relation between the parts of the same whole (I *have* three colleagues, I *have* a brother, etc.).

And the child, in effect, sometimes says : " I have three brothers " instead of " We are three brothers," or " I am my sister," and in this he is confusing the possessive relation with the attributive (taken in its widest sense) ; sometimes, as when he says, " I have two brothers," but denies to each of his brothers the possibility of having more than one brother, the relation is almost that of possession (as when one says " I have a father, but I am not a father "), and not that holding between the several units of one and the same whole.

CHAPTER III

THE GROWTH OF RELATIVITY IN IDEAS AND NOTIONS

> Yet let me ask you one more question in order to
> illustrate my meaning, added Socrates : " Is not a
> brother to be regarded essentially as a brother of some-
> thing ?—Certainly, replied Agathon.—That is, of a
> brother or sister ?—Yes." PLATO, *Symposium.*

THE last chapter gave us some idea of the importance
attaching to the logic of relations, since a simple relationship like that of brother still presented insurmountable
difficulties to the child of 9–10. The sequel will show us
anew that childish realism, *i.e.* the inability to grasp the
relativity of notions or ideas is one of the principal
obstacles to the development of childish reasoning.
For this realism stands in the way of that gradual improve-
ment in deductive power which would free the child from
the immediate ready-made reality of particular cases
which have nothing to do with each other. Before going
on to examine these consequences of realism, it will be
well to investigate some new data taken fresh from
the child's actual experience, and not drawn from what
are, after all, very artificial tests, such as those which we
have been analysing. We shall set out to verify the hypotheses put forward in connexion with the three brothers
test, by questioning the children of 4 to 12 about their
own brothers and sisters. We shall also study (in the same
children) the evolution of the notion of right and left,
which is an extremely interesting part of the logic of
relations ; then in a second part of the chapter we shall
study the definitions given of the notions of family and
country.

I. Some Tests in the Logic of Relations.[1]

When a certain number of children have been examined in conversation, one by one, the quality of the answers has always been obtained at the expense of their quantity, and the hypotheses which we proposed in the course of our study of the three brothers test needed to be verified by very extensive statistics. To this end we examined more than 200 children between 4 and 12 (180 of whom had brothers and sisters), following in our method the procedure of the test, *i.e.* asking a certain number of *ne varietur* questions in a fixed order. (This of course does not exclude making sure that the child has understood the question, so as to eliminate answers due to mere inattention and not to a fault of logic.)

Three of our previously reached conclusions will have to be verified in this statistical manner.

In the first place, when a child is questioned about his own brothers and sisters the answers given point to the same difficulties as were called forth by the test of the three brothers. We must now ascertain up to what point this phenomenon is universal, and whether the age when it appears corresponds in some measure—and when due allowance has been made for verbal difficulties—to the ages at which the Binet-Simon test is unsuccessful.

In the second place, we have interpreted these difficulties as due to the ego-centrism of child thought. The child reasons from his own point of view, and is unable to place himself at that of his brothers and sisters. This cause is obvious in the case of the child's own family, but we have extended it to cover cases in which the child talks about any family of which he is told the composition and about which he is asked to reason. It will be well to confirm the fact that these are two difficulties of the same order by showing, for instance, that the right solution of questions about the child's own family and that of ques-

[1] With the collaboration of Mlles Sophie Escher, Ulrike Hanhart, and Suzanne Perret.

tions about any family are correlative, *i.e.* are given at the same age.

Finally, we have extended this explanation of the child's inability to handle the judgment of relation by applying it to ideas which are apparently removed from the influence of ego-centricity, such as the ideas of colour, etc. In studying relations such as those of right and left, it will have to be shown that from the point of view of logical structure these relations develop along the same lines as were traced by the evolution of the brother and sister relations.

§ 1. METHOD OF EXPERIMENT AND NUMERICAL RESULTS. —We carried out individual examinations on about 240 children between 4 to 12, of whom 100 were girls, and we asked them the twelve following questions in the given order.

I. *Brothers and Sisters.*

1. How many brothers have you ?   And how many sisters ?   [Let us suppose that the child has a brother A and a sister B.]   And how many brothers has A ?   And how many sisters?   And how many brothers has B ? And how many sisters ?

2. How many brothers are there in the family ?   How many sisters ?   How many brothers and sisters altogether ?

3. There are three brothers in a family : Auguste, Alfred, and Raymond.   How many brothers has Auguste ? And Alfred ?   And Raymond ?

4. Are you a brother [or a sister] ?   What is a brother [or sister, according to the sex of the child] ?

5. Ernest has three brothers, Paul, Henry, and Charles. How many brothers has Paul ?   And Henry ?   And Charles ?

6. How many brothers are there in this family ?

II. *Right and Left.*

7. Show me your right hand.   Your left.   Show me your right leg.   Now your left.

8. Show me my right hand.   Now my left.   Show me my right leg, now my left.   [During these questions the experimenter must sit opposite the child.]

9. [A coin is placed on the table to the left of a pencil in relation to the child.] Is the pencil to the right or to the left ? And the penny ?

10. [The child is opposite the experimenter, who has a coin in his right hand and a bracelet on his left arm.] You see this penny. Have I got it in my right hand or in my left ? And the bracelet ?

11. [The child is opposite three objects in a row : a pencil to the left, a key in the middle, and a coin to the right.] Is the pencil to the left or to the right of the key ? And of the penny ? Is the key to the left or to the right of the penny ? And of the pencil ? Is the penny to the left or the right of the pencil ? And of the key ? [Six answers altogether.]

12. [The same questions as before with three objects in a row opposite the child, a key to the left, a piece of paper in the middle, and a pencil to the right. But the objects are only shown for half a minute and are then covered over with a copy-book, and the answers are taken down. The child is told] : Now listen, I am going to show you three things only for a tiny moment. You must look very carefully, and then afterwards tell me by heart how the things are arranged. Look out . . . (the experiment) . . . . Well now, is the key left or right of the piece of paper ? And of the pencil ? Etc.

When the answers are sorted out, no mistakes must be overlooked. None of the 12 tests can be considered as passed unless all the questions in it are correctly answered. (Naturally the decisive answer is the only one that counts when the child himself corrects any initial mistake due to inattention.) There are therefore no half mistakes. For in the questions of left and right the chances are two to one that the child will be right if he answers at random. In certain of the questions on brothers and sisters he stands a very good chance of answering correctly without paying attention. So that any test in which only one or two points are passed must be considered unsuccessful. For instance, if the child passes only in 2 or 4 out of the 6 points in test 11, then he has failed in test 11, unless of course he corrects himself in time. Naturally the experimenter must take his time so as to eliminate inattention, and he may even divide the examination into two or three parts when there are signs of fatigue on the part of the subject. Moreover, one should not ask very young children questions which are obviously beyond them, except of course where they show special aptitude.

For question 4 to be considered properly solved the child must state in one form or another that in order to be a brother one must oneself have a brother or a sister. It goes without saying that tests 1 and 2 cannot be applied to an only child.

Here, then, are the results to which all this led us. We have followed the accepted custom of considering a test successfully passed when at least 75% of the children of the same age have answered correctly.

Age.	Tests passed.
4	0.
5	Test **7**.
6	Tests **2** and 7.
7	Tests 2, 7, and **9**.
8	Tests 2, **3**, 7, **8**, 9, and **10**.
9	Tests 2, 3, **4**, 7, 8, 9, and 10.
10	Tests **1**, 2, 3, 4, **5**, 6, 7, 8, 9, and 10.
11	Tests 1–10, and **11**.
12	Tests 1–**12**.

We had hoped to discover a test of aptitude as well as one of age by sorting out the materials by the method of percentages, but we were prevented from publishing these results by two circumstances. In the first place we did not interview a sufficient number of children to establish homogeneous percentages, but above all we realized that there is no correlation between tests 1–7 and tests 7–12. The correlation varies according to age from 0 or even —0·2 to about 0·5. This means that we cannot use these tests as tests of aptitude, and that each answer is conditioned by personal circumstances, such as the number of the subject's brothers or sisters. At the same time it is obvious that if we confine ourselves to purely statistical considerations, the use of these tests is perfectly legitimate. The fact that there is no correlation among the individual answers is no reason for neglecting the conclusion that *on an average*, tests 1 and 5 or tests 8 and 10, which taken in pairs have the same logical meaning, are passed at the same ages respectively : the age of 10 for tests 1 and 5 and the age of 8 for tests 8 and 10.

Let us now turn to the analysis of what results we have obtained.

§ 2. BROTHERS AND SISTERS.—The first thing to note about these tests is that they are genuine tests of age, *i.e.* that the percentage of right answers given to each question increases regularly with age.

Here are the results of test 1 :

Years .	4–5	6–7	8–9	10–11	12
Percentage .	19%	24%	55%	87%	100%

Thus test 1, which is of particular interest to us as presenting a difficulty analogous to that of the Binet-Simon test, is solved unanimously only at the age of 12, and by 75% of the subjects only at the age of 11. There is no need for us to repeat the qualitative analyses of the wrong answers. All the observed cases were found to be identical with those which we quoted in Chapter II, § 3 (Raoul, Jacq, etc.). So that up to the age of 10, 75% of the children are incapable, through their inability to leave their own point of view, of saying how many brothers and sisters their own brothers and sisters possess. At the age of 8 only half the children succeed in doing so. This is an excellent confirmation of the value of the Binet-Simon test.

Question 2 (the number of children in the family) is far easier, since it is solved from the age of 6 by 75% of the subjects. The big difference existing between questions 1 and 2 thus confirms the usefulness of the distinction between the logic of classes (membership) and that of relations, and it shows how much easier is the former than the latter. For the child has far oftener had occasion to

H

take up the point of view of his family as a whole than that of each one of his brothers and sisters. It is to be noted, however, that up to the age of 10 there are a number of mistakes arising from the fact that the child does not count himself among his brothers and sisters, which is one of the commonest forms of the realistic delusion of children.

One curious thing is that among very young children it is not always the same who answer questions 1 and 2 correctly. In other words, the children who pass test 1 do not all necessarily pass test 2. But from the age of 8–9 it is different. It is not till the age of 10 that children are able to say simultaneously how many brothers and sisters there are in the family and how many brothers and sisters each member of the family has. Thus tests 1 and 2 combined give rise to difficulties which are identical with those of the Binet-Simon three brothers test. And since the latter is also not passed till the age of 10, we may conclude that our analysis of the materials supplied by this test is justified.

This impression will gain in strength if we now pass to an examination of the answers given by the child when he is questioned about a family other than his own by means of tests 3, 5, and 6.

Question 5 which has the same logical structure as question 1 (How many brothers have X and Y, etc.) gives comparable results. It also is solved at the age of 10. Below the age of 7, however, it yields less satisfactory results than question 1, which is only natural, considering the claim which it makes on the child's power of adaptation to such things as new names, etc. But after the age of 7–8 incidental circumstances cease to play an important part, and the logical difficulty alone comes into play, thus making this case analogous to that of test 1.

Question 6, on the other hand, is harder than question 2, and is solved only at the age of 10, like question 5, and not at the age 6, like question 2. But this is easy to explain. Before the interrogatory, the child has often thought about question 2 (the number of children in his family) and has done so independently of the point of view of each of his brothers. But question 6 calls for a certain effort of adaptation (new names, etc.) ; and above all it requires of the child that he should find the total sum of the brothers as a function of what he has just learned in connexion with question 5. Thus he will not add up the units directly as he does for his own family, but he will be forced to *construct* a judgment of membership with the judgments of relation taken from question 5. This construction is what constitutes the difficulty of test 6.

Tests 5 and 6 taken together reproduce, it should be noted, the difficulties of the Binet-Simon test, and it is once again only at the age of 10 that these tests (5 and 6) come to be solved.

Test 3, on the other hand, is solved from the age of 8. It is therefore easier than test 5 and even, curiously enough, than test 1. The only explanation of this seems to be the following. In the case of test 1 the child has more difficulty in entering into the point of view of his brothers than into that of the three brothers of the test 3, because in the case of his own family it is not enough for him to enter into the point of view of others, he must also look at himself from the point of view of others, which is twice as difficult. Now in test 5 the child is placed straight away at a privileged point of view, that of Ernest. The difficulty is therefore analogous in a sense to that of test 1. These considerations explain why test 3, which does not involve these peculiar difficulties, is found to be easier than test 1.

Be this as it may, the analogies presented by the results of tests 1, 5, and 6 are sufficient in themselves to confirm the interpretations given in Chapter II. It is the mental habits acquired in his reactions to his own brothers and sisters that explain the child's way of reasoning when he is dealing with purely logical problems such as the Binet-Simon test of the three brothers.

§ 3. DEFINITION OF THE WORD ' BROTHER ' (OR ' SIS-TER ').—We have one last counter-test to bring forward. If the difficulties we have described are really caused by an inability to handle the logic of relations, this same absence of relativity will have to be found in the definition of the word ' brother.' This will be shown to be the case by test 4.

In the first place it should be noted that the first part of the question (Are you a brother ?) hardly presents any difficulties after the age of 4–5. The correct definition, on the other hand, is not found till the age of 9, and by correct we mean that which implies in one way or another the idea that in order to be a brother one must have a brother or a sister.

The most primitive definitions consist simply in saying that a brother is a boy.

Jo (age 5) considers that a brother is ' a little boy.'— " Are all boys brothers ?—*Yes.*—Has your father got a brother ? — *Yes, and a sister.* — Why is your father a brother ?—*Because he is a man.*"

Lo (age 5) g. : " *A sister is a girl you know.*—Are all the girls you know sisters ?—*Yes, and all the boys are brothers.*"

Ba (6 ; 10) g. : " A sister is *a girl.*—Are all girls sisters ? —*Yes.*—Am I a sister ?—*No.*—How do you know that I am not a sister.—*I don't know.*—But I have got a sister, then aren't I her sister ?—*Oh yes.*—What is a sister ?— *A girl.*—What must you have to be a sister ?—*I don't know.*" (Ba has two sisters and a brother.)

Pi (age 6) : " A brother is *a boy.*—Are all boys brothers ? —*Because some of them are little.*—If anyone is little isn't he a brother ?—*No, you can only be a brother if you are big.*"

This is all the more curious because Pi has just said that he himself was not a brother. " Why not ?—*Because I haven't got any others, because I am alone.*" Implicitly, he seems to know what a brother is, but he has not become sufficiently conscious of the necessary characteristics to be able to give a definition. In such cases question 4 is naturally marked *correct.* But what shows very clearly that the conscious realization involved in definition is the thing to go by is that Pi is no better at handling the notion of brother than he was at defining it. He answers question 3 by saying that Auguste "*perhaps has two*" brothers, Alfred "*three*," and Raymond "*four*." Question 5 he answers by saying that Paul "*perhaps had three brothers*," Henry "*one*," Charles "*four*," and there were altogether (question 6) three brothers in the family.

Sob (age 7) considers that all boys are brothers.—" Is your father a brother ?—*Yes, when he was little.*—Why was your father a brother ?—*Because he was a boy.*—Do you know your father's brother ?—*He hasn't got a brother* (or a sister)."

Kan (age 7½) : " *It's a boy.*—Are all boys brothers ?— *Yes.*—Is your father a brother ?—*No.*—Why ?—*Because he is a man.*—Isn't your father a brother ?—*Yes.*—Why ? —*Because he used to be the same as little boys.*"

Bo (age 8) : A brother, "*why, that's a boy, it is some-one.*—Are all boys brothers ?—*Yes, and then there are cousins and nephews as well.*—Has your father got a brother ?—*Yes.*—Why is your father a brother ?—*I don't know.*—What must you have to be a brother ?—*I don't know. That's very hard.*"

Po (8½) g. : " *A sister is a girl.*—Are all girls sisters ?— *Yes.*—Are you sure ?—. . . *A sister is a girl.*—Aren't there some girls who are not sisters ?—*No.*"

Pon (age 9) and X (age 10) also consider that all boys are brothers.

A second stage in definition is reached by those subjects who know that in order to be a brother there must be several in the family, but who do not assign the title to all the children.

So (age 8) is not sure if he is a brother (he is an only child). A brother : *That's when someone has a child, well the child who comes next is a brother.*" So cannot answer either question 5 or question 6. Question 3 on the other hand is correctly solved.

Hal (age 9) : " *When there is a boy and another boy, when there are two of them.*—Has your father got a brother ? —*Yes.*—Why ?—*Because he was born second.*—Then what is a brother ?—*It is the second brother that comes.*—Then the first is not a brother ?—*Oh no. The second brother that comes is called brother.*" It would be impossible to show more clearly the absence of relativity from the word ' brother.'

There are other kinds of false definition, but they have no logical interest because they are simply incomplete :

Cour (age 9) : *" A brother is a little person who lives with us.*—Are all the boys who are with you brothers ?—*No, it must be a boy who is always with us."*

Pon (age 9) : *" A brother is a boy who is in the same flat."* In such cases the child should be probed in other ways so as to find out whether or not he has realized that it is a question of children being in the same family.

The correct definition is therefore that which implies the idea that there must be at least two in the same family for there to be a brother or sister. The child often knows this without being able to express it straight away, in which case he must be helped to make his idea explicit. There is a good proportion of such correct definitions from the age of 7 onwards (average of 60%).

Mi (7½) : A brother is *" a boy.*—Are all boys brothers ?—*Yes.*—Is a boy who is the only one in the family a brother ?—*No.*—Why are you a brother ?—*Because I have sisters.*—Am I a brother ?—*No.*—How do you know ?—*Because you are a man.*—Has your father got brothers ?—*Yes.*—Is he a brother ?—*Yes.*—Why ?—*Because he had a brother when he was little.*—Tell me what a brother is.—*When there are several children in a family."*

We were perhaps helping the child too much when we asked " Is a boy who is the only one in the family a brother," but here are other cases.

Fal (age 7) : " Are all boys brothers ?—*Yes.*—All of them ?—*No, there are some who have no sisters. To be a brother you must have a sister."*

Fa (age 7) : " Are all boys brothers ?—*There must be two boys together, a mother and two boys."*

Sait (age 7) : *" A brother is a little boy who has another little boy with him."*

Rey (age 10) : *" A brother, why, that's when there are two children."* Bern (age 10) : *" A brother is a relation, one brother to another."*

It is a remarkable thing that there is no noticeable difference between only children and others.

Although they are not directly derived from the judgment of relation, these definitions furnish a very useful counter-test by showing us that the relativity of the notion of brother comes to be realized very slowly. At first the notion is not relative at all : one is a brother as one is a boy, in the absolute sense of the term. During the second stage, relativity is guessed at, but the child still indulges in specifications, singling only one child out of the family and thus making all genuine relativity impossible. The peculiar interest which this second stage possesses for us will now be clear, since it gives a clue to the strange calculations indulged in by children of the first and fourth types in connexion with the Binet-Simon test. If, in the subject's opinion, all the children in a family are not brothers, then it is only natural that each brother should not have the same number of brothers as the others. Anyhow, such specifications in the notion of brother are sufficient to prevent the formation of any correct judgment of relation. Finally, the fact that the correct definition does not appear on an average until the age of 9 will enable us to understand why such simple tests as 1 and 5 are not passed until after this age.

§ 4. RIGHT AND LEFT.—We must now look for the third confirmation which we had hoped to find, and see whether the progress made by the child in handling a notion like that of right and left is also due to the gradually decreasing ego-centrism of thought, as was the case in the brother relation. And we shall do this by showing that the idea of right and left in so far as it is a relative notion passes three successive stages which correspond to three successive points in the desubjectification or socialization of thought : the first stage (5–8) in which left and right are considered only from the child's own point of view ; the second (8–11) in which they are also considered from that of the other person, of the person who is speaking to him ; finally, the third stage (11–12), which marks the moment when right and left are also considered from the point of view of the things themselves. Now these

three stages correspond exactly to the three social stages
we established before : the age of 7–8 marks the decline
of primitive ego-centrism and that of 11–12 the discovery
of formal thought which reasons from every point of view
at once. But let us turn to the facts before us.

The Binet-Simon tests tell us that the age of 6 is that
at which a child can show his left hand and his right ear.
But this does not necessarily mean that at that age right
and left are known and handled *as relations*. These
notions may very well still be ' absolute,' *i.e.* there may
be a left and a right ' in themselves,' just as for the Greeks
there was a ' high ' and a ' low ' independently of weight.
The child's own body would naturally determine this
absolute right and left to begin with, and an enormous
amount of adaptation would still be necessary before the
child could realize, first that there was a right and left
for every one else, and later that objects themselves can
be to the right or the left of each other even though their
disposition in space is relative to us.

Now this is exactly what our experiments proved to be
the case. We began by trying to find out at what age
the child knew *his* left and *his* right hand (test 7). In
the poorer districts of Geneva in which we worked it
was at the age of 5, according to the 75% rule, which it
is customary to use.[1] But the following fact is evidence
that at this age left and right are only the names for a
particular hand or a particular leg, and that the child is
incapable of bringing these notions into relation with the
different points of view of his interlocutors. When the
experimenter stands opposite the child and says : " Show
me your left hand. . . . etc." (test 8),nearly three-quarters
of the children are unable to do so. This test is not passed
until the age of 8. Seeing the importance of this question,
we decided to control the result by means of another test.

[1] It is interesting to note that according to Decroly's test (a Loto
game in which the counters have to be moved to the right or the left),
studied by Mlle Descœudres at Geneva (*Le développement de l'enfant
de deux à sèpt ans*, Delachaux et Niestlé, 1922, p. 219), the age of
correct orientation is also 5¼.

Now test 10 contains exactly the same problem under a different wording ; and here again it is at the age of 8 that it comes to be solved. We can therefore say that it is only at the age of 8 that the child is able to place himself at the point of view of others with regard to left and right, *i.e.* three years after having succeeded in dealing with these notions from his own point of view. And, be it said once again, it is precisely at the age of 7–8 that ego-centrism undergoes a considerable diminution (L.T., Chap. I).

The relativity of left and right in connexion with the actual objects emerges far more slowly, and here again we must beware of being misled by appearances when we begin to question the children. Thus question 9 (finding whether a coin is to the right or the left of a pencil) is solved at the age of 7 (nearly 70% at the age of 6). But it is obvious that in such cases the child is judging objects only in relation to himself. The adult does the same, and all logicians know that the notions of right and left cannot be defined without referring implicitly or explicitly to the position of one's own body. But the difference is that when the coin and the pencil are presented to the adult, he will say that the coin is *to the left of the pencil*, whereas the child will simply say that it is *to the left*, in the absolute sense of the word. The shade of difference is not verbal but from the logical point of view essential, and its importance is proved by the fact that the child does not pass test 11 before the age of 11 precisely because he does not understand the expression *to the left of* as applied to the relation between two objects. The success of test 9 at the age of 7 is therefore in no way a proof that the child has realized the relativity of the ideas of right and left in connexion with objects taken by themselves.[1]

One ought to have asked the child—this did not occur

[1] M. H. Delacroix has observed data which tally completely with ours. *Cf. Le Langage et la Pensée*, Alcan 1924, foot-note on p. 550. We take this opportunity of expressing our regret at not having been able to deal in these pages with M. Delacroix's admirable volume which was published after we had gone to press.

to us until after the experiment had been completed—
to go to the other side of the table after having said that
the coin was to the left of the pencil and to have added,
" Now is the penny to the left or to the right of the pencil ? "
It would be interesting to repeat the experiment along
these lines. The proof of the non-relativity of the notions
of right and left is therefore supplied by the results of tests
11 and 12. By placing three objects in a row before the
child and asking him to state exactly how these objects
stand to one another, we force him to discover the relativity of the ideas of position. The key, which is between
the coin and the pencil, can no longer be said to be ' to the
right ' or ' to the left ' in the absolute sense of the word ;
it is to the right *in relation to* the coin and to the left *in
relation to* the pencil. Left to himself, the child will say
that the key is ' in the middle,' but we then ask him
more explicitly : " Is the key to the left or to the right of
the penny? And of the pencil? " If the child is not accustomed to make use of the notions of left and right in
relation to objects taken by themselves, this expression
' to the left *of*' will be unintelligible to him. And this is
precisely what proves to be the case in experiment.
This test is not passed till the age of 11. At 9 only about
15% of the children understand it at all.

The age of 11 is therefore very important as marking
complete assimilation of the notion of right and left as
applied to objects in themselves. Test 12, it is true, is
not passed until a year later, but this interval is easy to
explain. For test 12, having the same logical structure
as test 11, calls in addition for retention of the data by
means of a certain topographical memory (knowing the
position of three objects in a row which have been presented for half a minute). It is simply a matter of imagining the relations instead of merely seeing them.

It is interesting to note that tests 11 and 12 supply a
complete confirmation of the results previously obtained
by means of Burt's test, and which were summarized in
Chapter II, § 4 : " Edith is fairer than Suzanne ; Edith is

darker than Lili. Which is the darkest of the three,
Edith, Suzanne, or Lili ? " Now this test bearing upon
colour and our tests 11 and 12 have exactly the same
logical structure, viz. the comparison of the middle unit
of a series of three to the two extreme members of the
series. We have been criticized however for making use
of this test of Burt's, for it is one that requires a considerable effort of attention, even on the part of adults, if
the phenomena which it brings under observation are
to belong to the psychology of logical relations and not
merely to the psychology of attention. Our answer
to this was to point to the facts and to show how once
the child has read the test often enough, once he has it
sufficiently engraved upon his mind and difficulties of
attention no longer exist, the logical difficulty still subsists
of understanding how a little girl can be at the same time
fairer than a second and darker than a third. We are
now, moreover, in a position to give a still better answer
to prove the child's inability to deal with the logic of
relations, and that is the answer suggested by tests
11 and 12, or at least by test 11 alone. This test is very
simple from the point of view of attention. To begin with,
it must be played instead of being spoken, *i.e.* the child
has the objects before his eyes as he speaks. In the
second place—and this is most important—there is no
need during the whole of this test for the child to think
of the three objects at once. He is asked six successive
questions, which he answers separately : " Is the pencil
to the left or to the right of the key ? . . . etc." At
the same time this test has the same logical structure as
that about the colour of the girl's hair.

Now the answers obtained were found to be the exact
equivalents of those obtained by means of the Burt test.
In the first place, the Burt test is successful on the average
between the years of 11 and 13, if the child is given time
to think ; and this age corresponds with that of our tests
11 and 12. But the analogy is most striking from the
point of view of the mechanism of the answers. In

the case of the colours, the child's fallacy (in logical parlance) consists in treating the relations, 'fairer than,' etc.
as judgments of membership (Edith is fair or dark,
Suzanne is fair, Lili is dark). Exactly the same thing
happens in the case of the right and left. The child asserts
that the coin is to the right and the pencil to the left, but
these terms are not in any sense relational. Consequently
in the case of the colours the child does not know what to
do about Edith—she is both fair and dark! Similarly
in the present case the child cannot understand how the
key (the middle object) can be both to the left of the coin
and to the right of the pencil. He simply states it to be
'in the middle.' If he is forced to be more precise and is
made to say whether the key is to the left of the coin,
he will also say that it is to the left of the pencil. If one
begins with the pencil, and the child pronounces the key
to be to the right of the pencil, he will answer the question :
" Is the key to the left or to the right of the penny ? "
by saying that the key is also to the right. In a word, the
key is to the left or to the right in the absolute sense of the
word, and cannot be both at the same time. Thus the
analogy is complete between Burt's test and our tests
11 and 12. The evolution of the ideas of right and left
is as complex as that of other relative notions, and obeys
exactly the same laws.

What conclusion can we draw from these facts ? Do
they admit of the proposed explanation which consists
in tracing the non-relational character of childish ideas
back to the ego-centricity of thought ? It would seem that
we can. There are three very definite stages in this evolution of right and left. During the first the child places
himself at his own point of view, during the second at
the point of others, and during the third at a completely
relational point of view in which account is taken of objects
in themselves. The process is therefore precisely that of
the gradual socialization of thought—ego-centrism, socialization, and finally complete objectivity. The curious
thing is that the three stages are determined by ages

which happen to correspond to the ages of important changes in the child's social life, viz. 7–8, diminution of ego-centrism, and 11–12, the stage of rules and of thought which has become sufficiently formal to reason from all given points of view. Later on we shall show that these three stages also mark three phases in the development of reasoning properly so-called : ' transduction ', primitive deduction, and completed deduction.

Even if these ages come to be modified by subsequent research, the order in which the stages follow on one another will remain the same, and this order of succession is the only important consideration for general psychology.

II. Some Definitions of the Ideas of Family and Country given by Boys between Seven and Ten.[1]

So far we have been examining the difficulties felt by the child in thinking about and handling ideas as apparently simple in character as those of brother and sister, right and left, which difficulties were found to proceed from the child's inability at a certain age to grasp the relational character of these ideas. The following sections though extending over a realm of subjects apparently unconnected with the logic of relations will serve nevertheless as a complementary study. In the family we touch upon a notion closely related to that of brother and sister ; and we shall see how children come to grips with the relational idea of family kinship. In the definition of country, town, or district we are faced with difficulties arising from the relation of part to whole which is again a relation of fundamental importance for the child. Finally, between the idea of family and that of country there are connexions which will appear more or less clearly, for both are bound up with the idea of a group or whole.

We need hardly tell the reader that our enquiry was never thought out in so systematic a fashion. Otherwise,

[1] With the collaboration of Mlle Lisa Hahnloser.

we might rightly be suspected of having forced the facts. On the contrary, our results were obtained, as before, through an accident of research. M. Bovet, in search of information on the social conceptions of children, had asked in the classes for definitions of such words as *country*, *family*, *uncle*, *cousin*, *stranger*. About 200 'children between the ages of 8 and 10 answered these questions. But instead of answers with affective tone, he obtained hardly anything but verbal answers requiring analysis. We carried out this analysis on about 30 boys from 7 to 10 who were examined individually. In the case of each definition we followed the line of thought adopted by the child, using conversation to get beyond the purely verbal character of the process.

Children's definitions are always interesting, but they are not easy to interpret, for all definition is conscious realization. Now Claparède's law of conscious realization (*prise de conscience*) tells us that the more automatically an idea is handled, the harder is the process of its conscious realization. Ask even an educated adult what is the difference between ' because ' and ' since ' ! Even though he is perfectly capable of assigning different though slightly overlapping uses to these terms, this does not mean that he can realize the difference straight away. And even though children are perfectly capable of only using the words ' uncle ' or ' country ' in sentences which make sense, this does not mean that they can define these words. That is why, in studying a child's definition, a careful distinction should be made between conscious realization and the actual idea which the child possessed unconsciously in a sense, or at any rate implicitly, but was unable to express.

It is our belief, with this reservation, that the ideas of country and family are still verbal between the ages of 7 and 9. This means that the actual idea which the child possesses implicitly and of which he becomes more and more aware as he comes to define it, is an idea occasioned by adult thought and not by direct or spontaneous experience.

To put it in another way, the child is constantly hearing the words ' country,' ' family,' etc. and he makes them correspond to a certain more or less syncretistic schema in which he incorporates an image ; and it is not the image that has given rise to the schema but conversely. Our study will therefore be concerned with verbal intelligence and not with concrete or practical intelligence, *i.e.* that which is directly brought into play by observation of the external world.

For by verbal thought we mean the child's faculty for adapting himself, not to actual reality, but to the words and expressions heard in the mouths of adults and other children and through which he tries to imagine reality. And just because verbal thought is partly divorced from reality, the pedagogue must refrain from cultivating it in the child, except with certain necessary precautions. But to the psychologist it is of the greatest interest, often showing as it does the schematism of the child's thought more clearly than in the case of concrete ideas. When the child hears the word country, for example, he is free to entertain what idea he chooses, and what idea he chooses to entertain is far less dependent than one would think upon environment. Whatever the child has heard, since it is not bound up with any concrete perception, is distorted and selected from according to laws of thought peculiar to each stage in the child's development. It will be sufficient for our purpose if we know exactly what we are doing in dealing with verbal thought, and if we distinguish this form of mental activity very clearly from that which is the direct outcome of perception.

§ 5. THE FAMILY.—It is our intention to show that definitions of the family supply a useful counter-test of the conclusions of our study of the brother and sister relation, in as much as before the age of 10 these definitions take no account of the blood-relationship. These definitions go through three stages. During the first stage the child calls family all the people who live with him, he is not interested in blood-relationship and defines the family by the house or the name. In the second stage the child makes use of the idea of blood-relationship, but limits the family to those members of it who are in his immediate vicinity. Finally, in the third stage, the definition is generalized so as to include all blood-relations.

Here are examples of the first stage :
Bet (age 7) :   "*It means people who live together in the same flat.*" Uncles and aunts are not in the family. Bet questions the fact of the experimentor having a family. Jacq (age 7) : "*It means people, it means that there are lots of people.*" This definition has the same meaning as the first.

Ku (7 ; 7) : A family is "*when they are all together.*— Is this a family ?—*No, when they both have the same family name.*" But cousins and aunts are not in the family "*because they do not live with us.*—If your aunt lived with you would you say she was in the family ?—*Yes.*"

Bus (8 ; 6) gives the same definition. A cousin does not belong to the family. "*If he was in the family he would live with us.*—If I lived with you, would I be in the family ?—*Yes.*" The grandmother is in the family "*because she used to live with daddy.*" This last remark belongs implicitly to the second stage, although the only explicit appeal is to the fact of ' living with.'

Bon (age 9) denies that his brother is in the family : "*No, he is in Savoy.*" Then after a little reflection he widens the scope of the family : "*He is in the family but he is in Savoy.*" The ' but ' shows clearly that Bon sticks to his original conception, otherwise the phrase would have no meaning. Bon's grandfather is not in the family but in the family of Bon's father, "*because when [my father] was little he lived with grand-papa.*" (Same remark as Bus.)

Lev (10 ; 9) defines the family by saying : "*They are all in the same flat.*" Then he adds the idea of a common name.

We need not multiply our examples. At this stage the child defines the family by the circumstance of living together, with or without addition of a clause about a common name. Cousins, grandparents, and brothers are in the family when they live with the child and not otherwise. It must not be thought that children are ignorant of blood-relationship. A proof to the contrary is to be found in the definitions of the words ' cousin ' and ' uncle ' which we asked the children to give and which they supplied with varying degrees of generality, but always with accuracy : " An uncle is a brother of Father's or Mother's, etc." " A cousin is the son of an aunt, etc." But just as a child can know of which parents his brother is the son and yet not be led to the reciprocity of the relation of brother, so in attempting to define his family he gets no further than the point of view of the moment. Though he knows who are his real relations, he calls family only those who are actually near him. This realistic line of thought is worth noting, for though it does not lead in this case to actual ignorance of relations, it does at least explain how by pursuing just some such line of thought as this, many of the most serious delusions can arise out of childish realism. It will be remembered that the correct definition of the word ' brother ' was not given till the age of 9.

During the second stage the idea of relationship intervenes but does not yet supplant the fact of living together.

Matt (9 ; 3) defines his family: "*A father, a mother, and children.*" But neither his father nor his mother have a family. " *When daddy was little he had a family* " (*Cp.* Bon). Mar (9 ; 7) after having defined the family as " *It is parents,*" goes so far as to say that " *Daddy isn't quite in the family.*"

Viq (age 11, backward) : The family "*is a group of relations.*—How many are there in your family ? — *Three . . . in my family, but there can be more.*—Why three ?—*Those who have dinner together.*"

Chav (12 ; 9, backward) : The family " *is a succession of people.*—How many are there in your family ?—*Four, because my sister is away.*"

Vo (age 9), speaking about his grandfather, who is still living, makes the following remark which is worth noting : " *He was my mother's daddy.*"

Family relationships are therefore not yet thought of by the child as independent of time and place. Even

I

when the child refers explicitly to the idea of relationship, at the back of his mind he is still thinking of the family from the immediate or realistic point of view.

Finally, in the third stage the child discards this realism and defines the family solely by relationship, and at the same time he almost immediately substitutes the wider sense of family (grandparents, uncles, aunts and cousins) for its narrow denotation (parents and children).

Pro (age 8, forward) : " *It means all the relations together.*" Pio (12 ; 3) : It is " *a generation,*" etc.

In conclusion, this rapid sketch of the evolution of the definitions of the family confirms our analysis of the brother relation. Owing to his ego-centric habits of thought the child does not attempt to go beyond his immediate perception of things. The family is thought of as the whole collection of people who surround the child, independently of the idea of relationship. This immediate point of view is realistic in the sense that family kinship, not having been separated from the circumstances of time and place in which the child is living, is not yet conceived in the nature of a relation. And this immediate point of view is intimately connected with an indifference to existing relations, as has been sufficiently emphasized by our study of the brother relation.

As to the nature of this realism, which in this particular case seems to be exclusively visual, it looks as though the image of the flat or of ' living together ' were the predominant factor in the simple definitions we have enumerated. As a matter of fact, images are always present in the child's mind ; but this does not mean that we can describe his characteristic realism as visual, without any further qualifications. The whole problem is to know what the image replaces and what it stands for : causal relations, spatial relations, simple juxtaposition of terms thought of without synthesis, etc. Now, in the case of the

family the image, however visual, however remote from
the logical fact in question (family relationships), is none
the less comparable to the form of realism which leads
the child when he is drawing a bicycle, for example, to
replace spatial relations (symbolizing causal sequence)
by juxtaposition of the parts which are conceived as
simply ' going together.' In this connexion, to define the
family by saying " they all go together " is to give proof
of a realism comparable to the intellectual realism which
produces juxtaposition in the drawing.

The ages at which our three different stages are reached
are approximately 9 for the second and 11 for the third.
If subsequent research leaves these ages unaltered, it
will be desirable to establish synchronisms with the age
when the brother relation and relations in general are
properly handled.

§ 6. COUNTRY.—We have often had occasion, independently of the enquiry with which we are concerned
at present, to ask the school children whom we were
examining : " Are you Swiss ? " Very frequently the
answer was as follows : " No, I am Genevan.—Then you
are Swiss ?—No, I am Genevan.—But your father is
Swiss ?—No, he is Genevan." We then made it our
custom to ask : " Are you Genevan ? " But the child,
even if he comes from Geneva, will sometimes answer :
" No, I am Swiss." Finally we asked a large number
of Swiss schoolboys from all the cantons : " Are you
Genevan (or Vaudois, etc.) ? " then, " Are you Swiss ? "
or in the reversed order, then, " Can anyone be both
Swiss and Genevan ? " Up to the age of 9, three-quarters
of the children denied the possibility of being both Swiss
and Genevan (or Vaudois, etc.).

What does this come from ? Is it perhaps due to
local patriotism ? We never discovered any trace of it.
Neither the children from Geneva nor those from Neu-
chatel, the Vaux, the Valais, nor even from Berne showed
the slightest signs of pride of district. It was not because

they had thought about the question that the children answered it in the negative. It was simply one that had never occurred to them. Òften it even struck them as eccentric.

It may be suggested that this was due to ignorance, to defective information which would rob such judgments of all their interest. And indeed the claim might be made that since there is no school teaching as to what is meant by Switzerland and the cantons until the age of 9–10, the child talks of Switzerland as he would talk of China. It is a country that is ' further away.' But this is a point for experiment to decide. In certain cases (such as we shall meet with in the first stage) this claim may be conceded. When this happens, it is always interesting to ask the child what Switzerland or any other country is, just to see how much he has assimilated or selected of the snatches of conversation which he may have chanced to hear in his family or in the street. But the child's answer will be of no direct interest to logic. In other cases, however, it is quite obvious that the child has some exact information about Switzerland or about other countries, but his tendency to deny the possibility of being both Swiss and Genevan, survives the information. One boy tells us that Switzerland is "*all the cantons taken together.—*Then you are in Switzerland ?—*No."* Others will know that Geneva is in Switzerland, but deny that they themselves are Swiss. This second group of cases is therefore by far the more interesting, for we are faced here, not with a deficiency in information but with a difficulty of schematization.

The initial difficulty consists in creating a visual representation, a schema with the right connexions ; but even when this schema has been attained, the child has still to understand how it is that a part inserted into a whole really forms part of the whole, and that a man who is fixed inside the part remains none the less within the whole. The difficulty in question will perhaps be made clearer by the answer of this child Bel (9 ; 2), which may serve

as a prototype. Bel knows that Geneva is in Switzerland
and that Switzerland is bigger than Geneva, but he
cannot realize that even though one is in Geneva one is
nevertheless also in Switzerland. We then draw him a
large circle containing several small ones, and explain
that the big circle stands for Switzerland, and that one
of the little ones stands for Geneva, the other for Vaud, etc.
and we point out to him that by being in the little circle
one is also in the big circle. But he has so failed to grasp
the schema that when we ask him whether anyone can
be both Genevan and Vaudois he promptly answers yes,
since both Geneva and Vaud are in Switzerland.

In short, the child's difficulty arises from the fact that
he juxtaposes territories but does not connect them.
He realizes that Geneva is in Switzerland but not that it
' forms a part ' of Switzerland. The difficulty lies in the
relation of part to whole, and this is our reason for including the question of the definition of the word ' country '
in a chapter devoted to the child's use of relations.

Three stages mark the evolution of the idea of country.
During the first, country is simply a unit along with
towns and districts, and of the same magnitude as these.
Switzerland is therefore alongside of Geneva and Vaud.
During the second, town and districts are in the country
but do not form part of it. Thus Switzerland surrounds
Geneva and Vaud. These are in Switzerland but do
not really ' form part of ' Switzerland. Finally, in the
third stage the correct relation is discovered.

Here are some examples of the first stage :

Schla (7 ; 11) : A country " *is another town,*" Le Salève
is " *a mountain in another town,*" that is to say " *in a big
village, France, like la Chaux-de-Fonds.*" Savoy is " *a
smaller village.*" A town is " *a pile of houses.*" Schla
seems to give his answers out of pure ignorance. For
it is the most natural thing for the child, unless he has
been specially told the contrary, to juxtapose country,
towns, and villages on the same plane instead of making
them form part of one another. And the interesting thing
is that Schla knows how to use the correct verbal formulæ :

He tells us spontaneously that " *A town is part of a country.*" " *A country is for travelling.*—What is there in a country?—*Houses, gardens, trains, trams, people.*— And towns?—*Yes. . . . No.*"

In other words, Schla has heard enough to form a correct schematization. If the idea of part were really understood by the child, the expression " *the town forms part of the country* " would imply the enclosure of Geneva inside Switzerland. But the tendency to juxtaposition is too strong, and Schla goes on thinking of Geneva as alongside of Switzerland, and of countries as identical with towns.

Jacq (age 7) comes from Vaud, but thinks that one cannot be both Vaudois and Swiss. For him Switzerland is a district or a country on a level with Geneva. He knows, however, that a canton is bigger than a town. Like Schla he can use the correct verbal expressions, but fails nevertheless to reach the schematization of part and whole.

Bos (6 ; 9) can say that " *Geneva is in Switzerland,*" but he conceives Geneva, Switzerland, and France as juxtaposed cities. Switzerland is " *further away* " than Geneva.

Bus (age 8) presents a similar case. He also says that Geneva is in Switzerland. We make him a drawing of Geneva in the form of a circle and ask him to show us where Switzerland is. He then draws another circle alongside of the first. Switzerland is also " *further away.*"

Tié (age 10) is the same. Geneva is in Switzerland (but next to it). You cannot be both Genevan and Swiss, because the Swiss are " *in Switzerland.*"

These five examples are significant, as the children in question do not err through lack of information. They know how to make use of the correct verbal formulæ, but they translate them into a schema of juxtaposition. Of course there are in addition to these all the children who do not spontaneously use these formulæ, and in whom juxtaposition is simply the result of ignorance. For this schema is after all the most economical. It would even be strange if children were to begin by seeking for a hierarchy of part to whole among the units they hear named—Switzerland, Geneva, Vaud, France, etc., instead of simply juxtaposing them so as to make a collection of towns, whether contiguous or otherwise. The interesting thing, however, is that this schematism of juxtaposition, natural as it is, should be sufficient to hamper verbal adaptation in the child, *i.e.* should prevent him from understanding expressions used around him and from which he would otherwise have derived correct notions of reality. Nearly three-quarters of the children at this stage, even if they are not as explicit as Schla, are able to say that Geneva "is in Switzerland." But even so, the habit of juxtaposition proves strongest, so that Switzerland is imagined as situated "further away" than the cantons.

During the second stage we meet with an even more curious conflict between the tendency to juxtaposition and the relation of part to whole. Geneva is now definitely "in Switzerland," actually and not merely verbally; only—and the interest of the phenomenon lies here—Geneva does not form part of Switzerland, it is like a piece of land enclosed in a foreign country, and one cannot be both Genevan and Swiss at the same time. The paradox is of course not always as clearly marked as this, and along with the unmistakable cases there are a great many that are vague and fluctuating. In the following examples, however, the phenomenon is quite obvious.

Stu (7 ; 8) says that "*Geneva is in Switzerland*," and that "*Switzerland is bigger* [than Geneva]." But Genevans are not Swiss. "Then where must you come from to be Swiss ?—*From Switzerland*." We draw a circle representing Switzerland, and ask Stu to put the cantons in their places. Instead of alongside of it (like Bus) Stu inscribes within the circle three or four smaller ones—Geneva, Vaud, etc., but he still maintains that Genevans are not Swiss people. The Swiss are the inhabitants of the big circle.

Max (9 ; 7) is not familiar with the nomenclature, and makes of a country "*a part of a canton*." But even so,

it is obvious that he applies the partitive relation to
countries, at any rate in his language. " *It is Switzerland
at Geneva, no rather Geneva is in Switzerland.*" But this
is a purely verbal relation, for Max subsequently denies
that Genevans are Swiss. We point out the contradiction
to him : "You thought we were in Switzerland.—*No, I
knew we were in Geneva !* " In other words, Geneva may
be " in Switzerland," but there is still no genuine hierarchy of part to whole.

Let us recall the very clear case of Bel (9 ; 2) quoted
at the beginning of this paragraph and belonging to this
second stage. Bel begins by telling us that he is not
Swiss but Vaudois. Switzerland " *is a country,*" Vaud
" *is a canton.*" A canton, so Bel informs us, " *is smaller.*"
We draw a large circle for Switzerland and ask Bel to
draw Geneva and Vaud. He puts two smaller circles
inside the large one, which so far is correct. " If a man
is in the canton of Vaud, then he is in Switzerland ?—
Yes.—And he is in the canton of Vaud ?—*No . . oh
yes, he is* [Bel seems to have understood].—Can anyone
be both Genevan and Vaudois ?—*Yes, if he is in Geneva
he is in Switzerland, and if he is in Switzerland he can also
be Vaudois* [pointing to the circle designating Vaud] ! "
Bel has therefore failed to grasp the relation of part to
whole.

Ober (8 ; 2) says he is from Freiburg but is not a Swiss.
" Do you know what Switzerland is ?—*The whole country.
The twenty-two cantons.*" " Is Geneva in Switzerland ?—
Yes, it is a tiny little country in Switzerland." Ober seems
to have understood, but he still denies that he is a Swiss.
"What is a Swiss ?—*They live in Switzerland.*—Is Freiburg in Switzerland ? — *Yes, but I am not Fribourgeois
and then Swiss.*—And those who live in Geneva ?—*They
are Genevans.*—And Swiss ?—*I don't know. No, its like
me. I live in Freiburg which is in Switzerland, but I am not
Swiss. It's the same thing for the Genevans.*—Do you know
many Swiss people ?—*Not many.*" " Are there any Swiss
people ?—*Yes.*—Where do they live ?—*I don't know.*"

Mey (9 ; 5) : Geneva is in Switzerland, and Switzerland is bigger than Geneva (correct schematization),
but you cannot be in both at the same time.

As we have said, the schematization of this second stage
is naturally not always so clear. It is even probable
that the obviously visual schematism of the subjects just

mentioned was occasioned by our questions—which is not the same thing as to say that it was suggested by them. In the unexpressed thought of the child, things seem to happen more or less as follows. In the first stage the child, having no concrete notion of Switzerland and the towns he hears people talking about, simply juxtaposes them. At the third stage he grasps the correct notion. Between the two stages he learns that Geneva really is in Switzerland and that it belongs to Switzerland. He then establishes between Geneva and Switzerland an undifferentiated relation which is neither one of part to whole nor properly one of possession, but a relation which fluctuates vaguely between these two interpretations. It is therefore the relation of ' property ' about which we spoke in Chapter II (§ 4).

Finally, it should be recalled that the third stage marks the advent of correct schematization. A country, says Wi (10 ; 10), is the whole of the cantons, and Geneva forms part of Switzerland. One can be Genevan and Swiss at the same time.

§ 7. CONCLUSION.—These observations on the schematism of the idea of a country will enable us to complete the conclusions which were adumbrated with regard to the notion of family ; through them we shall be able to examine and check the bond which unites absence or relativity and childish realism.

In what way, to begin with, does the style of thinking which we have been describing reveal difficulties in the use of relations ? Obviously in so far as Geneva, though conceived as a ' part' of Switzerland or as situated ' in Switzerland ' does not really constitute ' a part ' in the adult sense of the word. In an earlier work [1] we have endeavoured to show how complicated is the evolution of the partitive relation in the child. We did not study the partitive relation in itself, i.e. as it is used in concrete

[1] J. Piaget, " Essai sur quelques aspects du développement de la notion de partie chez l'enfant," *Journ. Psych.*, vol. 8, 1921, p. 449.

observations through the activity of the mind in perception. We confined ourselves, as in the present enquiry
to the verbal expression of the idea of part, *i.e.* to that
decomposition into parts and a whole which is effected by
the mind with regard to objects which are spoken of but
not seen. Taking a Burt test and modifying it slightly
for our purpose we asked the following question : " Jean
says to his sisters : Part of my flowers are yellow. Then
he asks them the colour of his posy. Marie says : All
your flowers are yellow. Simone says : Some of your
flowers are yellow. And Rose says : None of your
flowers are yellow. Which of them is right ? " Now
the curious thing is that most of the boys of 9 and 10
answered : 1° That Jean's posy was all yellow ; and 2°
that Marie and Simone were saying the same thing.
In other words, the expression ' part of ' or ' some of '
is not understood. The expression ' part of my flowers '
therefore means " my few flowers which form a partial
posy, or a little posy." We have here a special sense
attributed to the preposition ' of ' which has already been
discussed (Chapter II, § 4). But we also have something
more, and this is the point we wish to drive home. We
have the child's capacity—at least on the verbal plane,
which is the only one that concerns us here—of thinking
of the part independently of the whole, without trying to
find the whole or to make the partitive relation more
definite.

" A part is something that isn't quite whole " (*loc. cit.*,
p. 466). " *A half is something that is cut*," says Ben
(7 ; 1). " And the other half ?—*It has been thrown away.*"
" *It means that it* [the posy] *is half yellow.*—And the other
half ?—*There isn't any more* " (p. 467). The posy " *is a
part.*—And the yellow flowers ?—*No, it is the part that
is with the posy* " (p. 471).

What interpretation are we to put upon these data ?
They would seem to be due both to an incapacity for
logical multiplication and to an incapacity for the logic
of relations. On the one hand, when the child is faced

with two or more logical classes (in this case a posy ×
yellow flowers) he does not look to see whether they
interfere, but tends from the first to juxtapose or to
confuse them (see below, Chap. IV, § 2). On the other hand,
if this tendency to juxtaposition in preference to multiplication or interference is so strong, this is due to the child's
invincible habit of thinking about things absolutely, and
not in relation to each other. This will show us very
clearly how dependent is the logic of classes upon that
of relations. Classes are only snap-shots of the moving
play of relations.

These same phenomena recur in connexion with Switzerland. Even the children who define Switzerland as the
whole of the cantons or as a whole of which Geneva ' is
a part,' or again as a country ' in which ' Geneva is
situated, do not grasp the relation of part to whole before
reaching the third stage. Either the whole is for them an
abstraction (*e.g* the case of Rey and especially that of
Dup who regards Switzerland as smaller than Geneva) ;
or else it is something less than the sum of the parts, as
in the opinion of Stu, since he places ' the Swiss ' in the
part of the large circle which surrounds the cantons and
extends beyond them.

In short, the data we have been analysing clearly reveal
a tendency to think of the part by itself, though it is
known to be a part, and to forget the whole, which then
becomes either an abstraction or another part. The
same facts meet us if we analyse the development of the
idea of fraction in the child, and above all, if we analyse
children's drawings ; the various parts of the same whole
(manikin, house, motor-car, etc.) are always drawn,
i.e. conceived independently of the whole, before being
correctly synthesized. This is a very wide-spread phenomenon, which points once more to that universal tendency
on the part of the child to avoid relations and to replace
them by notions that can be thought of in themselves
as something absolute.

What are the factors with which this tendency is

connected in the particular case before us ? Undoubtedly, with that realistic tendency which makes the child take his own immediate point of view as the only real one, and prevents him from bringing this point of view into relation with the experiment. But what is this immediate point of view ? It is not visual nor spatial. The children we examined seemed to have no geographical interest whatever. Not only were they ignorant of the location of the places about which we talked to them, but they had not the slightest notion of distances. When one is 7 or 8, Africa is not very much farther away from Geneva than Switzerland or Lausanne. This lack of interest might even serve as an objection to our enquiry, for as a general rule it is useless to question children on subjects which do not interest them. In such cases the child either answers at random or invents. But in this particular case the objection is not valid, for countries do interest the child. They do so, however, from a point of view which is very different from that of spatial realism, and this is just what explains the absence of relativity from the child's conceptions, and more especially the absence of the relation of part to whole.

This point of view is above all that of nominal and artificial realism. What interests the child is the name. A large number of children defined a country as " *A piece of land that has a name.*" In other words, the same thing happens here as in the drawings, where it is also an intellectual or even nominal realism that produces juxtaposition of the pieces and absence of definite spatial relations. For example, before reaching the age of 7–8 the child, when he draws a bicycle, knows that he must have ' wheels,' ' pedals,' a ' cord ' or ' chain,' a ' little wheel,' etc. He is therefore content to draw these side by side and to think that these various pieces ' go together,' but he does not trouble himself with their mode of contact. Since they exist and have a name, they are necessary, but there is no need to bother about their reciprocal relations. Similarly, in the case of a country : a country

is really a group of houses and a piece of land which have
been built and had their boundaries fixed by a ' man '
and to which the ' man ' has given a name so as to distinguish them from other territories. According to the
' man's ' good pleasure these countries maintain with
each other more or less complicated relations of possession.
And these are the only relations the child has in mind
when he says that Geneva ' forms part of ' Switzerland, or
' is in ' Switzerland. But by the mere fact of having a
name, Switzerland exists somewhere, further away, independently of the cantons. The child loves accumulating
names in his memory (the ' Gex country ' is often put on
the same level as Switzerland, France, and America), and
his interest consists not in locating the newly-named
country nor in thinking of it as really ' part ' of another
(even when his verbal expression would seem to indicate
this), but in conceiving of it as existing anywhere, after
having been manufactured alongside and at the expense
of the others.

Thus, in this particular case, as in many others (*e.g.* drawings), the absence of any relation of part to whole corresponds to the intellectual and nominal realism of the child.

This is not the place to examine children's ideas on the
origin of countries, which is a completely different subject,
but here are a few examples of these conceptions, which
show how far removed from spatial relations is the interest
of the child.

Schla (7 ; 11) considers that " *France belongs to another
man* [than Switzerland].—And does Switzerland belong to
a man ?—*No, yes, to the man who wanted to give us pass-
ports.*" According to Stu (7 ; 8) a country is " *a big
flat surface.* — What is that ?—*A drawing.* — Does it
really exist ?—*In earth.*" According to Fröh (age 7)
building contractors make countries as the need for them
arises. Pro (age 8) says that you recognize countries by
their railway stations " *because it is written in the stations.*"
Similarly Cont (age 9), " *It is marked* [in the stations].—
And if you walk there ?—*It is on the roads, it is marked
up, there is a sign-post.*"

In a word, just as in regard to his family the child made no attempt to get outside his own immediate point of view, so here he posits as something absolute his purely nominal conception of what is meant by a country. He is then led by this nominalistic realism to locate a country, not on a spatial plane capable of sustaining the relations of part to whole, but on an imaginary plane where things are thought of as absolute in themselves and without relations one to another, or at any rate without any beyond such vague and undifferentiated relations as those of ' property ' (" this going with that ").

In the case of country as in that of family, of brothers, and of right and left, realism, due to the ego-centric habit of sticking to the immediate point of view, entails a complete lack of relativity, or what comes to the same thing, a complete inability to handle the logic of relations.

III. CONCLUSIONS

What conclusions about the child's capacity for reasoning can we draw from these facts ? In the discussion on the ideas of brother, of right and left, of family and country we were concerned only with the schematism of judgment. The task that now confronts us is the synthesis of all this material with the material contained in Chapters I and II.

The chief conclusion of Chapter I was that the child, owing to the difficulty he experienced (a difficulty due to ego-centrism) in becoming aware of his own thought, reasoned only about isolated or particular cases ; generalization and consequently any sustained deduction do not come naturally to him. He juxtaposes successive judgments instead of connecting them, so that there is a lack of internal necessity about his thought. Even when the child comes to generalize and deduce with less difficulty, formal deduction is still a closed book to him, because he cannot shake off his personal beliefs nor reason from assumptions suggested from the outside.

Our subsequent study of the judgment of relation gave complete confirmation of these results by showing their universality from a different angle.

The conclusion to which we are finally led is this. The child does not realize that certain ideas, even such as are obviously relative for an adult are relations between at least two terms. Thus he does not realize that a brother must necessarily be the brother of somebody, that an object must necessarily be to the right or left of somebody, or that a part must necessarily be part of a whole, but thinks of all these notions as existing in themselves, absolutely. Or again he defines a family, not by the relation of kinship which unites its members, but by the space they occupy, by the immediate point of view from which he sees them grouped around him in a house. It should be noted that such behaviour is universal, and that the list of examples might have been added to indefinitely. We are indebted, for example, to the kindness of Mme Passello, a Geneva schoolmistress, for the knowledge of the fact that at the age of 7 the notions of ' friend ' and ' enemy ' are still devoid of relativity. An enemy is " *a soldier*," " *someone who fights*," " *a horrid person*," " *someone who is horrid*," " *someone who wants to hurt you*," etc. It is therefore not a person who is an enemy in relation to someone else, but an enemy in himself. Similarly for a friend.

We discovered innumerable examples of the same kind with Mlle Hahnloser in connexion with the word 'foreigner'. At the age when children can say that foreigners are people from another country (about 9–10), they are still ignorant of the fact that they are themselves foreigners for these people. All the more reason therefore for their ignorance of the reciprocity of this relation when the term is reserved for people coming from another country but living in Geneva. Such examples could be multiplied indefinitely.

M. Reichenbach, schoolmaster at La Chaux-de-Fonds, has been kind enough to send us the following observation.

Some of his scholars (aged about 10–11) told him that Berne was ' in the north ' because the north wind came from Berne (which is true at Chaux-de-Fonds). He then asked them where the north was for Bâle, and where the north wind came from at Bâle. The children replied unanimously that the north wind still came from Berne and that Berne was still in the north. We have ourselves observed that Parisian school-children of 10 or 11 still hold that Versailles is situated ' to the west ' in an absolute sense, as much to the west of Bordeaux as to the west of Paris. And we have known children in Geneva who were unable to understand how Switzerland could be both north of Italy and south of Germany. If it is north it is not south ! The points of the compass are absolute values.

Now such a tendency as this—realistic because it is ego-centric—helps just as much as failure in conscious realization of thought, which is equally the outcome of ego-centrism, to confine the reasoning process of the child to individual or particular cases. For why does the inability to become conscious of thought lead to a form of reasoning that concerns itself only with individual objects ? Because, by leaving in the unconscious the motives which guide his thought, and the consciousness of which alone would lead him to general propositions, ego-centrism functioning unconsciously as it inevitably must, leads the child to reason about immediate data only, about such or such an object given without any relation to other objects. And it is obvious that we are led to exactly the same result, from another angle by the childish realism which we have been examining. Just because he fails to grasp the relativity of a notion such as that of brother, or of right and left, the child will be unable to generalize it.

This is why he cannot succeed in finding which is the darkest of the three little girls who are compared to one another by colour relations, nor which is the most to the right of the three objects in a row before him.

Even when he is reasoning about single objects, the

child cannot generalize relative notions sufficiently to apply them to all possible cases. Here again we have a spurious generality in place of true generalization. The child unconsciously extends his own immediate point of view to all possible points of view (realism), instead of consciously generalizing a relation which he has conceived clearly as relative and reciprocal (relativism).

Realism is therefore a kind of immediate, illegitimate generalization, while relativism is a generalization that is mediate and legitimate.

With regard to generalization then our study of the logic of relations confirms that of the logic of classes. In both cases the apparent generalization of childish logic comes from a particular and immediate schema being unconsciously applied to all the objects that will more or less fit into it, and in both cases the unconscious and uncontrolled character of the application prevents the actual formula of the reasoning from extending beyond the particular cases. In both cases, in short, the realistic or immediate character of the reasoning process prevents the establishment of relations and stands in the way of generalization. (See note on page 134.)

In addition to this, childish realism, as opposed to adult logic of relations, also leads to a confirmation of the results we reached in studying formal reason. We saw there that until the age of 11–12 children were incapable of entering sufficiently into the point of view of their interlocutors to be able to reason correctly about the latter's beliefs, *i.e.* that they were incapable of reasoning from pure assumptions, of reasoning correctly from premisses which they did not believe in. Now, this age of 11–12 at which such reasoning becomes possible is likewise the age when the relations of brother and of right and left are beginning to be completely mastered. This may be more than a mere coincidence, for the mastery in both cases has the same trait—desubjectivation of thought and the power to see relations as such and handle them in an objective manner.

Our study of the logic of relations thus confirms that

K

of the logic of classes and of more general logical relations. Both of them show that the thought of the child passes from a state of ego-centric immediacy, in which single objects only are known and thought of absolutely, and made to bear no relation to one another, to a state of objective relativism in which the mind extracts from these objects innumerable relations capable of bringing about the generalization of propositions and reciprocity of different points of view.

We shall return to these conclusions in greater detail in the following chapter and from a new angle. Chapter I, by showing us how the child juxtaposes his judgments, instead of making them employ one another, made it clear that childish logic is lacking in necessity. Chapters II and III, by showing the child's inability to handle the logic of relations, led us to the very root of this defect. It is because he fails to grasp the *reciprocity* existing between different points of view that the child is unable to handle relations properly. We have yet to show the inner structure of a mind whose thought is ignorant both of logical necessity and of the logic of relations. We shall see that necessity and reciprocity constitute an essential character of logical thought—its *reversibility*. We shall therefore endeavour to show that the most general character of reasoning in the child is what may be called its irreversibility.

M. Claparède has achieved the following remarkable formula for the conscious realization of unconscious schemas : " En réalité nous constatons un double mouvement : de la généralisation implicite et inconsciente à l'individualisation inconsciente ou consciente : puis de cette individualisation à la généralisation consciente." *Arch. de Psych.*, Vol. XVII, 1919, p. 77.

CHAPTER IV

HOW THE CHILD REASONS

In the foregoing chapters we have tried to emphasize certain features in the structure of childish judgment by dissociating ourselves as much as we could from the usual framework of the logical text-books. For it is not by taking the ready-made schema of adult reasoning (and of explicit scientific or legal reasoning at that) and by submitting this schema to, say, syllogistic tests so as to see whether the child conforms to our practical and scholastic habits of thought, that we shall succeed in finding the true nature of child logic. It is rather in connexion with certain problems raised by the child himself, in connexion with his language, and especially with the evolution of the meaning which he attaches to certain expressions of logical relation (conjunctions, relational substantives, prepositions, etc.) that the most significant and the most unforeseen features will be discovered. But a certain looseness inevitably attaches to this indirect method, and after three preliminary studies we are left with very fragmentary results which would have to be classified and interpreted in the light of fresh facts in order to yield the outline of a psychology of childish reasoning.

We made no special enquiry into the structure of reasoning in children for the obvious reason that any direct method of investigation would have been artificial, seeing that we knew neither what we were looking for nor in what terms to state the problem. The only legitimate method, at least in the beginning, is the indirect one, viz. the comparison of results collected on the spot in our previous or in any other enquiries. Our materials will therefore be taken partly from preceding chapters of this book, partly from documents compiled in view of a study of children's ideas (physical causality, idea of force, animism, etc.) or of the development of the idea of number. These studies are unfortunately neither published nor even completed. We shall collect them into one or two volumes devoted to the contents and not to the structure of child thought. It is regrettable no doubt that we should have to anticipate by referring to childish reasoning about causality although—we repeat it—our concern is solely with the structure of children's reasoning not with the content of their ideas. But in the first place we should have been depriving ourselves of interesting data by eliminating such useful observations for the description of childish reasoning, and in the second place we should, by publishing a study of the ideas of children before showing how children reason, have been guilty of an even graver mistake, for such a reversal in the order of exposition would have undermined any actual understanding of our material. All we ask of the reader is that he will take our word for the generality of the facts to which we shall refer later on.

The course we intend to adopt is as follows. In the first section we shall try to show the difficulty experienced by the child in becoming conscious of his own thought (thus verifying the results obtained in Chap. I). The second section will describe one of the consequences of this by showing the difficulty which children have in giving definitions or in handling logical addition and multiplication. In a third section the following important deduction will be made : children do not know how to avoid contradicting themselves nor do they wish to do so. Finally, we shall attack the question of the actual nature of childish reasoning, or, as it has been called, of 'transduction.'

§ 1. Is the Child capable of Introspection ? [1] The fact that the child thought is less conscious of itself than is ours has already been hinted at in Chapter I. For ego-centrism of thought necessarily entails a certain degree of unconsciousness. Anyone who thinks for himself exclusively and is consequently in a perpetual state of belief, *i.e.* of confidence in his own ideas will naturally not trouble himself about the reasons and motives which have guided his reasoning process. Only under the pressure of argument and opposition will he seek to justify himself in the eyes of others and thus acquire the habit of watching himself think, *i.e.* of constantly detecting the motives which are guiding him in the direction he is pursuing.

Is it possible to go beyond these simple assumptions and to show by means of an appropriate technique the capacity for introspection of which the child gives proof at the different stages of his development ? Theoretically, it can be done by any test of reasoning. It is sufficient after the child has given his answer—whether right or wrong it is of no matter from the point of view of introspection—to ask him : " How did you find that out ? " or " What did you think so as to find that out ? " In practice, nothing is so well fitted for this study of childish introspection as simple problems of arithmetical reasoning. On the one hand the adult will see by the child's answer what line he has followed in his reasoning (which are the operations that have taken place), and on the other hand introspection does not require any considerable verbal facility on the part of the child, since it is sufficient for him to say : " I took that away " or " I added that."

Now what struck us in studying some fifty boys between 7 to 10 by means of these little arithmetical problems, spoken or treated as a game, was the child's initial diffi-

---

[1] In collaboration with Mlle Marcelle Roud.—Some of the following pages have been written by Mlle Roud, and are based on material which we collected together in view of a study on the notion of fraction and of elementary arithmetical operations. This study will appear in a future volume, and remains independent of any remarks which we shall make about children's capacity for introspection.

culty in telling us how he obtained a solution (whether right or wrong is of no importance here). Either the child is incapable of retracing the steps he has taken, or else after the operation is over he invents an artificial series of steps and becomes the dupe of illusions concerning the perspective of his own thought, taking as the starting-point what was really the final goal. In a word, everything happens as though the child reasoned in the same way as we do ourselves when we solve a purely empirical and partly manual problem (a puzzle, a trick-box), viz., when we are conscious of each result (failure or partial success) but do not direct or control our movements, and above all, are incapable either by introspection or by retrospection of recapturing the successive steps which our mind has taken. Of course we only came upon this difficulty of introspection in the child indirectly. Our aim being at first solely the study of the notion of number, we asked the children what steps they had taken to obtain each of their answers, and this was all the more necessary as the answer was often incorrect, and we had at first some difficulty in grasping what it was. For the children would recount their own reasoning process in so fanciful a manner, so totally unfitted to throw any light upon what had really taken place in their minds, that we were thus led indirectly to ask the question in the slightly biassed form which we have given it above.

Before turning to the facts we must distinguish between two phenomena, one of which undoubtedly gives rise to the other, but which must nevertheless be kept strictly apart. We mean difficulty in introspection and difficulty in giving a logical reason. When we ask : " Why do you say 5 ? " of someone who has given that answer to the question : " It takes 20 minutes to walk from here to X. Bicycling is 4 times as fast. How much is that ? " the answer may be : " Because I divided 20 by 4 " or " A quarter of 20 is 5." In the first case the speaker limits himself to an account of what he has done, to a retrospective view of his own reasoning process. In the second case he gives the logical reason. When we maintain that children cannot make their own reasoning process the object of introspection, all we mean to say is that it is extremely difficult for them to give an account of the psychological ' how ' of this process, quite independently from the question whether or not they can give a logical reason for the result they have obtained. But we shall see (as was hinted at in Chapter I) that is just this unconscious attitude towards his own thought which explains the child's difficulties in dealing with logical justification.

To turn to the facts. Three stages can be distinguished in the evolution of childish introspection. During the first the child, if he is presented with an easy question, immediately finds the answer by quasi-automatic adaptation, but is incapable of saying how it was done. During the second, the child has to search and grope for the solution, but he is still incapable of retrospection or even of immediate introspection. During the third stage introspection becomes possible.

Here are examples of the first two types. We give them as they come (though they may later on be subjected to a rough classification, for each partakes of several types, and it would be arbitrary to make the divisions too rigid). Thus the answer is sometimes immediate (1st stage), with or without manual operation, sometimes it requires prolonged fumbling (2nd stage), either manual or mental.

Weng (age 7) : " This table is 4 metres long. This one three times as long. How many metres long is it ?— 12 metres.—How did you do that ?—*I added 2 and 2 and 2 and 2 and 2 always 2.*—Why 2 ?—*So as to make* 12. — Why did you take 2 ? — *So as not to take another number.*" " This window is 4 metres high. Another window half as high would be how many metres ? —2 metres.—How did you do that ?—*I took away the other 2's.*" " Here are 12 matches. Make me a pile three times as small." After fumbling about a little, Weng makes a pile of 10 matches (by subtraction : 12—3, with a mistake of calculation into the bargain). " How did you find 10 ?—*I added 4 and 4 and 2.*"

This case of Weng's is very typical. Weng gets the result automatically. When he is asked how he found it, he starts from the result and reconstructs it anyhow, by means of any arbitrary expedient. Unable to recover his own reasoning process he invents a device which will somehow lead to the same result.

With other children the retrospective description given of their own reasoning also presupposes the result, but the description is better :

Ferr (age 8) : " There are 10 matches here, and there, three times as many. How many are there there ?—40 : *There, there are 10, and there are three times as many.* —How did you find that out ?—*I counted* 10, 20, 30, 40." " Here are 20 matches. There, there are twice as many.—60.—Why 60 ?—*I counted.*" " A wall is 12 metres high. Another wall is twice as small ?—*That makes 9 . . . I counted up to 9.*"

Gath (age 7) : " You are 3 little boys and are given 9 apples. How many will you each have ?—*3 each.*—How did you do that ?—*I tried to think.*—What ?—*I tried to think how much it would be.· I tried to think in my head.*—What did you say in your head ?—*I counted.*—What did you count in your head ? . . .*" Gath only gives answers like " *I guessed, I counted.*" " *I tried to see how much it was and I found* 3." With practice, however, he begins to see what is wanted. Only the first introspections he gives us manifestly reverse the actual order of things and presuppose the result obtained : " It takes me 20 minutes to walk to Carouge. I go twice as fast on a bicycle. That will be ?—*You'll take* 10 *minutes.*—How did you do that ?—*I took away* 10.—Why 10 ?—*To find out.*—Why did you take away 10 ?—*Because there were* 20.—Why 10 ?—*Because it takes you* 2 *minutes longer* (=twice as fast)."

Here are some more examples :

Bel (9 ; 2) : " It takes you 50 minutes to walk to Carouge. On a bicycle you get there five times quicker. How long does it take you on a bicycle ?—*45 minutes.*—How did you count ?—*I said* 50 *minus* 5, *then I went down to* 40 *and I saw it was* 45." Spie (9 ; 3) gives 25 in answer to the same problem, but cannot explain how he has done it : " *I can't explain, but I know how to count,*

it's easy, but not to tell anyone." As a matter of fact he
has, like many of the other children, simply taken half
of 50. Mey (9 ; 5) answers 35 and maintains that he
found 35 because he said to himself : 5 × 7 = 35. Trec
(9 ; 6) gives 10 as an answer (dividing 50 by 5). "How
did you find 10 ?—⅕ of 5 *is* 1, *then I added an 0.*—
Why? . . ."

Thus in no case is the child able to explain what he was
looking for nor what he did to find his answer. Instead
of giving an accurate retrospect he starts from the result
he has obtained as though he had known it in advance
and then gives a more or less arbitrary, method for
finding it again.

But we have every right to be suspicious of these answers.
They are obviously fanciful. Either they show that
the child does not know how to handle introspection and
therefore answers just as he pleases, or else they prove
that he has not understood what was required of him.
Sometimes, for example, the child will imagine that he is
being asked a school question on arithmetic, and proceeds
to recite additions or to produce devices for the simplifica-
tion of difficult multiplication, *e.g.* to find 4 × 6 you take
(4 × 3) + (4 × 3). The only way of being sure that the
answers in question are genuine examples of faulty
introspection is to take cases where the child is obviously
his own dupe, or rather the victim of an illusion in
mental perspective, taking systematically as a point of
departure what is the result of his calculation.

Here are such cases.

Bis (9 ; 6) : "One little boat costs 3 francs. How
many could you buy with 18 francs ?—6.—How did you
get at 6 ?—*I did 3 times, I did 6 times 3.* . . . [He is
therefore taking the result as a starting-point, instead of
saying 'I divided 18 francs into 3.']—*I counted, and then
I found that it made 6.* . . .," etc. Only at the end of a
long discussion does Bis declare : "*I looked to see how
much it would be to go up to 18.*" Thus, in attempting to
gain a retrospect of his reasoning, Bis has thoroughly
inverted its order.

Bon (9 ; 6) presents an even clearer case, for we heard him counting to himself. We asked him to find three-quarters of 16 matches. He then mutters to himself : " A quarter of 16 =4 ; 3×4 =12," and hands us the matches with the answer : " 12.—How did you find 12 ?—*I said 4 times 3 =12. To go up to 16 makes 4. I took 4* [matches from the pile of 16] *and I gave back the rest.*" Bon has therefore completely reversed the correct process which he had muttered to himself and presents us with a line of reasoning devoid of logical direction.

There is no need to add any more of these examples, for they are all alike. It will be sufficient for our purpose to arrange them according to the following schematization. During the first stage or at least when he first attempts to handle a notion, the child either fumbles with his fingers, as when he tries to divide a pile of matches into two halves, or else applies automatically the ideas resulting from these manual operations. In both cases reasoning consists of a succession of operations either manual or mental, but neither of them directed by a mental process that is entirely conscious. In such cases, of course, introspection is not possible. During the second stage the problem becomes more difficult, and instead of being solved by automatic adaptation, it calls for a certain direction of thought and control of judgment. But it is a question not only of reasoning, but of reflecting on one's reasoning, or of relating it, which comes to the same thing, since all reflection is a narrative told mentally to oneself ; and here again we find introspection to be deficient. Either the child remembers only a few terms of his reasoning, and then combines them as best he can, arbitrarily and regardless of gaps and additions, or else he reverses the whole process, starting from the conclusion and arguing towards the premisses as though he had known from the first whither these premisses were leading him. Finally comes the third stage in which introspection enables him to reflect upon the whole course of his reasoning.

When does this third stage appear ? It is hard to say, because estimates of this kind depend upon such delicate shades of distinction. Nor should the reader take things too literally and conclude from our examples that childish reasoning is unconscious. From 7 onwards we find cases of first-rate introspection.

Mour (7 ; 10) : " It takes you 50 minutes to walk to Carouge. Bicycling you go 5 times as fast, so that would take?—*It doesn't take a minute.*—Why?—*50 minus 5 times* [50], *50 minus 50 makes* o." (This is the definition which several children give of the expression " *x* times less." Whether the definition is correct need not concern us here.)

Ober (age 8) gives 25, then 45 in answer to the same question : " How did you do that ?—*I took* 25 *from* 50, *no* 5, *then* 5 *times as fast would be* 45. *I thought of taking* 25 *from* 5. . . . *I took half of* 50 ! "

Any statistical treatment of our material would be misleading, as the types under observation are not sufficiently pronounced, but we may say in conclusion that up to the age of 7, introspection seems to be completely absent, and that from 7–8 until 11–12 there is a consistent effort on the part of thought to become more and more conscious of itself.

The question may now be raised as to the causes and the consequences of the difficulties which the child experiences in knowing the motives and directions of his own thought. The explanation is simple. M. Claparède has shown in a remarkable contribution to the subject[1] that we become aware of the relations which have been woven into the texture of things by our action in so far as automatic usage fails, and some new mode of adaptation is forced upon us. The child cannot express the relations of resemblance between a bee and a fly, for example, although he is perfectly conscious of the differences between them. This is because when in relation to the bee he goes through reactions which he has acquired in relation to the fly, he is only performing an automatic

[1] Ed. Claparède, " La conscience de la ressemblance et la différence chez l'enfant," *Arch. de Psych.*, Vol. XVII.

act which requires no conscious realization, whereas when
he reacts differently in response to a special feature (the
discovery one day of yellow flies which he has heard
people call ' bees '), his experience is not automatic and
consequently entails a certain degree of consciousness.
The ' law of conscious realization,' as M. Claparède calls
it, can therefore explain why introspection is so difficult
for the child. For introspection is really a variant of
conscious realization, or rather it is conscious realization
in the second degree. And if we try to generalize Claparède's law we are inevitably led to the view that the things
which call forth a new adaptation on our part, and which
consequently excite consciousness in us are always changes
occurring in the external world in contrast to the inner
vagaries of mental activity. If the difference between
objects strikes us sooner than their resemblance it is
because their resemblance is subjective, it is the product
of our own thought, or rather of the identity of our
reaction to these objects. Difference, on the other hand,
is objective, *i.e.* is given by the things themselves. From
this angle it becomes obvious that all introspection is
extremely difficult, for it requires that we should be conscious not only of the relations which our thought has
woven, but of the actual activity of thought itself. If
consciousness is directed entirely to the unadapted, the
new, its exclusive focus will necessarily be the external
world and not thought as such.

Now the ego-centric character of childish thought only
reinforces these circumstances which are already important
for the adult. Never without the shock of contact
with the thought of others and the effort of reflection
which this shock entails would thought as such come to
be conscious of itself.

Let us now turn to an examination of the consequences
of this inborn unconsciousness of thought towards itself.
They are numerous, and this is why we opened this chapter,
which is devoted to the psychology of childish reasoning,
with a section on the difficulties of introspection. For

subconscious thought is 1° far less inclined to reasoning and more allied to action than is ours, and 2° much further removed than ours from the need for logical justification and the deduction of judgments one from the other.

The first point is of the utmost importance, but it is very difficult to deal with, because of the poverty of the existing psychological vocabulary. We shall therefore be as brief as possible. What is thought which has little or no consciousness of itself? Can one really speak of unconscious reasoning? To our mind, if the greatest ambiguity is to be avoided, it must be allowed that unconscious thought merges into action. An unconscious thought is a series of operations, not actual but potential, not manually performed but none the less outlined in the organism. Ribot's view that this unconscious life can be resolved into movements is the most intelligible that has yet been put forward. These movements and operations are a preparation for conscious reasoning in so far as they reproduce and prepare anew the manual operations of which thought is a continuation. They obey, moreover, a logic of their own in that they do not merely reproduce previous actions, but recombine them according to special laws (the Pleasure principle or *Lustprinzip* as regards dreams, laws of economy and assimilation between various operations, etc.). But to attribute logical implications to these movements, to say that their functioning is controlled, in short to assign to them all the features of spoken and fully conscious thought would be to take a wholly unwarrantable step. Thus the only kind of implication of which we can talk in connexion with subconscious thought is one which merges into the determinism which unites one action to another; it is internal and of a nature intermediate between physical and logical necessity; we may call it psychological or mental necessity.

So that everything we have said in this work to show that the thought of the child is less conscious than ours has *ipso facto* led us to the conclusion that childish thought is devoid of logical necessity and genuine implication ; it is nearer to action than ours, and consists simply of mentally pictured manual operations,. which, like the vagaries of movement, follow each other without any necessary connexion. This will explain later on why childish reasoning is neither deductive nor inductive ; it consists in mental ' experiments ' which are non-reversible, *i.e.* which are not entirely logical and not subject to the principle of contradiction.

Our second remark in connexion with the child's difficulties in conscious realization was that for a type of thought that is not conscious of itself logical justification is impossible. This view has already been argued in Chapter I. We saw how hard it was for the child to find a logical reason for the judgments he expresses. Either he gives up the attempt to justify them logically and gives a psychological motive, where only an intellectual reason would be in place, or else he tries to justify his statements, but for lack of having consciously realized the factors which guided his thought, he succeeds in giving only a very incomplete logical justification. The reason for this is now apparent. The logical justification of a judgment takes place on a different plane from the invention of this judgment. Whereas the latter is the unconscious result of previous experiences, the former requires reflection and thought, in a word introspection which will construct on top of spontaneous thought a ' thinking about thinking ' which alone is capable of logical necessity. The proof of this is that among the children quoted above, those who were incapable of introspection were also those who were prepared to give a fantastic and illogical justification of any of their statements (Weng, Gath, Tiec), whereas those more skilled in introspection also showed greater aptitude for demonstration (Mour and Ober).

§ 2. THE DEFINITIONS AND CONCEPTS OF CHILDREN ; LOGICAL ADDITION AND MULTIPLICATION.—We do not propose to deal with the problem of children's definitions by itself. We shall merely discuss it, in so far as it touches upon the problem which we have set ourselves in the last section, and especially in so far as the subject of definitions serves as an introduction to the study of elementary logical operations (logical addition and multiplication) and consequently to the discussion of the problem of contradiction.

With regard to the first point, if children really have consistent difficulty in grasping the progress of their own reasoning by means of introspection, they must experience the same difficulty in giving definitions, at any rate exhaustive definitions ; for from the psychological point of view, definition is the conscious realization of the use which one makes of a word or a concept in the course of a process of reasoning. In this connexion the stage which will interest us most, *i.e.* during which this difficulty will be most apparent is the stage beginning at 7–8 and which marks the first appearance of logical definition.

Previous to this stage, *i.e.* up to the age of 8, inclusively according to Binet and Simon,[1] exclusively according to Terman, children are either incapable of defining, and simply point to the objects or repeat the word to be defined (a table . . . is a table), or else they define things " by their uses." Thus, when the child is asked, " What is a fork ? " he answers : " *It is to eat with.*" " What is a mother ? . . .—*For cooking the dinner.*—What is a snail ?—*It is to crush.*" Constantly in the course of our enquiries we came across definitions of this type, characterized by the words ' it's for.' A mountain, " *It's for climbing on to*", a country, " *It's for travelling*", rain " *It's for watering,*" etc. The reader will readily perceive that such a method of definition is prior to any logical habits of thought if he refers to our analysis of precausality (L.T., Chap. V). For to the question : " What is it ? " as to the question ' Why ' ? the child gives an answer which is neither causal nor physical (rain is the result of . . .) nor logical, viz., *i.e.* an answer

---

[1] Binet, A., et Simon, Th., *La mesure du developpement de l'intelligence chez les jeunes enfants*, Paris, 1917.

which will define the concept by the use to which it is put in a sentence (rain is water that falls from the sky). The answer he gives is equally far removed from physical causality as it is from logical definition, and appeals to a notion situated midway between these two extremes—viz. to the notion of motive or utility : " Rain is for watering." Definition by usage, like the abundance of ' whys ' which is contemporary with it, is therefore really a sign of the phenomenon of precausality, or what comes to the same thing, of an interest which is midway between the psychical and the physical. Thus the real nature of an object lies neither in its physical cause, nor in the concept one has of it, but in a reason or in a motive for its existence which imply both a directing intelligence and a physical realization. At this stage clearly there can be no question of making the child conscious of logical definition, *i.e.* of the use which he has made of a concept in his reasoning. Thought at this stage remains entirely realistic ; the mind projects it into things and confuses it with them. Owing to the phenomenon of precausality the child will be unable to distinguish between concept and object, since things do not yet form an independent order but are still permeated with intention and finalism. Or to put it in another way the child will fail to distinguish between logical justification (since all definition whether logical or conceptual, consists in a justification of the use made of a concept in reasoning) from explanation. For explanation at the precausal stage is still harnessed to justification and not yet differentiated from it. So that, unable to distinguish between justification and explanation, the child is consequently debarred from consciously realizing what use he is making of a concept in his reasoning : hence the absence of logical definitions at this stage.

After the age of 7–8, on the contrary, as the decline of precausality sets in, the child begins to distinguish thought from things, and logical justification from causal explanation ; from this moment he begins to be conscious of his reasoning process as it unfolds itself. At this age

we meet with the first logical definitions, *i.e.* definitions
according to the formula by genus and specific difference
(*e.g.* A mother is a lady who has children). When these
definitions are perfect and exhaustive they presuppose
conscious knowledge 1° of a general proposition (" All
mothers are ladies ") ; and 2° of an interference or
' multiplication ' of two general propositions (All ladies
are not mothers, nor are all people with children mothers :
mothers therefore entail the interference of these two
conditions). But these logical definitions do not appear
in perfected form from the beginning. At first and up till
the age of about 11–12 the child is incapable of giving
exhaustive definitions : he simply defines by the genus
(A mother is a lady), or by a feature that is particular but
not specific (A cousin is the son of an aunt or an uncle)
without generalization of the notion.[1] If the reader will
recall the conclusions we reached in Chapter I, showing that
the child is for a long time incapable of reasoning about
general propositions, and the conclusions of Chapters II
and III showing that the child always forms his judgments
from an immediate and ego-centric point of view which
makes him incapable of grasping the relativity of ideas
to the extent of being able to generalize them, the statements we are now making about children's definitions
will seem perfectly natural to him. We are drawing attention to these facts again in order to show how they arise
from the difficulties which occur when children introspect,
and to what incessant contradictions they lead when
children reason. For if, on the one hand, children are
incapable of exhaustive logical definitions, this is because
they are not conscious of the meaning which they assign
to the concepts and words which they use, and on the
other hand this unconsciousness is what involves them
in incessant contradiction. For if the child were conscious
of the meaning of a given word he would *ipso facto* transfer
this meaning to the plane of reflection where it would

---

[1] *Cf. L'intermédiaire des Educateurs*, Vol. I, pp. 69–75 (1913). M. Bovet
places definitions by genus only chiefly at the age of 9.

acquire a fixity that would admit of generalization. But so long as the meaning is only implicit it remains subject to all the fluctuations of subconscious thought, *i.e.* to all the particular and irreversible cases of pure action or of elementary ' mental experiments.'

The first of these two phenomena shows with particular clearness in definitions of such notions as ' alive ' or ' strong ' (force), concepts which the child frequently uses in his spontaneous questions and explanations. We have already shown (L.T., Chap. V) the importance of questions about life and death, and no very searching enquiry need be made to see that in his explanations of how boats float on the water, how motors move along the road, how trains run, how bodies act mechanically on each other, how rivers flow, etc. the child is constantly invoking the idea of ' force ' : a pebble has ' force,' the wind has ' force.' The question may therefore be raised whether the children who spontaneously use these ideas realize the meaning which they themselves attach to them. For this reason we have undertaken, with the help of certain ladies, a systematic enquiry into the nature of childish animism and the idea of force. Our results will be published later on from the point of view of the ideas themselves, *i.e.* of the contents of the thoughts. But without prejudicing the result of our labour by dealing with these ideas as such, we can nevertheless draw conclusions from them which are essential not to their contents but to their form, *i.e.* to the manner in which children define to themselves the notions of which they made use in their talk.[1]

Naturally, there is no question of asking the children : " What is life ? " or even " What does ' being alive ' mean ? " This would be to expect them to possess the power of making abstractions, and it would be absurd to conclude from the lack of such power to the inability to

---

[1] The examples which follow are taken from a study of animism in collaboration with Mlles H. Krafft and S. Perret and from a study on the idea of force in collaboration with Mlle J. Guex and Mme V. J. Piaget. These studies will appear in a later volume.

be conscious of meanings and to give definitions. The following method, on the contrary, raises no such difficulties. You give the child a list of familiar objects, asking about each in turn, " Is it alive ? " and adding after the affirmative or negative reply, " Why is it (or is it not) alive ? " The only thing to avoid is suggestion by perseveration. In view of this it is best to begin with objects that are obviously alive or obviously inanimate, and then only after making sure whether there is or is not a definite systematization in the child's mind, can he be questioned about objects which strike him as doubtful. The order to be observed is therefore roughly as follows : a dog, a fish, a fly, then a pebble, a table, a bench, then the sun, the moon, the clouds, the rivers, fire, wind, a marble, a bicycle, a train, a boat, etc.

Now in using this method which seems to call only for a very limited power of abstraction, the following phenomenon immediately becomes apparent. The child cannot define the idea which he has of the words ' to be alive,' or to put it differently, he assigns life to the sun and denies it, say, to a boat. He is not conscious of the apparently consistent meaning which he attributes to the concept ' life.' One group of children, for example, confine the word ' alive ' to everything that seems animated by its own movements, thus excluding from the category of living beings objects to whom movement has been communicated. But these children will not be able to express this condition, to say, for example, that the sun is alive ' because it moves by itself.' It is we who grope towards the discovery of the child's unconscious intention and sometimes succeed in making him indirectly own to it. Left to himself the child will simply say ' because it moves ' and will be greatly perplexed when he has to explain why a motor-car, which also moves, is not alive.[1]

[1] We say nothing here on the subject of childish animism. The fact of children saying that the sun is alive does not mean that they also attribute to it consciousness and intention. A far more delicate method is required to detect the features of animism in the child.

This will show that the difficulties bound up even with implicit definition are closely related to what we saw (Chap. I) of the child's inability to give complete logical justifications or reasons.

Here are some examples.

Grand (age 8) assigns the quality of being ' alive ' to fishes " *because they swim*," to flowers " *because they grow*," to the moon " *because it comes back in the evening*," to the wind " *because it can blow*," to fire " *because it burns*," but he denies it to clouds, bicycles and watches, etc, When we came to analyse some of Grand's answers, such as this one : " *Water is not alive, it hasn't got any hands, it can't run on the grass*," and especially when we compare his answers with most of those given by children of his age, we see that he regards as living those objects which have a movement of their own, whereas he denies this quality to clouds, because they are driven along by God, to machines because they are worked by men, to rivers because their movement is regulated by the slope of their bed and especially by their banks, etc. But the interesting point is that Grand is not conscious of this implicit conception. When he explains why certain objects are alive, Grand certainly says that they move (they swim, fly, blow, come back, drive along), but never that they move ' by themselves.' In his explanations of why certain objects are not alive, however, Grand has no fixed definition at his service. He says of clouds that they are not alive " *because they don't move*," but he admits that they very often do move. In Grand's language then " They don't move " obviously means " They don't move by themselves," " The wind makes them move," etc. But he is not explicitly conscious of this shade of meaning which however plays an important part in his implicit thought, as is shown by his choice of objects classed as alive and of objects classed as inanimate. Rivers also are not considered to be alive by Grand, ostensibly because they do not run about and have no hands. But neither sun nor fire have hands, and yet they are allowed life in so far as they have movement. Grand begins by saying of a watch that it is alive " *because it goes*," but he adds immediately that it is not alive. There is therefore a momentary and purely superficial conflict between his deep conviction (it is not alive) and the

incomplete definition of the word ' alive ' (life = movement and not self-movement) which alone is in his mind.
In a word, Grand conceives life as the power of self-movement, but he defines it consciously simply as movement.
His definition does not cover his conception, or more
precisely, his *prise de conscience* does not extend to the
full use which he makes of the word ' alive.' Grand has
not yet become conscious of his own thought.

Schei (6 ; 6) is in the same case. He defines life by
movement ; clouds are alive " *because they move,*" a table
is not alive " *because it does not move.*" But he is thinking
of self-movement and not of movement in general (he
does not think like Grand that clouds move because
God pushes them, but that they travel by themselves).
He refuses life to motor-cars, etc. but cannot say why :
" Is a motor-car alive ?—*No.*—Why not ?— . . . —Does
it move ? Why is it not alive ?—*Dunno.*" Same attitude
with regard to bicycles, rivers, etc.

Horn (6 ; 3) regards animals, sun, moon, clouds, and
wind as alive, because " they move," but not motor-cars
nor bicycles, etc., but is unable to say why.

Cal (age 5) says that to be alive means " *that you move,*"
but denies that motor-cars, etc. are alive.

In short, out of a large number of children who conceive life as autonomous movement, hardly one can give
a proper definition of the word ' alive ' nor even say why
such and such an object is or is not alive. Every now and
then an isolated case (Barb 5½ says that to be alive is " *to
move by yourself*") shows that this *prise de conscience*
is possible among the most intelligent, and also confirms
the validity of our interpretations ; but the bulk of the
children under 7–8 are incapable of reaching this stage.

So far we have chosen the simplest case, that in which
the child implicitly assigns a single meaning to the word
' alive,' viz. self-movement. But it goes without saying
that this is not always so. The concept of life frequently
subsumes a number of heterogeneous qualities. For
example : movement, the fact of having hands, a face,
blood, or some activity useful to man, etc. What takes
place in such cases ? To the difficulties of simple conscious realization which we have just been analysing

are now added the difficulties of becoming simultaneously conscious of two or more elements. This is a difficulty of synthesis which will form an additional obstacle to adequate definition on the part of the child. Let us examine one or two examples which will show us wherein these phenomena differ from the mental processes that take place in the educated adult.

Duss (age 9) conceives life as determined by two heterogeneous qualities : activity and the fact of having blood. Thus a lizard is alive " *because he has blood*," a tree " *because it has sap* " (*cf.* blood), the sun is also alive " *because it lights* " (activity), the cloud " *because it makes rain* " (activity), fire " *because it burns* " (activity). But Duss varies in his judgments according as he thinks of blood or of activity. Thus immediately after having said that the sun was alive because it lights, he declares that it is not alive " *because it has no blood.*" The same applies to clouds and fire. Consequently Duss has no satisfactory definition to give of life. He hesitates between blood and activity without achieving a synthesis between the two.

Im (age 6) subsumes three heterogeneous notions— activity useful to man, the fact of giving heat (perhaps a variant of the first), and movement. In this way clouds, sun, moon, stars, and wind are alive if considered from the angle of movement or activity (clouds are alive " *because they show us the way* ") but are not alive if viewed from the angle of heat. For after telling us that the sun is alive " *because it warms us* " and the wind because it blows, Im says that fire is not alive " *because it warms us and then it burns us*" (non-useful activity), and neither is wind : " *It blows, but it is not alive.—Why ?—Because it makes us cold.*"

Thus Im's three ideas of useful activity, heat and movement clash. Wind is said to be alive when Im is thinking of its movement, and not alive when he is thinking of the cold which it causes. In this way Im never succeeds in giving a fixed definition nor in becoming simultaneously conscious of the various factors which determine his thought at each moment of the interrogatory.

Pig (age 9, backward) considers that the sun and the moon are alive because they move, but not a bicycle,

" *because it has to be pushed,*" nor fire, " *because it has to be made,*" nor rivers " *because the air makes them move along.*" It would seem then that Pig presented a typical case of a child who identifies life with self-movement. But he denies life to the North wind although it moves by itself. It is not alive " *because it doesn't talk.*—But fishes don't talk and they are alive ?—*They swim.*"

Pig's case is therefore very clear and very representative. Life according to him is characterized by two heterogeneous qualities—self-movement and speech. But Pig has not become conscious of these two conditions simultaneously, and he fluctuates between the two, unable to synthesize them. If life were characterized by addition (self-movement) + (speech), the North wind would have to be regarded as alive ; if life were defined by interference between two conditions (=objects endowed both with speech and with self-movement) fishes would have to be excluded from life. In both cases therefore Pig would be inconsistent. To put it more simply, we can say that Pig has never asked himself the question, because he has never been conscious of this dualism. The same thing is true of the two children studied before Pig, and of all those who could be quoted.

The same phenomenon comes out very clearly in connexion with definitions of force. To obtain these definitions we proceed in exactly the same way, giving the child a list of objects and asking him whether they have force, and why. Now here, even more than in the case of life, the child's conceptions are the outcome of various heterogeneous factors, but here no more than in the previous case can the child achieve consciousness of this multiplicity nor consequently arrive at a synthesis which alone would make definition possible. Here is an example.

Hellb (8 ; 6) hesitates like most of his companions between two separate ideas of force : force as cause of movement and force as resistance. Force he tells us is " *when you carry a lot of things.*—Why has the wind got force ?—*It's when you can move along.*" Hellb's opinions

are therefore frequently changing according to the point
of view he adopts. At one moment of the interrogatory
the wind has force because it moves, at another it has none
because it does not carry anything. The same phenomenon appears as regards water. Rivers have force
" *because it* [water] *runs, because it goes down.*" A moment
later water has not got force because it carries nothing.
Again, a moment after this a lake has force " *because it
carries boats.*"

From the point of view of form, all these conceptions
resemble one another. It is therefore needless to multiply
examples, especially as these will be found, though
treated from another point of view, in our forthcoming
studies on children's ideas.

Two fundamental conclusions can be drawn from these
considerations. The first is concerned with conscious
realization in thought, the other with the arrangement of
notions and ideas into a hierarchy. On the one hand,
when the child has to deal with complex conceptions
(such as those in which the notion in question is determined by several heterogeneous factors) he is, as is only
natural even less conscious of the definition of the concepts
than when he makes use of simpler notions. This can
be very clearly seen in a case like that of Hellb. Hellb
defines force as resistance even when he has just behaved,
and will again immediately behave, as though force were
to be defined solely by activity and movement.

On the other hand—and this is fundamental for what
follows—this inability to become conscious of the guiding
factors of one's own thought entails a second phenomenon
which is of the utmost importance for the psychology
of childish reasoning, and in particular for the analysis
of contradiction in the child. We mean the absence of
logical hierarchy or of synthesis between the different
elements of the same conception. For most of our ideas
too are determined by several heterogeneous factors
and even by factors which are often the same as those
used by children. Thus we, like children, define life as

self-movement, as the fact of having blood (or sap, or any kind of circulation), etc. We also define force as activity and as resistance. Where we differ from the children we have just been discussing is that we always have the component parts of the concept *simultaneously* in mind. Thus we say that a river has force because it flows fast, but we do not deny that a bench has resisting force even though it makes no movement. The child, on the contrary, thinks, not simultaneously, but *alternately* of the two determining factors. When he is thinking of resistance he denies force to rivers because a pebble sinks to the bottom of the water, and when he is thinking of motor force he denies force to a bench because it moves neither itself nor anything else.

We find ourselves here in the presence (under a new form) of the phenomena of juxtaposition and syncretism which have already been sufficiently dealt with (see L.T., Chap. IV, and Chap. I of this volume, especially the conclusion). We can say that childish conceptions are the result of the juxtaposition and not of the synthesis of a certain number of elements, which are still disparate and will only gradually come into relation. Thus ' life ' is for Duss a juxtaposition of two concepts—activity and the fact of having blood. Now by the very fact of these childish concepts being the product of juxtaposition and not of synthesis, their apparent unity will be that which syncretism gives to a diversity of elements, viz. a subjective unity which cannot be made to serve as a foundation for logical reasoning. The proof of this is that the moment the children we have quoted begin to apply their conceptions, they contradict themselves to no slight extent. Once again, therefore, we find verification of that necessary bond of union between juxtaposition and syncretism which was so carefully emphasized in the conclusion of Chapter I.

This strange phenomenon of concepts by conglomeration may be compared to what, in a totally different sphere, has been called ' over-determination ' of images. It is well known that Freud, when he was studying the images and symbols which occur in dreams, day-dreams, and imagination, in short in undirected, autistic thought, was led to the view that each one of these images was the resultant not of one content which alone could determine it, but of several contents which insert themselves into the image with various degrees of complexity. Thus a man will dream that he is looking for a room. If the association of ideas evoked by this image be analysed, it will be found that the image is related to the actual situation (the subject happens to be looking for lodgings), but also that in view of this situation the dream is the depository of numerous circumstances in which the subject also has actually looked for a room.

So that from the point of view of this person's psychology, the image has not one content but a large number of contents. It is in this sense that an image or a symbol is said to be ' over-determined.' Now this is a phenomenon which we always find in primitive, ill-directed thought. The mind always begins in chaos. Simplicity is an effect of art and is in nowise given in the complex that forms the beginning of mental activity. The childish conceptions which we have been analysing are therefore very rarely a sign of simplicity. Each is the product of an over-determination of factors. The word *life* is over-determined by a list of factors piled upon each other without order or hierarchy—movement, the fact of speaking, of having a face, or blood, of being useful to man, and so on.

Children's explanations often point to the same phenomenon.[1]

It might be thought that these over-determinations were identical with what takes place in our case, for each of our concepts is determined by an enormous number of heterogeneous components. But, we must repeat it once again, what distinguishes over-determination from

[1] J. Piaget, " La pensée symbolique et la pensée de l'enfant," *Arch. de Psych.*, t. XVIII, p. 296.

this sort of determination, or rather what distinguishes disorder from complexity is that in the case of over-determination there is no hierarchy, no real composition among the factors. And the child never having become conscious simultaneously of these factors, they act upon his reason in alternation with one another, penetrating the field of attention at different moments in time. The concept therefore resembles a metal ball that is attracted successively and in no fixed order by six electro-magnets, and jumps without rhyme or reason from one to the other. Because thought has not first become conscious of itself in every direction, over-determination is an unstable system of equilibrium, or to take a chemical image, it is a case of false equilibrium, like a state of apparent rest due simply to adherences or viscosity (syncretism). The complexity of an adult concept on the other hand does not exclude equilibrium. The mind has become conscious of each factor, not in isolation from, but in relation to the others, so all these factors act on the concept at once; there is synthesis and hierarchy.

These phenomena of psychological equilibrium can be translated into the language of formal logic. In terms of this language the child is incapable, both of systematic logical addition and multiplication. The reader is doubt-less familiar with these terms. Let us take concepts in extension, or two classes such as the class of vertebrates and the class of invertebrates. Logical addition consists in finding the smallest class that will contain them both, viz. the class of animals. Therefore (animals) = (verte-brates) + (invertebrates). Take two other classes, say that of Protestants and that of Genevans. Logical multiplication is the operation which consists in finding the largest class that is contained in both these classes, or in other words the sum total of elements that are common to both, viz. the class of Genevan Protestants, or that of Protestant Genevans. Therefore (Protestant) × (Genevan) = (Genevan Protestant). In the example of vertebrates and invertebrates there is no common element, no invertebrate-vertebrate. So (vertebrate) × (inverte-brate) = 0. To multiply is always to exclude. For to find the sum total or to determine the concept of Genevan Protestants is to exclude 1° Non-Protestant Genevans, 2° non-Genevan Protestants.

The reason why adult concepts are in a state of equilibrium is that they are the products of logical addition or multiplication. If moving objects (like rivers) have force, and resisting objects (like a bench) also have force, then the concept of force will result from the logical addition of these various classes : (Objects animated with force) = (moving objects) + (resisting objects) + . . ., etc. But the children we quoted above never add up these factors or classes of objects. They think of them alternately, without bringing them together, and that is why they cannot define the word. They do not say : " Force is when one can support things and *also* or *or else* when one can move along." But they say, like Hellb : " It is when one can support things," and once they have forgotten this initial proposition, " It is when one can move along." Thus a bench sometimes has force because it ' supports ' things, sometimes it has none because it does not move. There is no logical addition of the factors in question, there is only chaotic over-determination.

In the same way the adult, like Duss, defines life, at least among the animals, by self-movement and the fact of having blood. But he multiplies these two factors by each other. In other words he defines life by the fact of having *both* blood *and* self-movement (and not by one *or* the other, as in logical addition). Thus for the adult the sun is not alive, because it has no blood but only self-movement, and a corpse is also not alive because it has only blood but no self-movement. The child on the other hand reasons like Duss. He does not multiply the two factors but considers them separately. He says that the sun is alive because it moves, forgetting that it has no blood. Or even if in limiting cases the child thinks of this second clause, it will not disturb him in his affirmation that the sun is alive (though bloodless) so long as he keeps the idea of self-movement before his mind. In a word, logical multiplication does not take place, and the factors involved are not compounded; each works separately on its own.

It is interesting to note that these facts, which were obtained by simple talks with the children, entirely confirm the results previously reached by a far more artificial method.[1] By applying and modifying a test of Burt's we found that children were incapable of logical multiplication even in apparently very simple cases. Here is one of these cases. The child is shown the following test, written on a piece of paper which is left before him : " If this animal has long ears, it is a mule or a donkey. If it has a thick tail it is either a horse or a mule. Now this animal has long ears and a thick tail. What is it ? " Now experiment shows that among very young children (up to the age of 8, the period that especially interests us in this chapter. and which we have elsewhere called the unreflecting stage) the two conditions cannot be held before the mind simultaneously, nor even collected into a single mental act, Sometimes the child thinks of the long ears, but as he forgot that the animal must also have a thick tail, he cannot see why the animal in question should not just as well be a donkey as a mule. Sometimes he thinks of the tail but forgets that the animal must have long ears, so that he cannot see why the animal should be a mule rather than a horse. It therefore matters very little whether the animal is a horse, a donkey, or a mule. Now what is still more curious is the fact that even at the age when the child succeeds in thinking of both conditions at the same time, the habit of thinking by simple juxtaposition still holds the field and prevents him from making a logical multiplication. For example, Fourn (9 ; 10), in spite of four long readings cannot decide between the

---

[1] J. Piaget, " Essai sur la multiplication logique et les débuts de la pensée formelle chez l'enfant," *Journ. Psych.*, Vol. XIX (1922), pp. 222–261.

horse, the donkey, and the mule, because " *It might be a donkey since it says : if the animal has long ears, it is a donkey or a mule. And it might be a horse since it says : if the animal has a thick tail it is either a horse or a mule,*" etc. There is no logical multiplication and exclusion (either . . . or) has not taken place.

The child's inability to perform logical multiplication therefore seems fairly general, since in addition to these experiments which are specially designed to reveal it, it is implied in the very common difficulty which he experiences in giving definitions that cover the whole of the object to be defined.

We have just seen, moreover, that the lack of hierarchy in children's concepts is more far-reaching than we had thought, since it affects logical addition as well as logical multiplication. At the time of writing the article quoted above, we thought that the children simply had a tendency to replace logical multiplication by logical addition. But, as a matter of fact, they have not even added the conditions ' long ears ' and ' thick tail ' in the test in question ; they have simply juxtaposed them. Otherwise, we might be able to say, in connexion with the definitions of force, for example, that the child replaces logical addition by multiplication ; in reality, he is equally incapable, at least systematically, of both these operations. This is only natural, since logical addition and multiplication are closely bound together.

It should be pointed out from the first that this difficulty in handling elementary logical operations goes through the whole structure of childish reasoning, for without logical addition or logical multiplication, except of the simplest kind, reasoning can only proceed from particular to particular. The syllogism rests mainly upon the right use of general concepts or classes which are the product of additions and multiplications of more elementary classes ; and even if the syllogism does not play the part which has been assigned to it in deduction, it is at least necessary for the verification of new cases by old ones. Moreover, if the child is ignorant of logical multiplication, this involves the use of alternation and exclusion, for to multiply two classes is, in most cases at any rate, to exclude something from each. If, on the other hand, the child cannot exclude with any consistency, the door is open to every kind of contradiction. All these are funda-mental phenomena which we shall now proceed to examine. This throws new light upon the results obtained in Chapter I, namely, the child's deeply-rooted inability to use the terms and relations of discordance. To insert discordance between a cause and an effect presupposes consciousness of the expression of a rule. Expression is exclusion, and if the use which the child makes of exclusion depends upon his capacity for logical multiplication, it follows that the possibility of discordance depends upon that of this fundamental logical operation. This will enable us to understand why the relation of explicit discordance is so late in appearing.

§ 3. CONTRADICTION IN CHILD THOUGHT.—It will be clear from the above analysis that until he reaches a certain age (7–8 at least) the child is insensible to contra-diction. If he is really incapable of defining even such notions as are unequivocally determined, this already supplies an element of contradiction. The particular use which he makes of a concept being unconscious, there will be throughout his reasoning a constant oscillation between the implicit conception which he possesses and the partial definition which he gives. And if his complex notions are really due to an over-determina-tion of factors such that the child can neither add nor multiply these factors logically, i.e. can never have them all simultaneously in his mind, this will constitute an even more important source of contra-diction. To show this in greater detail we shall begin by classifying the different types of contradiction which occur in the child.

These could be grouped by means of a table with double entry, two headings referring to the structure of the contradiction, and two to the subject-matter of the judgment. The structural types may be called *contradiction by amnesia* and *contradiction by condensation* (or by over-determination of which it is a product). The types classified by subject-matter are contradictions about *concepts* and judgments of classification, and contradictions about *explanations* and judgments of causality.

Contradiction by amnesia is not a specifically childish type, but it is far more abundantly represented in the child than in us for the following reason. The child hesitates, as we often do ourselves, between two opinions, as for example that the moon is alive and that it is not. He has very good reasons for each, but instead of choosing or of suspending his judgment, the child affirms each one in turn. For instance, he will maintain that the moon is alive. A few days or even a few moments later, when he is questioned again, he will quite sincerely deny that this is the case. Now after each *volte-face* the child really forgets his previous belief. He remembers what he said, but forgets his reasons for believing it ; he can no longer enter into a state of mind that is past. The same thing happens to us, not in purely intellectual problems (for then we know that our beliefs are changing, and we do not forget what we have rejected) but in problems where judgments of value play an important part. In ethical or religious questions, for example, the adult often behaves like the children we have spoken of : he may completely forget a belief which he held sincerely only a few minutes before, and then return to it a few moments later.

This form of contradiction is, however, far more frequent in the child, especially in view of the two following circumstances.

In the first place, as we have pointed out elsewhere (L.T., Chap. V, § 9), modality of judgment is a very different thing for us from what it is for the child. For us reality is always, if not distributed on one plane, at least unified, coherent, and submitted to a hierarchy by means of a single criterion—experience. For the child, on the contrary, there are several heterogeneous realities ; there is play, there is what is immediately observed, there is the world of things he has heard and been told about, and so on ; and these different worlds are more or less chaotic and independent of each other. So that when the child turns from a state of belief to a state of play, or from a state of submission to adult talk (verbal reality built up upon faith in what adults say) to a state of personal investigation, his opinions are apt to undergo singular transformations ; he may deny what he has just affirmed, and so on. In this mutability or rather this remarkable instability of belief we have a very important factor in contradiction by amnesia. There is even no paradox in maintaining that the child's belief varies as a function of his environment. According as he is with his parents, with his school-teachers, by himself, or with his companions, the child may very well have three or four interchangeable systems of belief. I have seen children of 8 years old state in all seriousness and with a degree of conviction that admitted of no doubt that there were ogres near Geneva on the Salève, and then, the moment they saw me smile, assure me that they never believed in them. Obviously there are two groups of contradictory beliefs, and when he is with strangers like us the child does not know at first which to adopt. Besides, this mentality survives in a great many adults, and it would not be hard to find working people who believe in the Devil when they are in church and cease to do so when they are in their work-shops.

A second circumstance in favour of the frequence of this type of contradiction is the very general character of childish amnesia. It is curious to note what illusions of perspective children are subject to with regard to their own thought, and to what lapses of memory with regard to what they have said and believed. A child will affirm, for example, that all rivers have been dug by the hand of

M

man. Somebody corrects this opinion and explains to him that water can bore out its own bed. Shortly or even immediately after this explanation, the child thinks that he has reached this newly-learned idea by himself and that he has always believed it. A large number of boys of 6 to 8 believe that one thinks through one's mouth or that thought is a voice inside one's head. The word ' brain,' when they know it, is always a recent acquisition. But as soon as they know it, they completely forget their former ideas, they claim never to have dreamt of thinking through one's mouth, and believe themselves to have discovered the word and the concept ' brain.'

For example, Reyb (8 ; 7) states that we think " *with our brains.*—Who told you ?—*No one . . .*—Where did you learn that word ?—*I've always known it.*—What is a brain ?—*Tubes in the head.*" A moment later : " Who told you it was tubes in the head ?—*No one.* Did you hear some one say it ?—*No,*" etc.

A child of the same age who has been asked to tell us what the moon is made of, says he doesn't know. We show him our watch and ask him what it is made of. Answer : *Gold.* " And the moon ?—*Also gold.*—Since when do you know that ?—*I've always known it.*—Did someone tell you or did you find out alone ?—*I found out alone.*—Since when ?—*I've always known,*" etc.

We have dwelt sufficiently in an earlier work [1] on the chaotic nature of memory and attention in children of 7–8, to allow ourselves to be very brief on the subject of these phenomena of amnesia. We need only recall the fact that these difficulties are closely bound up with the child's inability to become conscious of his own thought. It is because the child is not accustomed to notice the progress of his own thought, that the latter is subject to these illusions of perspective, these amnesias and consequently these contradictions.

---

[1] See *Arch. de Psych.*, Vol. XVIII (1921), p. 167. What we have called the ' implicit stage ' of the solution of logical problems is the stage when the child cannot hold two or three elements together in his mind without immediately forgetting at least one of them.

Belonging to the same type of contradiction are those arising from the fact that the child has no conscious grasp of definitions which have been determined by a single factor. It is obvious that this discordance between the definition of a concept and the use to which it is put must lead to contradiction. Thus Schei (6 ; $\frac{1}{2}$), as we saw in the last section, considers a cloud to be alive because it moves, but not so motors, although they also move. Theoretically, *i.e.* when we know the reason for these fluctuations there is no contradiction, but actually the children do not know the cause of their own inconsistency, and if we take account only of what they say and think, there is contradiction. This contradiction is not really due to amnesia, but to something analogous, viz. an inadequate *prise de conscience*.

Contradiction by condensation is much more important theoretically, because it is peculiar to the child ; unless indeed one regards it as the characteristic of all concepts in process of formation, and compares it to those contradictions to which scientists are sometimes driven when they are dealing with concepts whose full elaboration has not been completed (such as were for a long time the concepts of cause, force, action at a distance, the ether, and so on). Most childish concepts are, as we saw, over-determined by a large number of heterogeneous factors, as, for instance, resistance and activity for the concept of force, blood and activity for the concept of life, and these factors are simply thrown together by the child without being submitted to logical addition or multiplication. Such a lack of selection and hierarchy necessarily leads to contradiction, and this over-determination points not to any mystical capacity for dispensing with the principle of identity, but simply to an inability for restraint and for elimination. In this way the child is constantly faced with alternatives, both of which, for lack of the power to perform logical multiplication, he accepts simultaneously, and is consequently involved in contradiction. Condensation is therefore the result of over-determination ; a concept formed in this way is not a system but a heterogeneous and contradictory conglomeration, the result of simultaneous participation in several different realities.

It is easy enough to detect this phenomenon in the examples given in the last section in connexion with over-determination, and it is not necessary to add to these, for they are all alike. Duss (age 9), for example, looks upon the sun sometimes as alive, sometimes as not alive, according as it is determined by one of the component factors (because it gives light) or by the other (because it has no blood). In Duss's mind this concept is therefore a conglomeration, a contradictory condensation. Similarly, Imh regards the wind as sometimes alive and sometimes not, the concept ' life ' being for him a contradictory condensation of the quality of having movement (blowing) and of that of giving heat. Pig, Hellb, Berg, etc. present analogous cases.

These children's ideas of ' force ' and ' life ' are therefore genuine contradictory condensations. Such contradictions abound before the age of 7–8, and can, moreover, be produced by experiment. Thus, in the Burt test quoted above (Chap. II, § 4) '' Edith is fairer than Suzanne, Edith is darker than Lili : Which is the darkest of the three ? '' we made the following discovery. The child cannot conceive of a girl being both fairer than one and darker than another. In a sense then he seems more eager to avoid contradiction than we do. But this is so only in appearance, and is due to the fact that the child fails to make proper use of the judgments of relation. The proof of this is that the child who thinks that Suzanne is fair and Lili dark ends by finding contradictory (and accepting) the solution which assigns a ' darkish brown ' to Edith. So that Edith is both darker than Suzanne (who is dark) and fairer than Lili (who is fair) ! The enormity in this case is of course only momentary, and due to the conditions of the experiment, but the fact that children experience so much difficulty in controlling

their hypotheses shows us what must be going on in
their minds from day to day.

In addition to these contradictions by condensation,
which affect concepts and judgments of classification or
of simple relations, we can constantly note the occurrence
of contradictions in causal explanations either by amnesia
(to which we need not return) or by condensation. Here
is an example.

To ($7\frac{1}{2}$) thinks that boats float " *because they are wood.*—
Why does wood stay on the water?—*Because it is light
and the little boats have sails* [over-determination].—And
those that have no sails why do they not sink?—*Because
it is light.*—. . . And how about big boats?—*Because
they are heavy.*—Then heavy things stay on top of the water?
No.—Does a big stone?—*No, it sinks.*—And big boats?
—*They stay because they are heavy.*—Is that the only
reason?—*No.*—What else?—*Because they have big sails.*
—And when these are taken away?—*Then they are less
heavy.* — And if the sails are put on again?—*The same
thing happens. They stay* [on the water] *because they
are heavy.*"

Theoretically, *i.e.* if we look for To's unconscious
tendencies, the contradiction is perhaps not quite so
flagrant as it appears to be, for it may be that To
regards weight as a sign of strength. Big boats would
float because they were strong and little ones because
they were supported by the water. But To says
nothing about this and is in no way conscious of it.
Actually, *i.e.* on the plane of conscious formulation,
there is contradiction.

We shall meet with more examples later on in connexion
with transduction. Moreover, these contradictions occurring in explanation do not differ in structure from those
contained in simple fragments of classification or logical
relation.

§ 4. THE PSYCHOLOGICAL EQUIVALENT OF NON-CON-
TRADICTION AND THE NOTION OF MENTAL REVERSIBILITY.
—It will now be of interest to enquire into the psycho-
logical significance of childish contradictions. The prob-

lem is important and should be clearly stated if the subject of reasoning in the child is to be approached in its widest aspects.

What is contradiction between two judgments or within one and the same concept ? From the point of view of logic it is an ultimate and indefinable notion which can only be described by showing the mental impossibility of affirming contradictory propositions simultaneously. But from the psychological point of view we have here a problem because we cannot see how it comes about that the mind wishes to avoid contradiction nor what are the conditions of non-contradiction. We cannot say straight away of the psychological (as opposed to the logical) structure of thought any more than of the structure of any other natural phenomenon that it is non-contradictory. For it is only too obvious that there is within the organism, for example, a host of antagonistic tendencies existing in an unstable condition and such that the growth of one involves the decay of the others. Mental life in its primitive, instinctive, or affective aspects will naturally obey the same laws. There is not a single emotion that does not contain a hidden bi-polarity or, as Bleuler has called it, an ambivalence which from the point of view of consciousness is a contradiction. How then are we to characterize from the psychological point of view behaviour or mental states which are the concomitants of logical non-contradiction in distinction to those other forms of behaviour which, if they were translated into fully explicit judgments, would be contradictory ? Such is the problem which we wish to deal with in the very briefest outlines.

Broadly speaking, we may make the following fundamental distinction : non-contradiction is a state of equilibrium in contrast to the state of permanent disequilibrium which is the normal life of the mind. For, as every one knows nowadays, sensations, images, pleasure and pain, in short all the ' immediate data of consciousness ' are borne along on a continuous ' stream of consciousness.' Exactly the same thing applies to the immediate data of the external world ; they constitute Heraclitus' eternal becoming. A certain number of fixed points stand out in contrast to this flux, such as concepts and the relations subsisting between them, in a word, the whole universe of logic, which in the very process of its formation is independent of time and consequently in a state of equilibrium. We can therefore say that every notion, while still in the making, contains a certain amount of contradiction, and that on reaching a state of equilibrium or immobility it is enabled to eliminate this element of disharmony.

But this is only a rough approximation to the facts. It is not true to say that notions are immobile. Every idea grows, finds fresh application, becomes generalized and dissociated. These operations, which are due to the incessant work of the judging activity, do not necessarily lead to contradiction, and though the permanence of an idea may be an index of its logical identity, identity and non-contradiction certainly do not cover the same ground. Mathematical equations are not identities, and yet they escape contradiction. The balance we are trying to determine therefore presupposes something permanent, but it cannot be defined as the absence of all movement ; it is a ' moving equilibrium.'

This equilibrium can be quite shortly defined as the *reversibility* of the operations in the balance. A non-contradictory operation is a reversible operation. This term must not be taken in the logical sense which is derivative, but in the strictly psychological sense. A mental operation is reversible when, starting from its result, one can find a symmetrically corresponding operation which will lead back to the data of the first operation without these having been altered in the process. Thus to extend, as does the child, the notion of ' force = activity ' to the notion of ' force =resistance ' simply by means of syncretic condensation devoid of logical addition is not to perform a reversible operation ; the condensed notion resultant upon the operation alters both the original notions. The child therefore becomes involved in the contradictions which we pointed out. Logical operations, on the contrary, are reversible. If I divide a given collection of objects into four equal piles, I can recover the original whole by multiplying one of my quarters by four : the operation of multiplication is symmetrical to that of division. Thus every rational operation has a corresponding operation that is symmetrical to it and which enables one to return to one's starting-point. Contradiction may therefore be detected in the irreversibility of any particular process, in the fact that no exactly symmetrical relation could be found whereby to control the original operation.

This description is so obvious from the logical point of view that it seems absurd to lay so much stress upon it, but a logical truism may very well conceal serious complexities of a psychological order. The child will naturally not prove capable of reversible operations from the first, and the psychological conditions of reversibility will have to be closely analysed if we are to grasp the full significance in the history of thought of the desire to avoid contradiction.

Let us begin by confining the problem to the sphere of directed thought. For it is obvious that non-directed thought, *i.e.* that in which the individual has set himself no real problem, but seeks only to satisfy some desire which is not conscious, or not wholly so—it is obvious that such thought is by its very nature irreversible. This feature is even what constitutes its chief originality. A train of associations is irreversible, because association of ideas is nearly always directed by an affective tendency which nothing obliges to remain the same. Thus if from the idea of ' table ' I am led by the interests of the moment to the idea of ' Napoleon,' it is extremely unlikely that I shall travel back along the same route and by means of the same connecting stations (table, castle, Malmaison, Napoleon) when a few hours later I am asked to associate

my ideas to the word ' Napoleon.' The path I shall follow
is far more likely to be the irreversible stream of my own
spontaneous thought. Similarly, in dreams we have an
irreversible procession of images guided by a desire or
an unconscious tendency, which is akin to the work of
imagination in simply retracing the various phases of
an event. Here there are no logical or causal relations,
no implications, none of those ' if . . . then's ' which
alone would enable the dreamer or the day-dreamer to
really work upon his cinematograph, *i.e.* to reconstruct
previous images by means of present ones, and thus in a
measure to travel back up the stream of time. In a word,
we have here a stream of images devoid of reversible
relations. If we want reversibility, we must have proper
operations, *i.e.* either a manual or a mental process of
construction or decomposition whose aim it is to anticipate
or to reconstruct phenomena. A mere succession of
images with no other direction than that imposed upon
it by an unconscious desire is therefore not sufficient to
create a reversible process.

But in thought that is really directed, that obeys
conscious direction, what are the conditions to which the
mental operations will have to be submitted in order to
be really reversible ? The thought of the child, like every
other kind of thought, is swayed by two fundamental
interests whose interaction is precisely what determines
this reversibility. These are *imitation* of reality by
the organism or the mind, and *assimilation* of reality
by the organism or the mind. *Imitation* of reality is the
fundamental tendency of childish activity to reproduce,
first by gesture and then by imagination, the external
movements to which the organism is compelled to adapt
itself, and later and more generally the succession or partial
successions of events and phenomena which call for the same
adaptation. Imitation is the self's desire to be always
repeating the history of things so as to become adapted
to them ; it matters little whether this reproduction is
corporal or mental. Now there is nothing reversible about

thought as an organ of imitation.[1] The order in nature of phenomena is clearly reversible, except for certain mechanical successions which the mind only succeeds in grasping very late, and thanks to certain experiments intended to secure the very reversibility which he was hoping to find. Thus such and such a word which the child is imitating will be pronounced by his parents with different inflexions and used in a different sense on separate occasions. Such and such an old man whom the child is trying to imitate in his play or in his drawing will be dressed one way one day and differently on the next. It is therefore only natural that imitation should not immediately produce reversible mental operations, so long as imitation does not link up with genuine assimilation of reality to the self. That boats should float one day because they are light, and the next day because they are heavy appears to be a matter of course so long as the mind does no more than recall a set of disconnected stories—such as the story of the little boat put into the basin, or of the heavy boat made to sail on the lake. Imitation of reality cannot therefore lead to irreversibility short of combining with the assimilative faculty.

At first sight the assimilative tendency shown by thought seems sufficient to secure stability in judgments. To assimilate, in psychology as in biology, is to reproduce oneself by means of the external world ; it is to transform perceptions until they are identical with one's own thought, *i.e.* with previous schemas. Assimilation is therefore preservation and, in a certain sense, identification. Thus the child, feeling himself to be alive, also regards animals, stars, clouds, water, and wind as alive : these disparate phenomena are all assimilated to a single schema. Within the constant stream of particular experiences and stories of which imitation recalls the image, assimilation seems

[1] The ' circular reaction ' by means of which M. Baldwin has attempted to define imitation (*Mental Development in the Child and the Race*, London, 1907) does not seem to us to characterize imitation pure, but is already the result of a combination between imitation and assimilation.

to create a fixed element, a uniform manner of reacting to the flux of becoming.

The facts show, however, that this process of assimilation has a far more complicated history in the child's mental life than at first appears to be the case. If assimilation is really the fusion of a new object with an already existing schema, this fusion may very well have originally been a kind of reciprocal destruction : the object, because it is new and until this moment unknown, will remain irreducible to the schema, and both will be altered by being identified with one another. The object, in other words, will lose its specific character, and the schema will be not only widened and generalized, but fundamentally changed.

Now, a large number of facts show us that this is actually what happens in primitive or, as in this sense we may call it, in ' deforming ' assimilation. In undirected thought, assimilation is always deforming to begin with. At least this is how we can interpret the constant condensation in dream and imagination described by Freud. To condense two images is to fuse them into one composite image (as, for example, one person combining the features of two distinct persons) ; it is not to subsume them under one schema which will leave them their respective individuality, but to force them into a schema which is the result of their confusion. In the child's directed intelligence, on the other hand, there are several phenomena analogous to this deforming assimilation. There is, for example, the phenomenon of syncretism which we have shown elsewhere (L.T., Chap. VI) to be exactly half-way between ' condensation ' of undirected thought and the generalization of directed thought. In the experiments we dealt with then, the child reads a given sentence A and a given sentence B, and although for us the sentences have nothing in common, the child, whose task it is to find two sentences meaning the same thing, actually fuses the two sentences into a common schema built up out of all the given elements. Assimilation is therefore present, but here again it is clearly ' deforming,' in the sense that if A digests B, A also deforms B (the child would have understood B quite differently if he had not previously read A) and is in its turn digested and deformed by B. ' Over-determination,' of which we spoke in the last section, is simply a special case of syncretism, and consequently of deforming assimilation. But in this case the various components are not completely assimilated, but remain partly estranged from one another ; it is only for a moment that one component disfigures another or is disfigured by it.

In short, the tendency of thought to assimilate the external world cannot, in the first place, lead to the reversibility of mental processes. On the contrary, in its early stages, as is shown by the phenomena of con-densation and syncretism, assimilation tries to be too thorough, and destroys both the assimilated object and the assimilating schema. Now once the object and the schema have been altered in this way, the mind cannot, after the act of assimilation, turn back and dis-assimilate them, so to speak, so as to find them identical with what they had been. Take, for example, the two sentences of which we spoke just now, or the two terms of a condensed image, or again the two components of an over-determined concept. In such cases the schema A and the object B do not give rise to a synthesis $(A + B)$ or $(A \times B)$ as would be the case with us, but to something which partially or totally destroys both A and B. The process is therefore not reversible. It is not $A + B \rightarrow C$ in such a way that one can retrace one's footsteps $C \rightarrow A + B$. It can only be schema-tized as follows : $A + B \rightarrow C$ such that $C \rightarrow A' + B'$ or $\rightarrow A + B'$, or $\rightarrow A' + B$.

In conclusion, neither the imitative nor the assimilative tendency is sufficient by itself to secure for child thought a reversibility that will render it free from contradiction. Left to themselves, each will lead either to dream or play, both of them activities in which the irreversibility of thought is practically complete.

What then is necessary for the presence of reversibility in mental operations ? The answer is that assimilation and imitation will have to collaborate instead of pulling in different directions as they do in the early stages of mental growth.

After all, wherever thought has reached a certain degree of development, imitation and assimilation constitute two opposite poles. If a new phenomenon takes place within an organism, the organism can adapt itself to it, and in so doing breaks away from its previous habits of reasoning or imagination in order to create a new and original image which will faithfully copy the unknown phenomenon. This is the imitative tendency, which consists in reproducing objects by means of gesture or thought, and consequently in deforming earlier thought and gesture as a function of the new-found objects. Or else the organism can force the new phenomenon into the habitual motor or intellectual schemas, as happens in children's games, in childish syncretism of thought or in the condensation of dreams. This is the assimilative tendency, which consists, not in reproducing things by gesture or thought, but in feeding and reproducing personal motor tendencies or earlier schemas of thought by means of things, and consequently in deforming the new-found objects as a function of earlier thought or gesture. This shows that at root imitation and assimilation are fundamentally antagonistic.

And this antagonism is really what produces the irreversibility of thought. For why does assimilation in fusing an object B and a schema A deform both one and the other ? It is because at the moment when the mind is assimilating, it ceases to imitate ; in other words imitation ceases to preserve in all their specificity the images corresponding to A and to B. If in spite of assimilating B to A the mind could preserve intact the images subsumed under A, it is obvious that the process $A + B \rightarrow C$ would be reversible and that $C = A + B$. The element C would then represent the synthesis and not the confusion of A and B. In short, the necessary and sufficient condition for assimilation to constitute a reversible process is that it should go hand in hand with an imitation of phenomena which shall be directly proportional to their assimilation. And why, conversely, does imitation, by confining itself to the reproduction in action or imagination of the history of things, constitute an irreversible process exactly similar to the flux of becoming ? It is because the child, imitating one day the phenomenon A and the next day phenomenon B, gives up the attempt to assimilate them one to another. In logical parlance, he does not try to generalize his experiences and his observations. The condition for a reversible imitation is therefore that there should be a corresponding proportion of assimilation.

In so far, then, as imitation and assimilation are antagonistic to one another, there is irreversibility of thought, and in so far as these two tendencies succeed in harmonizing with one another there is reversibility. From the logical point of view these are only truisms, but for the psychologist there is a certain interest in analysing the conditions of a systematization as difficult for the child as that which will give rise to logically reversible processes of thought. By showing that logical contradiction is the result of the conflict (fundamental from the genetic point of view) of imitation and assimilation, we have at least a psychological picture of the logical structure of thought, and such presentations of the facts are never wholly devoid of utility.

And now we may ask what are the factors which will bring about the solidarity of imitation and assimilation ? To appeal to the presence of a desire for unity would be to involve ourselves in a vicious circle, and to explain non-contradiction by itself. But in order to escape from this circle (supplied in this case by the facts themselves) we must bear in mind that imitation and assimilation involve one another from the moment that they begin to function. For it is impossible for the mind to assimilate without a factor of differentiation which will in a measure keep apart the objects to be assimilated, in other words, without a certain degree of imitation ; and it is impossible to imitate a new phenomenon without *ipso facto* creating in oneself a process that tends to perpetuate and to reproduce indefinitely the image of this phenomenon, which henceforth ceases to be new, and enters the domain of assimilated objects. This is why Baldwin, in trying to characterize imitation, brings in a definitely assimilative element into his description (circular reaction). If assimilation and imitation remain antagonistic for so long, this is solely due to the pressure of external reality and to the excessive novelty and change of the images which it is constantly bringing before the mind. But as soon as reality is assimilated, an increasing solidarity comes to be established between assimilation and imitation.

When does this binding process become sufficiently powerful to produce genuine reversibility in thought ? At the moment when the solidarity in question ceases to be mechanical, and becomes logical or mental, and is regulated by definite and conscious judgments of value. Here again, social factors enter into the development of thought, and join themselves to the biological factors whose work they bring to completion.

The ego-centrism of thought which characterizes the early life of the child entails a consistent antagonism between assimilation and imitation. In the first place, an ego-centric mind will assimilate everything to itself and to its own point of view. Syncretism, the non-relativity of childish concepts, etc. are all due to this ego-centric assimilation. Now it goes without saying that this assimilation deforms its objects, *i.e.* that it has no respect for their specific nature. Imitation is therefore not sufficient. In the second place, in virtue of his very ego-centrism the child is not conscious of his own thought, he has not the feeling of his own ego ; consequently, he is always imitating things and people, owing to that sort of confusion between self and others which Janet made the characteristic feature of imitation. At such moments imitation is complete, but is not accompanied by assimilation.

Such, then, are the two antagonistic poles between which the child is constantly fluctuating : deforming assimilation due to his ego-centrism, and imitation devoid of assimilation due to his lack of consciousness of self arising from ego-centrism.

But as soon as thought becomes socialized, a momentous factor comes into play ; imitation and assimilation are transformed, solidarity is established between them, and thought becomes increasingly capable of reversibility. For the capacity for leaving one's own point of view and entering into that of other people robs assimilation of its deforming character, and forces it to respect the objectivity of its data. The child will henceforth attempt to weave a network of reciprocal relations between his own point of view and that of others. This *reciprocity* of view-points will enable him both to incorporate new phenomena and events into his ego, and to respect their objectivity, *i.e.* the specific characters which they present. Gradually, this same reciprocity of view-points will accustom the child to the reciprocity of relations in general. Henceforth, imitation of reality will find its completion in assimilation of reality by the mind.

Social life, by developing the reciprocity of relations side by side with the consciousness of necessary implications, will therefore remove the antagonistic characters of assimilation and imitation, and render the two processes mutually dependent. Social life therefore helps to make our mental processes reversible, and in this way prepares the path for logical reasoning.

§ 5. TRANSDUCTION.—The preceding pages may have seemed to the reader to be very far removed from the psychology of childish reasoning. But this is not the case, for the child's contradictions and the irreversibility of his thought are precisely the factors which will explain the nature of transductive reasoning. The whole structure of childish reasoning before the age of 7–8, and even in a certain measure up to the appearance of real deduction at the age of 11–12 can be explained by the fact that the child reasons about individual or particular cases between which he does not enquire whether there is contradiction or non-contradiction, and which give rise to mental experiments which are as yet not reversible.

Here is an example.

We show Mull (age 8) a glass of water into which we put a pebble, and then ask him why the level of the water has risen. Mull tells us that it is because the pebble is heavy. We show Mull another pebble and try to make him foresee what will happen. Mull says about the pebble: " *It is heavy. It will make the water go up.* —And this one [a smaller pebble] ?—*No.*—Why ?—*It is light.*"

Mull seems to be carrying out a syllogistic argument which consists in applying a general law to particular cases : " Heavy objects raise the level of the water. . . . Now this pebble is heavy, or light . . . therefore it will, or will not raise the level of the water.' If we bear in mind what has been said about conjunctions of causality and of logical sequence (Chap. 1) or about the unconsciousness of childish reasoning (present chapter, §§ 1 and 2), we certainly cannot suppose that Mull is conscious of the general proposition : " All heavy objects raise . . .," but this is of no consequence : Since Mull behaves logically as though he had this general law in his mind, we can admit that he has reasoned by implicit syllogisms, in short, by enthymeme. This conclusion gains in strength from the fact that Mull's explanation is that of practically all the boys of his age. Up to the age of 9 three-quarters of the children say that the pebble raises the water because it is heavy, because it weighs on the water, etc.[1] But to return to the experiment.

" Is this piece of wood heavy ?—*No.*—If it were put in the water would it make it rise ?—*Yes, because it isn't*

---

[1] We have borrowed this example from an enquiry into the development of physical causality which was carried out in collaboration with Mlle L. Hahnloser, and the results of which will appear in a subsequent volume devoted to the study of explanation in the child.

heavy.—Which is heaviest, this wood or this pebble [a small pebble and a large piece of wood] ?—*The pebble* [correct].—Which will make the water rise highest ?—*The wood* —Why ?—*Because it is bigger* [because it has more volume than the pebble].—Then why did the pebbles make the water rise just now ?—*Because they are heavy.*—If I put that in [a handful of pebbles] ?—*It will run* [the water will run over].—Why ?—*Because it is heavy.*"

This example shows the mechanism of childish reasoning very clearly. In the first place, there has been no syllogism. Not only is Mull in no way conscious of the general proposition we spoke of just now (" Heavy objects make the water rise ") but, what is more important, he does not apply it even implicitly. He claims, for example, that the wood makes the water rise " because it is not heavy," immediately after having said that the pebble did so " because it is heavy." Now where does this illogicality come from ? Clearly, from the factors which we have just been studying, and in particular from the fact that the subject is not conscious of his own thought. For Mull has not contradicted himself for the pleasure of doing so ; he simply had several things in his mind at the same time. On the one hand, he thought that heavy objects, as such, caused the water to rise, and not in their capacity of bigness. On the other hand, he knew implicitly that large, voluminous objects caused the level of the water to rise. Unconsciously guided by this schema, he affirms that the wood will make the water rise " because it is not heavy," but he only becomes conscious of this reason a little later and under pressure of the comparison which we force him to make between a large piece of light wood and a small heavy pebble. This conscious realization is, however, so weak that immediately after having said that the wood makes the water rise " because it is big," Mull once again maintains that the handful of pebbles will do so " because they are heavy." In short, Mull has in his mind the concept of volume and is occasionally guided by it, but he has only become conscious of the concept of weight, as though objects were heavy in proportion to their size. When discordance appears between volume and weight, Mull invokes sometimes weight and sometimes size in his explanations. The two following conclusions should be borne in mind. 1° Mull contradicts himself in his explanations of the rise of the water-level, because his explanations are over-determined by two heterogeneous factors (weight and volume), because he is not conscious of this dualism, and because in consequence of this he cannot submit these two factors to logical addition or multiplication. These phenomena have been analysed at great length in the preceding sections of this chapter. 2° Now (and this is the most important point for us at present) this absence of synthesis is what forces Mull, when he reasons consciously, *i.e.* when he makes his implications explicit, to reason only about individual or special cases. There is no (deductive) reasoning and no induction that is possible for Mull, because as soon as he tries to generalize an explanation he contradicts himself. So that he will either generalize and contradict himself, which is the same as not generalizing, or he will not contradict himself and will reason only about particular cases.

Mull's example is far from being unique ; it is the proto-type of all childish reasoning up to the age of 8 or more. With regard to the way children reason when they are being questioned, we found in the first place (preceding sections) cases of unconsciousness, of inability to give definitions, of inability to perform logical operations (addition and multiplication) and cases of contradiction. All these phenomena go to prove that the child does not reason by syllogisms, but by inferences from particular to particular, made without any logical rigour. In addition to this, the study of the spontaneous language of children and of the conjunctions of logical relations (Chap. I) leads us to exactly the same result. In their spontaneous reasoning children infer only from particular to particular. Or, to put it in a different way, all the reasoning processes that have been collected are 'mental experiments' carried out on individual cases without any attempt at generalization or appeal to laws previously generalized. *" I can shut my* [cardboard desk] *if I want to. That is why it doesn't stick. Afterwards* [if it sticks] *I shan't be able to shut it any more."* The list of spontaneous logical reasons enumerated in § 5 of Chapter I (in connexion with the word ' then ') is sufficient in itself to show how even spontaneous attempts at proof appeal to nothing beyond non-generalized mental experiments.

Children's reasoning, in short, does not move from universal to particular (All voluminous objects make the water rise, therefore this pebble makes the water rise because it has volume), nor from particular to universal (This piece of wood has volume and raises the water ; this pebble is smaller and raises the water less, therefore all voluminous objects raise the water-level), but from particular to particular : this pebble makes the water rise because it is heavy, therefore this other pebble will also do so because it too is heavy ; this piece of wood will make the water rise because it is large, this one will therefore do so because it also is large, etc.   To each object belongs a special explanation and consequently special relations which can only give rise to special reasoning. This of course is only natural, considering what we know of childish language and judgment, and it is a characteristic which has attracted the attention of every psychologist from John Stuart Mill and Ribot onwards.   Stern has christened this form of reasoning *transduction*, in contrast to deduction and induction.   But all we possess as yet is a description of this process of transduction ; an explanation of it has yet to be found.   To say that the child cannot generalize is simply to make a statement of fact.   The task still remains of bringing this statement into relation with what we have found to be the general conditions of child thought.

It should be noted, moreover, that transduction is not opposed to deduction in the sense that Stern supposed it to be. Stern simply adopted the definition of classical logic : deduction is a passing from the universal to the particular. But logicians themselves, and subsequently M. Goblot [1] have shown that deduction may very well deal with individual or special objects, as is often the case in mathematics, and so lead from the particular to the universal. For in order to prove that the sum of the angles of a triangle is equal to 180° we work on a single triangle, and only afterwards do we generalize about all triangles by modifying the figure on which we have worked. As M. Goblot says, quoting Mach, we simply ' construct ' by means of a mental experiment the conclusion that is to be proved. Wherein, then, does transduction differ from deduction ? Clearly by its lack of logical necessity ; mathematical deduction has a rigour which is absent from transduction. But wherein does this rigour consist ? According to M. Goblot, a mental construction leads to necessary conclusions in so far as it obeys rules, and these are not the rules of logic, but previously admitted propositions which are now applied syllogistically. The rules, then, are general propositions, but in this new interpretation, deduction does not consist in drawing the looked-for conclusion from these propositions ; it consists in applying these propositions to a mental or actual construction which will allow the desired consequence to be found. This solution, however, cannot meet the problem as we have stated it here, for it still remains to be determined how, from the psychological point of view, the child has been able to establish these propositions and to handle them with any degree of logical rigour.[2]

---

[1] *Traité de logique*, Paris, 1918.

[2] In order to dispose in a few words of this point of logic before resuming our analysis of transduction, we may be allowed to point out that M. Goblot's solution does not steer clear of all the difficulties presented by the problem. For either deduction is limited to drawing conclusions from previous propositions—which is a view that M. Goblot rightly rejects—or the strictness of the mental construction which gives rise to the conclusions is not due solely to the earlier propositions applied syllogistically to these constructions. For if the latter were the case, our original constructions, those for instance, which by

The problem is then as follows. Transduction is a form of reasoning which proceeds from particular to particular without generalization and without logical rigour. Deduction is a form of reasoning that proceeds from particular to particular, from universal to particular, or from particular to universal, but always with logical rigour. What are the relations between this rigour and these generalizations? Can we say that generalization leads to rigour, or is it the other way about? It will be our object to show that the absence of rigour from transduction is what prevents the child from generalizing, and that this lack of rigour is itself due, as we hinted in the last paragraph, to the irreversibility of thought.

Here, then, is a child who claims that a pebble raises the water-level because it is heavy, and that a piece of wood produces the same result because it is large. The child generalizes neither of these explanations, and does not feel them to be mutually contradictory. Why? Let the relation be one of cause and effect. " The water rises because the stone is heavy." Even in reasoning about this particular case a mind accustomed to handle deduction would conclude to the existence of a reciprocal

addition, subtraction, etc. give rise to positive or negative integral numbers, ought to be lacking in rigour for want of any previous mathematical propositions. It may be said in reply to this that the propositions on which these operations or constructions rest are the axioms and definitions of those same operations. But axioms and definitions are not external to construction. The operations or constructions which underlie the fertility of mathematics must therefore be their own guarantee, and must not be subject to an appeal to any earlier propositions. The axiomatic element of science only appears after the science in question, and does no more than to emphasize by isolating it the verifiable element which the constructions or operations of this science contained in themselves. This is why although we accept M. Goblot's profound criticism of the syllogism and his notion of construction which is so fertile from the psychological point of view, we feel that we must go one further and say that ' mental construction ' must itself furnish the explanation not only of the fertility but of the rigidity, rigour, and strictness of deductive reasoning. It is our opinion that a construction becomes rigorous to the extent that it is reversible, and that this reversibility of the operations is what makes generalization possible.

relation between the fact of the water rising and the weight
of the pebble. For each relation of cause and effect there
is a corresponding relation of effect to cause, and if such
and such a cause can be reconstructed surely such and such
an effect can be anticipated ; it is simply a matter of
altering the original data so as to know whether the
explanation was right, or of making a supplementary
experiment to confirm or invalidate the consequences
drawn from the hypotheses that had arisen during the
first. Thus our child could have said to himself, by simply
inverting the relations : " This pebble will make the
water rise because it is heavy : this piece of wood which
is not heavy will not make the water rise. If the water
does rise, then there is no necessary connexion between
weight and the rise of the water, etc." This shows clearly
that the discovery of a general law is bound up with the
possibility of using relations in all directions and of finding
the reciprocal counterpart to every relation. If the child
in this particular case has been unable to generalize, has
failed to find a ' law,' it is simply because the reciprocity
of the relations in question has escaped him. Otherwise we
could not understand why the child is unable to generalize,
seeing that his habits of syncretism, of immediate analogy,
etc. lead him to assimilate everything to everything else.

This hypothesis will seem very plausible if reference is
made to our analysis of the logic of relations (Chaps. II
and III). We examined at great length the persistent
difficulties which the child experiences in finding such
simple reciprocal relations as that of brother and sister,
of right and left, etc., and we saw that this lack of reciprocity is what prevents children from reasoning logically.
We may conclude from this that the absence of rigour
from transduction is due to difficulty in handling relations,
and particularly in grasping their reciprocity.

Now, as we saw in the preceding section this inability
to realize the reciprocity of relations is itself due to the
irreversibility of thought in the child. The child either
assimilates everything from the immediate point of view,

or else he juxtaposes a series of separate explanations. In both cases, thought is irreversible in the sense that it involves contradictions. In both cases, the reciprocity of the various perspectives is rendered impossible.

But the example of Mull which we have just been examining is not sufficient to make us grasp the exact difference between transduction and adult deduction. Mull juxtaposes a series of separate explanations, and this is why his reasoning is not reversible. It may be objected, however, that in each particular sphere Mull reasons deductively : " This pebble makes the water rise because it is heavy, therefore this one will do the same because it is heavy." This, at any rate, seems to be reasoning by partial analogy, and analogy is the starting-point of deduction.

But transduction is something different from reasoning by analogy, at least in its beginnings. Let us now quote a case of pure transduction, because it is more primitive, and will lay bare the mechanism of this reasoning without general laws.

Roy (age 8) tells us that the moon grows. ' Half ' of the moon (its crescent) becomes ' the whole.' " How does the moon grow ?—*Because it gets bigger.*—How does it happen ?—*Because we grow ourselves.*—What makes it grow ?—*The clouds.*—How did it begin ?—*Because we began to be alive.*—How did the moon make herself be there ?—*Because we made ourselves be there.*—And did that make the moon grow ?—*Yes.* — How ? —. . .— Why ?—*The clouds made it grow,*" etc., etc.   Roy also tells us that the wind walks along, " *because we also walk along,*" or that the sun is not trying to go away," *because sometimes we don't go away.*"

For us these words would simply have the following meaning : 1° The moon, the wind, etc. are analogous to us. 2° Now we grow and walk, etc., therefore they grow and walk, etc.   But for the child these propositions have a completely different meaning.   1° There is not simply analogy between the different objects Roy is talking about, there is syncretism. It is we who make the moon grow, etc., not materially, since the clouds do that, but ' precausally ' (through confusion of motive and cause. See L.T., Chap. V). The analogy is therefore felt, not only as a reason, but as an immediately given relation. Such cases are not rare. This is not the place to discuss them from the point of view of causality· This will be done in a later volume where the case of Roy will be analysed along with all analogous cases. It will be enough to say here that syncretism precedes and out-runs mere analogy. 2° There is therefore no general law. It is not in virtue of the law : " All living objects grow " that the moon grows ; it is quite simply and directly " be-cause we grow." The relation here is not merely causal, it is also logical. The moon is alive, " because we are alive.'

We can see now what transduction consists in. It is an inference from particular to particular without any general law. We can see, above all, why there is no general law. It is because there is syncretism, *i.e.* immediate fusion of the separate terms. Now this fusion is irre-versible. It takes place as the accidental outcome of new perceptions, and deforms what is acquired, instead of respecting it as genuine deduction would do. Thus, whether there is juxtaposition of separate explanations as with Mull, or syncretistic fusion of separate cases, as with Roy, in both cases we have irreversibility, and this irreversibility is what explains the absence of general laws.

In conclusion, reversibility of thought determines generalization, because this reversibility entails a certain necessity according as the phenomena to which the mind applies itself admit of more or less reversible experi-ments. The essence of thought is the attempt to make reality itself reversible. Thus a scientist faced with the hypothesis : " The water has risen because the stone is big, " will do his best, before knowing how to generalize, to find a completely reversible relation between volume and the water-level. He will vary the volume of the pebble until he has found between this volume and the water-level a relation that shall be no longer purely causal, but functional (which simply means reversible) according to which the level will vary " as a function of " the volume. This function will enable the scientist to foresee both the water-level, given the volume that has been immersed, and the volume of the pebble, given level that has been reached. From the moment that this necessity has been reached, even by means of only two or three experiments, the proposition in question can be conceived as entirely general. Generalization is therefore the product of constructions performed on particular cases, as M. Goblot maintains. But these constructions are directed not necessarily by previously admitted propositions but by the need for respecting the reciprocity of the relations that have been brought into play.

It goes without saying that in experimental constructions properly so-called (the physical sciences) the progressive generalization can be accompanied by logical necessity only in so far as the experiment succeeds in converting irreversible reality into a reality that is reversible. The peculiar property of purely mental constructions like those of mathematics is to be entirely reversible, and therefore entirely logical from the first.

One could not do better in selecting the distinguishing mark of transduction than to describe it as an elementary ' mental experiment,' or as Mach and Rignano have put it, as a combination in imagination of the relations presented to us by reality. Elementary mental experiment is not as yet a process of necessary reasoning ; there is nothing necessary about the observation of facts so long as the elements of reality so observed are not dissociated to the extent of supplying the material for the construction of a simpler and completely reversible reality. For mental experiment, arising as it does out of immediate perception, will necessarily contain syncretistic and consequently reversible elements.

How does the transition take place in the child from this primitive mental experimenting which is transduction to logical reasoning proper ? If we are willing to incur the risk of artificial classification, childish reasoning may be divided into three principal stages of development.

The first stage, which might be called ' the stage of pure transduction ' would extend up to the age of 7–8, and would be distinguished by the character of irreversibility which we have been describing.

During the second stage (ages 7–8 to 11–12) the mental experiments tend to become reversible, which does not mean, however, that they all succeed in doing so on the same plane of thought. This reversibility can be recognized by the diminishing number of contradictions, and is the result of an increasing awareness of the reciprocity of view-points and relations. After each mental experiment the child is impelled to travel back along the road he has taken, *i.e.* to find consequences as well as causes and proofs as well as explanations. In other words, logical or theoretical necessity appears upon the scene. The child is no longer content to explain one phenomenon by another simply by recalling their common history, he wants to connect the two phenomena by a necessary relation. Transductive reasoning yields before the increasing need for combined induction and deduction. Generalization has become possible.

But this primitive form of necessity and deduction is still only concerned with perception; these early deductions still bear only upon actual reality, upon premises which are given by direct observation and are immediately believed by the child, as opposed to hypotheses which are reasoned about in order to test them, or assumptions which are suggested by other people. Only during the third stage, *i.e.* after the age of 11–12 are these restrictions removed from deduction when thought becomes formal and is freed from immediate beliefs of the moment.

What, from our present point of view, is the distinguishing feature of this third stage to which we have already drawn attention in our analysis of formal thought (Chap. II) ? Pure transduction, as we have just seen, is a primitive mental experiment, a simple imagining or imitation of reality as it is perceived, viz. as irreversible. The second stage is that of full mental experiment in which imagination completes irreversible reality by a pictured whole of reversible relations or logical implications, such that from A we can infer B and vice versa. With those two types of mental experiment it therefore looks as though the mind had attained the measure of reversibility which it needed.   But this is not the case. If a mental experiment is to be completely reversible, it is necessary to substitute for the objects offered in perception other more intellectual objects which shall be defined in just such a manner as will allow of reversibility. Thus, in our recent examples, the child, in order to explain why the pebble makes the level of the water rise, begins by reasoning about ' weight,' as though this were an immediately given notion and bore an unequivocal relation to volume.   He soon notices, however, that a large object and a small object may both have the same weight. Absolute weight, *i.e.* weight conceived as directly indicated by volume will therefore have to give way to relative weight, and henceforward the child will reason from the idea of weight-volume, a relation which he will formulate more or less as follows : " Pebble heavy for its smallness " or " light for its bigness," etc.   Even if the child has no exact scale of measurement in mind there is already an advance in the evolution towards greater relativity (Chaps. II and III), and this presupposes definitions or concepts that are more and more removed from immediate reality.   Thus we saw the concepts of right and left gradually losing their primitive meaning and coming nearer and nearer to the state of well-defined relation. Now as soon as the mind has attained this degree of relativity ; as soon, that is, as it has discarded the naïve realism bound up with primitive mental experiments, the problem of reversibility appears in a completely new light.   It no longer consists in finding the reciprocal element to a given relation between two phenomena, but in finding the reciprocal counterpart to a general point of view. To put it differently, it is to find the key which will enable one to pass from the personal, momentary point of view to another point of view without contradicting oneself. Henceforth the mind is constantly faced with the following problem : how to choose suitable definitions, concepts or premisses, *i.e.* such that can be used from all possible points of view without contradicting either the results of immediate experience, or those of past experience or the experience of others ? In other words, how to select notions that will have the maximum amount of reversibility and reciprocity. This problem comes out very clearly in connexion with such reasoning processes as we have discussed in Chapters II and III. Take, for example, the question bearing upon the three objects in a row, of which one is to the left of the second and to the right of the third (Chap. III, § 4). At the earliest ages the child says that the first of these objects is ' in the middle,' and disputes the possibility of being both to the left and to the right. Later on, however—and our experiments showed this very clearly round about the age of 11–12—the child will acquire a sufficiently relative notion of the relations of right and left, one that is sufficiently removed from the immediate point of view, for the relation to remain the same, whatever the point of view. Henceforward, there is reciprocity of view-points, and consequently complete reversibility of thought.

Now, how will the mind be able to solve such problems consisting in the choice of definitions or relations, when these are not imposed upon it by reality itself ? By a ' mental experiment ' ? Certainly not, if mental experiment is really a reproduction or an imagining of this self-same reality or of the operations which can be carried out upon it. Reality never imposes a definition. Definition is always the result of a choice and a decision, and reality occasions but does not compel this choice. We have here an experiment which thought makes, not on things, but on itself, in order to find out what greater measure of fertility or of logical satisfaction it will gain from such and such a system of definitions or premisses. This experiment is of exactly the same order as that which Rauk has described in the ethical sphere. The individual adopts a certain rule as a hypothesis, to see whether by applying it he reaches a state of moral satisfaction, and especially whether he can remain true to himself and avoid contradiction. For in all questions of choice or definition of premisses the criteria of contradiction and fertility are not external, but internal or moral. The question is resolved by a chain of reasoning which aims at discovering, not what will happen in the external world (as is the case in the simple ' mental experiment '), but what will be the state of satisfaction or dissatisfaction of the will which has guided the thinking process. We have therefore decided to call this experiment *logical experiment*, and to put forward the view that formal thought, *i.e.* deduction dealing with any hypothetical or merely assumed hypothesis presupposes this logical experiment in addition to the reversible mental experiments which supply its raw material. For logical experiment alone enables a suitable choice to be made of the notions which serve as starting-points, and it consequently alone enables the mind to be in harmony with itself and thus achieve complete reversibility.

In conclusion, we may say that the first stage of childish reasoning is that of primitive or irreversible mental experiment, that the second is distinguished by a beginning of reversibility in the mental experiments, and that the third stage is marked by the appearance of formal deduction and logical experiment, the latter alone being capable of rendering the mental experiments completely reversible. Or again, we can say that during the first stage the reasoning mind does no more than to ' imitate ' reality as it is, without reaching any necessary implications ; during the second stage the mind ' operates upon ' reality, creating partly reversible experiments and thus reaching the consciousness of implication between certain affirmations and certain results ; finally, in the third stage, these operations necessitate each other in the sense that the child realizes that by asserting such and such a thing he is committing himself to asserting such and such another thing. He has at last attained to necessary implication between the various operations as such, and to a complete reversibility of thought.

§ 6. CONCLUSION : EGO-CENTRISM AND LOGIC.—The first conclusion to be drawn from our examination of the evolution of reasoning is the priority of the logic of relations.[1] True, the correct use of relations is what appears last, but what is last in chronological order is often first in the order of values. Indeed one may say that the possibility of reasoning logically is subordinate to that of handling relations correctly. In ordinary as in mathematical reasoning we deal only with particular cases, but by building up and combining with each other the different elements presented by these particular objects, we generalize the initial relations to the full extent that is required.

Logical classes are themselves dependent upon relations. The group of dark-haired or of fair-haired individuals is obtained by means of relations and of their multiplications. To forget the relations which form the basis of classification is to rob the latter of all its value. In logic as in mathematics we can talk of ' wholes,' but these have significance for us only in so far as we remember the law of construction which gave them birth. And the law of construction is a combination of relations.

The syllogism is therefore not reasoning proper, but a sort of abbreviated reasoning which consists in making use of the facts of inherence (membership and inclusion), while disregarding the relations which alone permitted the construction of these classes and the establishment of these facts. Consequently the syllogism is rigorous, but sterile. It is not deductive reasoning, but it allows

---

[1] We shall speak of relations (R) in contrast to facts of inherence (membership and inclusion).

of the rapid application of previous results. On this point we join issue with M. Goblot.

Logical addition and multiplication, whose use is, as we saw, not native to the child, are therefore *qua* constitutive of classes subservient to the logic of relations. To find the common element in two given classes is to construct the relations between the given individuals and through this construction to reach a classification.

In short, the fertility of reasoning is due to our unlimited capacity for constructing new relations, two given relations being always sufficient to find a third by multiplication, and so on. The logic of classes is a snap-shot of these constructions ; for each relation has its own ' domain,' and it enables us to pass at any moment from the point of view of relation to that of class and inherence. The most ordinary of everyday reasoning processes is that dealing with relations ; the syllogism or enthymeme consist only in the application of the results obtained. All this is current knowledge to-day.

The reason why the opposite view has survived for so long is that thought, in becoming conscious of itself, always reverses the order of things, and is last in reaching what had actually happened first. Thus classes struck the attention long before relations, because, being the residue of relations, they lingered in the mind and permeated elaborated verbal thought while the actual process of their construction remained unnoticed.

We are now in a position to define our genetic results more closely. Wherein does transduction differ from deduction, or what is the nature of primitive relations ?

Primitive reasoning, we are told, is a ' mental experiment,' *i.e.* an imaginary combination of relations given directly by reality. Now, primitive relations are always relations between the self and things, since reality in these early stages is a confused mixture of ' imitation ' and ' assimilation.' This means that the measuring factor which is the ego intrudes upon the measured entity which is the world, and every relation given by mental experi-

ment must originally bear the traces of these two inseparable terms. Now we have seen that the whole perspective of childhood is falsified by the fact that the child,
being ignorant of his own ego, takes his own point of view
as absolute, and fails to establish between himself and the
external world of things that reciprocity which alone
would ensure objectivity. There are undoubtedly certain
simple relations which, in so far as they are independent
of his ego, the child can handle correctly, so that many
childish transductions may be said to be valid. But this is
due to chance, or at any rate applies to the existence of a
privileged set of relations. Wherever relations, dependent
upon the ego, are concerned—and they are the crux
of the matter—the child fails to grasp the logic of relations
for lack of having established reciprocity, first between
himself and other people, and then between himself and
things.

What applies to the child is also true of science. So long
as Physics took absolute space and time as its domain
it reached a certain degree of development but came short
of any fundamental solution. But from the moment that
it was realized that the measurer was relative to what
he measured, the resulting relativity enabled physics,
thanks to the conditions of invariability and co-variability,
to attain objectivity. In the same way, so long as the
child thinks he can reason directly about things without
taking himself into account, he will succeed neither in
handling relations nor in reaching logical necessity. As
soon as he brings in his own ego as an element in these
relations, the child attains to the reciprocity of relations
and to logical strictness.

Transduction may therefore be defined as a combination
of relations woven between the organism and the external
world by action (the movements of the organism), but
without consciousness of its own processes on the part of
this action, and consequently without conscious realization of its own existence on the part of thought. Thus
the succession of relations constructed by the sum of

o

movements—whether performed, begun, or imagined—does present something that is equivalent to a reasoning process, but as these actions are not reversible, deduction has not yet appeared upon the scene. In short, *transduction is a combination of elementary relations, but without reciprocity of these relations amongst each other, and consequently without the element of necessity that would lead to generalization.* As soon, on the other hand, as relations become completely reciprocal, the fertility of relational multiplication knows no bounds, and generalization becomes possible. Nay, more, this reciprocity is what explains the reversibility of all deductions and consequently the character of strictness and necessity that is peculiar to the reasoning process. As in the case of mathematics (which are only a special case) all relations bear within themselves both their own verification and their own fertility.

CHAPTER V

SUMMARY AND CONCLUSIONS

THE PRINCIPAL FEATURES OF CHILD LOGIC.[1]

ROUSSEAU loved to say that the child is not a small grown-up, but has needs of his own, and a mentality adapted to these needs. Contemporary studies of the language and drawing of children have often emphasized the truth of this view. Karl Groos, in his ' theory of play' has given particular weight to this statement, and Claparède has developed it extensively from the functional point of view. The time, therefore, seems ripe for raising the question whether child thought, which differentiates itself from every other kind of thought, both by the interests which guide it, and by its means of expression, cannot also be distinguished by its logical structure and method of functioning. This is the view which we shall now attempt to develop, at least schematically, and without renewing any detailed discussion of the phenomena. For the purpose of attempting this synthesis, we have

[1] This chapter summarizes Volume 1 (*The Language and Thought of the Child*), and the present volume, which constitutes the conclusion of our ' Studies in Child Logic.' Given the loosely-knit character of these Studies, which were designed to follow the facts in all their complexity, we fear that the reader, having followed us so far, will experience, as we did, an impression of incoherence and obscurity. The present summary is intended to correct this impression. Starting from the beginning, we shall give a rapid and, if possible, complete exposition of what we consider to be the essential part of our results, as though the reader were not already familiar with the preceding chapters. In this way, we run a certain risk of needless repetition, in particular with regard to the chapters immediately preceding this conclusion, but we believe that by grouping the same subjects under new headings, we shall give a more synthetic view of our results.

in our possession a certain number of observations made
in the course of our own studies on the thought of the child,
or in the course of other enquiries, conducted by the
method of tests.   In addition to this, several works
dealing with the language, the drawings, and the perceptions of children have furnished us with first-rate information on the subject of his thought. The material collected
in this way can be grouped under a certain number of
headings : ego-centrism of thought, intellectual realism,
syncretism, inability to understand relations, difficulties in
using logical multiplication, etc, etc. The problem can be
stated as follows : Do these phenomena form an incoherent
whole, that is to say, are they due to a series of accidental
and fragmentary causes, unrelated to each other, or do
they form a coherent whole, and thus constitute a logic
of their own ?   The truth would seem to lie between the
two. The child's mind shows signs of having a structure
of its own, but its development is subject to contingent
circumstances.   The question is, where does the rôle
of the original structure end and that of the contingent
circumstances begin ? The only answer lies in the attempt
to explain the characteristics of child logic by each other.
If they can be synthesized in this way, even though
the method seem for the moment to involve us in a vicious
circle, it means that the thought of the child is coherent
and *sui generis*.

But what do we mean by explaining psychological
phenomena ? As Baldwin has shown in his subtle analyses,
without the genetic method in psychology, we can never
be sure of not taking effects for causes, nor even of having
formulated problems of explanation aright. The relation
of cause and effect must, therefore, be superseded by
that of genetic progression, which adds the notion of
functional dependence, in the mathematical sense of the
word, to that of antecedent and consequent. This will
give us the right to say of two phenomena, A and B,
that A is a function of B, as B is a function of A, and yet
leave us the possibility of taking the earliest phenomenon,

i.e. genetically speaking, the most explicative, as the starting-point of our description. What, then, are these explicative phenomena ? The psychology of thought is always faced at this point with two fundamental factors, whose connexion it is her task to explain : the biological factor, and the social factor. The mind becomes conscious of itself, and consequently exists psychologically speaking only when it is in contact with objects or with other minds. We have here two different planes, theoretically independent of one another, and which logically one would wish to keep separate ; but in practice, these two planes will always be associated, so long as the child has parents who represent Society to him, and so long as he experiences sensations which constitute a biological environment. Describe the evolution of thought from the purely biological point of view, or as threatens to be the fashion, from the purely sociological point of view, and you risk leaving half the real process in the shade. These two poles must both be kept in view, and nothing must be sacrificed ; but in order to make a beginning, we must needs choose one language at the expense of others. We have chosen the language of sociology, but wish to emphasize the point that there need be nothing exclusive in the choice. We reserve the right to revert to the biological explanation of child thought and to bring our present description into accordance with it. All we have attempted to do as a beginning, was to order our description from the point of view of social psychology, taking the most characteristic phenomenon as our starting-point, namely, ego-centrism of child thought. We have sought to trace most of the characteristics of child logic to ego-centrism ; though of many of these it might just as well be said that their presence explains ego-centrism. This is of no consequence to the object of our research ; all we need do is to point out that these characteristics form a compact group, for it is this very group that defines the logic of the child.

§ I. Ego-centrism of Thought in the Child.— Logical activity is not the whole of intelligence. One can be intelligent without being particularly logical. The main functions of intelligence, that of inventing. solutions, and that of verifying them, do not necessarily involve one another ; the first partakes of imagination, the second alone is properly logical. Demonstration, research for truth is therefore the true function of logic.

But on what occasions do we experience the need to verify our thought ? This need does not arise spontaneously in us. On the contrary, it appears very late, and for two reasons. The first is that thought puts itself at the service of the immediate satisfaction of desire long before forcing itself to seek for truth. Thought's most spontaneous manifestation is play, or at any rate that quasi-hallucinatory form of imagination which allows us to regard desires as realized as soon as they are born. All the writers who have concerned themselves with the play, the testimony, and the lies of children, have realized this. Freud has restated it with vigour by showing that the ' Lustprinzip ' is prior to the ' Realitätsprinzip.' Now the child's mind is full of these ' ludistic ' tendencies up to the age of 7–8, which means that before this age it is extremely difficult for him to distinguish between fabulation and truth.

But this is not all. Even when thought turns away from immediate satisfaction and play, and gives itself up to disinterested curiosity in things for their own sakes (and this curiosity appears very soon, certainly from the age of 3) the individual still has the peculiar capacity for immediate belief in his own ideas. It is, therefore, not for ourselves that we try to verify our statements. One of the most striking things one finds about the child under 7–8, is his extreme assurance on all subjects. When, according to one of the well-known Binet-Simon tests, a subject of 4 or 5 is shown two little boxes of the same volume, and is asked, " Which is the heaviest ? " he immediately answers, " That one," without even having felt the weight of the boxes, and it is the same in everything. " I know ! " . . . such is the only proof that is used for a long time in childish logic. True, the child is always asking questions, but up to the age of 7–8. a large number of the questions asked are rhetorical: the child knows his own answer, and often gives it spontaneously, without waiting for the other person to speak. Its strength of conviction characterizes what Janet has called ' the stage of belief.' [1]

It must be remembered, moreover, that experience itself does not undeceive minds orientated in this fashion. Things are in the wrong, not they. The savage who calls down rain by a magic rite explains his failure as the work of an evil spirit. He is, according to a famous saying, ' impervious to experience.' Experience undeceives him only on very special technical points (cultivation, hunting or manufacture) ; but even this momentary and partial contact with facts does not react in any way upon the orientation of his thought. This applies even more strongly to the child whose every material want is anticipated by his parents' care. Only in his manual games does the child learn to understand the resistance of objects. On the plane of verbal thought, every idea pictures a belief. Round about the age of 6–7, for example, what Mr Brunsch-vicg calls the ' artificialist ' explanations given by children, of natural phenomena, are very frequent : rivers, lakes, mountains, sea, and rocks have been made by man. Obviously, this does not require the slightest proof : the child has never seen people digging lakes or building rocks, but this does not matter. He enlarges sensible reality (a bricklayer making a wall, or a labourer making a ditch) by means of the verbal and magic reality which he puts on to the same plane. These things are not sufficient in themselves to make the mind feel any need for verification, since things themselves have been made by the mind. On the contrary, the child never really comes into contact with things because he does not work. He plays with them, or simply believes them without trying to find the truth.

[1] On the stage of ' pithiatic tendencies ' see *British Journ. of Psych.* (Med. Sect.), Vol. I, 1921, p. 154.

What then gives rise to the need for verification ? Surely it must be the shock of our thought coming into contact with that of others, which produces doubt and the desire to prove. If there were not other people, the disappointments of experience would lead to over-compensation and dementia. We are constantly hatching an enormous number of false ideas, conceits, Utopias, mystical explanations, suspicions, and megalomaniacal fantasies, which disappear when brought into contact with other people. The social need to share the thought of others and to communicate our own with success is at the root of our need for verification. Proof is the outcome of argument. All this, moreover, is common knowledge for contemporary psychology. P. Janet has laid great stress on the psychological origin of reflection. Reflection is the act by which we unify our various tendencies and beliefs, in the same way as conversation and social inter-course unify the opinions of individuals, namely, by giving due weight to each, and extracting an average opinion from the lot. Argument is, therefore, the back-bone of verification. Logical reasoning is an argument which we have with ourselves, and which reproduces internally the features of a real argument. Ch. Blondel has given an added importance to these views, by showing that pathological thought is the result of the given individual's inability to submit to social habits of thought. Discursive talk and reasoning are the product of inter-course between individuals. When a man cannot fit his personal thoughts and emotions into this schema, when he ceases to think socially, the mere fact of this isolation destroys the logical structure of his thought. Psycho-analysis arrives at a very similar result from a completely different angle, and it is to the lasting credit of this science that it has discovered two ways of thinking, one, social, communicable, guided by the need for adapting oneself to others, ' logical thought,' the other, personal, incom-municable as such, ' autistic thought.' Now Freud and his disciples have shown that by the mere fact of its

' autism,' this second way of thinking was bound to be confused, undirected, indifferent to truth, rich in visual and symbolic schemas, and above all, unconscious of itself and of the affective factors by which it was guided.

In order to understand child logic, we must therefore begin by asking in what degree children communicate their thought, and try to conform to that of others. In order to answer this question, the study of intercourse between children and adults will not at first be of very much use to us. Such intercourse is undoubtedly of fundamental importance, but it raises problems of its own, for the respective parts are not on an equality. The child feels he is inferior to the adult in every way, and is also for a long time under the delusion that the adult understands everything he says. Consequently, he never tries to express his thoughts clearly when he speaks to his parents, and conversely, he remembers only as much as he chooses of what is said by adults, because of his inability to enter into the world of ' grown-ups.' This is why we have no proof that childish beliefs held in solitude are the same as those which appear in his intercourse with adults. From this point of view, the unity of child thought is only a postulate. We shall, therefore, leave the question of intercourse between child and adult for the moment, and confine ourselves to the results of conversations between children ; for if the child really feels any need to socialize his thought, he must be able to satisfy such a need to the full with friends of his own age, whom he sees every day, and with whom he plays in freedom from restraint or self-consciousness. Now, experiment shows that the child's way of thinking occupies a place situated exactly between the ' autistic ' and the social. We have therefore given it the name of ego-centric, which indicates that this type of thought is still autistic in its structure but that its interests tend not merely towards organic or ' ludistic ' satisfaction as in pure autism, but towards intellectual adaptation as in adult thought. The ego-centric character of child thought has been demonstrated by three special enquiries.

In the first place (L.T., Chap. I), after making verbatim reports at the *Maison des Petits* (attached to the *Institut J. J. Rousseau* at Geneva) of the language of several children over a period of about one month each, we discovered that between the ages of 5–7, 44–47% of their spontaneous remarks were still ego-centric, although these children were free to work, play, and talk exactly as they chose. Between the ages of 3 and 5, the proportions were 54–60%. These ego-centric remarks, as opposed to question, orders, or adapted information, consisted, for the most part, of soliloquies, and of a kind of pseudo-conversation or ' collective monologue ' in the course of which the children speak to themselves and pay no attention to each other. The chief function of this ego-centric language is, therefore, to serve as an accompaniment to the thought or action of the individual. We have here something of a remnant of that ' cry accompanying action,' which Janet has spoken of in his studies on language. At any rate, we are very far removed from any genuine interchange of ideas. This characteristic of a large portion of childish talk points to a certain ego-centrism of thought itself, the more so as in addition to the words with which he marks the rhythm of his own action, there must be an enormous number of thoughts which the child keeps to himself, because he is unable to express them. And these thoughts are inexpressible precisely because they lack the means which are fostered only by the desire to communicate with others, and to enter into their point of view.

A second study (L.T., Chap. II) showed that even in the socialized portion of childish language, conversation passed through a certain number of primitive stages before becoming a genuine interchange of ideas. Not until about the age of 7–8, does argument, in particular, become what it is for the adult, namely the change from one point of view to the other, accompanied by the effort to motivate one's own and to understand that of the interlocutor. Before this, argument is nothing but a conflict of contrary affirmations, affirmations without understanding, and without motivation.

Finally, a third study (L.T., Chap. III) served as a counter-test and enabled us to specify the causes of this ego-centrism. If children talk so little to each other, and if, in particular, their best thoughts towards adaptation to adult thought and to the external world are performed in solitude, this may be for two quite separate reasons. It may be either that they prefer their own company, or it may be that they are permanently under the impression that they understand each other, and have no suspicion of the ego-centric character of their thought. As a matter of fact, the second solution is the right one. Not only do children believe that they are talking and actually listening to one another, but they also have a tendency to think that each of their thoughts is common to all the others, that they can all discern it, and understand it, even if it never finds distinct expression. For even if children are ego-centric, they are ignorant of the nature of thought, or rather by the mere fact that they talk only for themselves, they are saying aloud everything that they can express verbally, and therefore believe that they are always understanding one another.

One is tempted to wonder whether this habit which children have of always believing themselves to be understood, does not, in fact, prevent them from understanding each other when they take the trouble to explain themselves. Our third study was devoted to the solution of this question of verbal understanding between children of the same age. Naturally, when children are playing together, or are all handling the same material, they understand each other, because, however elliptical their language may be, it is accompanied by gesture and mimicry which is a beginning of action and serves as an example to the interlocutor. But it can be questioned whether verbal thought and language itself are really understood among children, whether, in other words, children understand each other when they speak without acting. This prob-

lem is of fundamental importance, since it is on the verbal
plane that the child makes the chief effort of adaptation
to adult thought and to the acquisition of logical habits.
Moreover, as it is partly from his verbal thought and not
as it is presented to him in direct sensation, that the child
views the world, the verbal plane permeates his whole
conception of reality.

For the solution of this problem, we chose fifty child-
dren from the same class, between the ages 6–7 and 7–8,
and we made them relate to each other in pairs, a set
story, and the explanation of a drawing showing the
mechanism of a tap and of a syringe. Now, it will be
remembered that although the child who had to explain
(and each did so in turn) generally had a clear idea of what
he was explaining, his interlocutor generally failed to
grasp this explanation, although of course he imagined
he had been understanding it perfectly well. We need
not recapitulate the numbers which enabled us to estimate
the degree of understanding between child and adult, and
between one child and another. We need only recall the
fact that lack of understanding between children is due
as much to faulty expression on the part of the explainer,
whose very language is ego-centric, as to faulty adaptation
on the part of the interlocutor who does not listen because
he thinks all along that he can understand everything,
and because he assimilates everything he hears to his own
point of view.

These are the three groups in support of the hypothesis
that the thought of the child is more ego-centric than
ours and that it is half-way between ' autism ' proper,
and socialized thought. Such a statement is indeed
hypothetical. There is still a great deal of work to be
done on the intercourse between children of different ages,
between brothers and sisters, and above all, between
parents and children. But the hypothesis is close to
common sense. However intimately the child may be
connected to his surroundings in his affective life, there
is still an enormous portion of his thought that is

incommunicable, partly because the adult cannot turn himself into a child, partly because the child cannot measure the limits of adult understanding, nor find language that will logically convey his various shades of meaning. The fact of childish ego-centrism, therefore, seems to us to be beyond dispute. The point is whether ego-centrism entails the difficulties in expression and the logical phenomena which we shall presently examine, or whether the reverse is the case. But surely from the genetic point of view, we must start from the child's activity, if we want to explain his thought. Now, this activity is unquestionably ego-centric and egotistical. The social instinct is late in developing. The first critical stage occurs at the age of 7-8, and it is precisely at this age that we can place the first period of reflection and logical unification, as well as the first attempts to avoid contradiction.

§ 2. THE DIFFICULTIES OF CONSCIOUS REALIZATION, AND THE SHIFTING [1] OF OPERATIONS ON TO THE PLANE OF THOUGHT.—Many adults are still ego-centric in their way of thinking. Such people interpose between themselves and reality an imaginary or mystical world, and they reduce everything to this individual point of view. Unadapted to ordinary conditions, they seem to be immersed in an inner life that is all the more intense. Does this make them more conscious of themselves ? Does ego-centrism point the way to a truer introspection ? On the contrary, it can easily be seen that there is a way of living in oneself that develops a great wealth of inexpres sible feelings, of personal images and schemas, while at the same time it impoverishes analysis and consciousness of self. The work done by M. Ch. Blondel constitutes a complete demonstration of this view. The concept of autism in psycho-analysis throws full light upon the fact

---

[1] French ' décalage,' which literally means the lowering of an object by removing wedges or supports from under it. The reader must therefore bear in mind that the metaphor employed describes a downward, dropping movement from one plane to another rather than the horizontal movement implied in the word ' shifting ' [Translator's note].

that the incommunicable character of thought involves a certain degree of unconsciousness. In short, the claim is not too bold that we became conscious of ourselves to the extent that we are adapted to other people. Our discovery that other people do not spontaneously understand us nor we them is the gauge of the efforts we make to mould our language out of the thousand and one accidents created by this lack of adaptation and the measure of our aptitude for the simultaneous analysis of others and of ourselves.

But how about the child ? Does his ego-centrism go hand in hand with a certain degree of unconsciousness which would explain of itself a large number of the features of childish logic ? The question is of interest only if it is raised within the realm of exact experiment. Unless the child's unconsciousness of himself is submitted to precise technical definition, its existence can naturally only be stated as one of the truths of common sense.

Now a study which we made of certain types of arithmetical reasoning (J.R.,[1] Chap. IV, § 1) brought us into close contact with a very interesting fact in this connexion. When we questioned children between the ages of 7 and 9 about little problems connected with the notion of fractions or about certain verbal expressions, such as ' x times more,' ' x times less,' we discovered that the very diverse answers we received obeyed a law of development which we were able to state more and more definitely. But it was a long time before we were able to give an immediate interpretation of the children's answers, precisely because the child was incapable of telling us how he had set about the task in each particular case. He appeared in a manner to be unconscious of his own reasoning process, or at any rate incapable of immediate introspection or retrospection. To recall an example : the expression ' 5 times faster than 50 minutes ' was sometimes identified with ' 45 minutes.' As such, this answer has no particular interest for us. But the method and the

---

[1] The initials J.R. designate the present volume.

degree of consciousness in the reasoning process are suggestive. As the number of questions was increased, analysis
showed that the child simply takes away 5 minutes, as
though " 5 times less " meant " — 5." But when he is asked
to explain what he has done, he can neither describe his
process of reasoning nor even say that he has ' taken
away 5 ' from 50. He answers, " I tried " or " I found
45." If we go on to ask " How did you find ? " and press
him to reveal the steps of his reasoning, the child invents
a new calculation which is perfectly arbitrary and presupposes the answer 45. One boy, for example, told
us : " I took 10 and 10, and then 10 and 10 and then I
added 5."

In short, as soon as the problem contains ever so little
complexity the child seems to conduct his reasoning
process much as we do ours in the course of a purely
empirical problem (such as a puzzle, etc.) ; *i.e.* he keeps
no record of his successive attempts, and his mind proceeds
by a series of fumbling movements, each of which is
conscious, but that does not easily admit of retrospection
as a whole. If after this is over we ask the child to
describe his search, all he gives us is a device for finding
the solution, and a device which presupposes the solution
in question. Never does he succeed in describing his
reasoning process as such.

The reader may consider these introspective difficulties
insufficient to prove the faint degree of consciousness
present in childish reasoning, but a number of other facts
lead us to the same conclusion. One of the clearest is
the inability of children to give definitions (J.R., Chap. IX,
§ 2). There are many children between the ages of 7 and
9 who regard as ' alive ' all self-moving bodies—animals,
sun, moon, wind, etc. But these children are usually
incapable of giving a reason for their choice. It is we
who have to make them aware of their own definition of
life by asking them, for example, why clouds are not alive
(answer : Because the wind pushes them). Spontaneously,
therefore, the child ' practised ' or ' acted ' his definition,

often even consistently, but without knowing it and without being able to express it verbally.

This feature of children's arithmetical reasoning and of their definitions shows in itself that childish reasoning cannot consist of a deductive sequence about which the subject knows how and why he is carrying it out. It consists of a series of discontinuous judgments which determine one another extrinsically and not intrinsically, or, to put it differently, which entail one another like unconscious acts, and not like conscious judgments. Childish reasoning before the age of 7–8 is in the strict sense of the word the ' mental experiment ' of Mach. It resembles a physical action during which one arm - movement will bring about another arm-movement, but in which the subject is unaware of the determinism of these successive movements. In other words, the operations remain unconscious, and the determinism which rules them has not yet become logical necessity. Of course, it may be objected that in this determinism there is virtually contained a logical implication. But of such the child is not aware, so that we have no right to speak of logical deduction. There is here, if one likes, a logic of action but as yet no logic of thought.[1]

Claparède has shown in some exceedingly interesting experiments that consciousness of resemblance appears earlier in the child than consciousness of difference. As a matter of fact, the child simply adopts an identical attitude to all objects that lend themselves to assimilation, but does not need to be aware of this identity of attitude. He ' acts ' resemblance, in a manner of speaking, before ' thinking it.' Difference between objects on the other

---

[1] The notion of ' unconscious reasoning ' is singularly elastic. Either we assign to the unconscious a logic similar to that of reflective thought in which we are making a gratuitous assumption, or else we are thinking of some special process analogous to that which will be described later on. But then the problem arises of how to distinguish this process from conscious ' reasoning,' and nothing but confusion can come from giving the same name at the outset to operations which are perhaps very different from each other.

hand creates disadaptation, and this disadaptation is what occasions consciousness. Claparède has taken this fact as the foundation of the law which he had called *loi de prise de conscience :* the more we make use of a relation the less conscious we are of it. Or again : We only become conscious in proportion to our disadaptation.

This law seems to us fundamental for establishing relations between the functional factors of childish thought, particularly between ego-centrism and the absence of social needs, and the structural features which define childish logic. For this ' law of conscious realization ' is alone in explaining why childish ego-centrism should involve the inability to be conscious of logical relations. For in so far as he is thinking only for himself, the child has no need to be aware of the mechanism of his reasoning (J.R., Chap. I, §§ 2 and 4). His attention is wholly turned towards the external world, towards action, in no way directed towards thought as a medium interposed between the world and himself. In so far, on the other hand, as the child seeks to adapt himself to others, he creates between himself and them a new order of reality, a new place of thought, where speech and argument will henceforth hold their sway, and upon which operations and relations which till then have been the work of action alone will now be handled by imagination and by words. The child will therefore have to become conscious to the same extent of these operations and relations which till then had remained unconscious because they were sufficient for the purposes of action.

How does this conscious realization take place ? Claparède's law is a functional law, and only indicates when the individual does or does not require to become conscious. The structural problem remains. What are the means and the obstacles to this conscious realization ? In order to answer this question, we shall have to introduce a second law, the law of ' shifting.' For to become conscious of an operation is to make it pass over from the plane of action to that of language ; it is therefore to re-invent it

P

in imagination in order to express it in words. As regards reasoning in particular, to become conscious of its operations means, as Mach, Rignano and Goblot have said, to re-make ‘mentally’ mental experiments that one has already made in action. Consequently, given this perpetual necessity for re-invention, whenever a child attempts to speak an operation, he will probably relapse into the difficulties which he had already conquered on the plane of action. In other words, the process of learning an operation on the verbal plane will reproduce the same incidents as had arisen when this operation was being learned on the plane of action ; a process of shifting will take place from one apprenticeship to the other. The dates will differ, but the rhythms will probably be analogous. This shifting from action to thought can be observed at every turn. It is of fundamental importance to the understanding of child logic and explains all the phenomena which have been the object of our enquiry. For example, the child has difficulty in realizing that a part or a fraction is relative to a whole. He has difficulty, when told that a given colour is both darker than one and lighter than a third, in discovering which of the three is the lightest. Now these difficulties still show very clearly on the verbal plane between the years of 7 to 11, whereas on the plane of action they have ceased to exist. But the way the child has to grope and feel in order to overcome these difficulties reproduces what a few years ago he had known on the plane of action. For on this plane too he was unable to divide a whole into two or four parts without forgetting the whole, and of comparing the features of three objects without committing the fallacies which reappear at a later date in his thinking. Thus, the mere fact of thinking an operation instead of actually carrying it out causes circumstances to reappear that had been forgotten long ago on the plane of action (J.R., Chaps. II and II).

This shifting of external experience on to the verbal plane has not always received due attention. To Associationism it is incomprehensible ; for if our conscious reasoning were the direct result of previous experiences, then, clearly, once these experiences were over, the individual ought to be able to re-enact them in thought or imagination upon the verbal plane. If, however, the mental experiment which appears at a given moment on the verbal plane is really, as Claparède maintains, due to a failure to adapt to new requirements, it will not be a mere translation of the subject's most recent and most highly evolved external experiments, but will, on the contrary, entail a whole process of learning over again. It is in this sense in which the past is shifted on to the present. The evolution of intelligence is therefore not, as was claimed in the Associationism of Taine and Ribot, continuous, but rhythmical ; it seems at times to go back upon itself, it is subject to waves, to interferences, and to ' periods ' of variable length.

All these statements are the merest truisms nowadays, but they are truisms which it is dangerous to neglect when we are analysing the reasoning processes of children. For we may either confuse verbal aptitude with an apti-tude for handling relations in action, or neglect the verbal element altogether, as though all the operations of logic had not at one time or another to be learnt over again on the plane of discursive thought, if they are to be of any use in social intercourse.

Most of the phenomena of child logic can be traced back to general causes. The roots of this logic and of its shortcomings are to be found in the ego-centrism of child thought up to the age of 7–8, and in the unconsciousness which this ego-centrism entails. Between the ages of 7–8 and 11–12 these difficulties are shifted on to the verbal plane, and child logic is reminiscent at this point of factors which were active at a period prior to this.

§ 3. INABILITY TO HANDLE THE LOGIC OF RELATIONS, AND NARROWNESS OF THE FIELD OF ATTENTION.—One of the first results of childish ego-centrism is that every-thing is judged from the individual's own point of view.

The child experiences the greatest difficulty in entering into anyone else's point of view. Consequently, his judgment is always absolute, so to speak, and never relative, for a relative judgment involves the simultaneous awareness of at least two personal points of view.

Moreover, we are not speaking of any logical relations in general but solely of what the logicians call a 'judgment of relation' in contrast to a ' predicative judgment.' Now a predicative judgment such as ' Paul is a boy ' only presupposes a single point of view, mine or Paul's, it does not matter which. A judgment of relation such as " Paul is my brother," on the contrary, presupposes at least two points of view : mine, for Paul is no one else's brother, not even his own, and Paul's, for in his mouth the judgment would change its form and become " I am the brother of. . . . " The same applies to all judgments of relation which connect at least two individuals and change in form according to the point of view of each. Now the child is so accustomed to thinking from his own individual point of view, and so incapable of taking that of anyone else, that such simple relations as those of brother and sister give rise in him to all sorts of difficulties, at any rate on the verbal plane. The child tends to deform relational judgments that are proposed to him, and to reduce them all to the simpler, because absolute form of the predicative judgment.

Two of our former studies (J.R., Chaps. II and III) showed us that the child has a tendency, in connexion with such statements as " I have brothers," to confuse the point of view of inclusion or of the predicative judgment (" We are x brothers ") with that of relation. It is to such causes as these that we must attribute the difficulties arising out of the Binet-Simon test of absurd phrases ("I have three brothers, Paul, Ernest, and myself": a 10–11 years' test, according to the district). In addition to this, up to the age of 10, three-quarters of the children are unable to indicate simultaneously both how many brothers and sisters there are in their own family and how many brothers and sisters each brother or sister possesses. The typical answer is as follows. The child says, for example, that there are two brothers in his family, which is correct. " And how many brothers have you got ? —*One, Paul.*—And has Paul got a brother ?—*No.*—But you are his brother, aren't you ?—*Yes.*—Then he has a brother ?—*No,*" etc. Such a phenomenon is clearly under the domination of ego-centrism. There is no reasoning in the real sense of the word. The child has never asked himself the question and makes no attempt to answer by reasoning. The phenomenon consists rather in what might be called an illusion of point of view. The habit of thinking solely from his own point of view prevents the child from taking up that of others and consequently from handling the judgment of relation, *i.e.* from realizing the reciprocity of view-points.

A further enquiry showed us that this explanation can be made to cover phenomena connected with more complex relations, such as those of right and left (J.R., Chap. III). A five-year-old child (in Geneva) can show his left and his right hand, but these qualities possess for him an absolute meaning. They are the names of the hands, and the names of all objects situated in a certain way in relation to the child's body. Thus, up to the age of 8, the child is unable to point to the left or right hand of anyone placed opposite him, for the same reason that his own point of view is felt to be the only one. At the age of 8, the child succeeds in adopting his interlocutor's point of view, but this does not mean that he can place himself at the point of view of the actual objects. If a pencil and a knife are placed on the table, he will be able to say whether the pencil is to the left or to the right of the knife, but this is still from his own point of view. It is not till he is 11 years old that he will know when presented with three objects in a row whether they are to the left or to the right of one another when they are taken in pairs. In short, his progress seems to run as follows: personal view-point, view-point of others, and finally, view-point of objects or of the relational judgment in general.

Ego-centrism seems therefore to be responsible for the difficulty which children experience in handling relative notions, and for their tendency to deform relational judgments by moulding them on the pattern of judgments of membership or inclusion.

In a recently published study [1] we had occasion to analyse in some detail a phenomenon of this kind in connexion with a Burt test. Take three little girls, of whom the first is fairer than the second and darker than the third. The question asked is which of the three is the darkest. The children whose reasoning processes we analysed make no attempt to compare by taking account of the relations that are indicated. They transform the relational judgments into predicative judgments, by means of a mechanism which may be schematized as follows. The first and the second of those little girls are fair, the first and the third are dark ; therefore the third is the darkest of all, the second is the fairest and the first stands midway between the two. The result is the exact opposite of what it would have been if the relational logic of the adult mind had been applied.

In order to explain this phenomenon, we simply appealed to the narrow field of attention in the child (although we reminded the reader that this was a static, and therefore a provisional way of describing things). For a far wider field of attention is required to handle a relational judgment than to handle a predicative judgment ; or at any rate, as Revault d'Allonnes would put it, there is need for more complex ' attentional schemas.' Every relation requires that the subject be conscious of at least two objects at the same time. P. Janet has often drawn attention to this point. Supposing the child's field of attention to be narrower, i.e. less synthetic than ours, this means that he will be unable to take in all the data of the test

---

[1] " Un cas de comparaison verbale chez l'enfant," *Arch. de Psych.*, Vol. XVIII.

at a single grasp. He will take the objects in one after another and not as a whole. This alone will be sufficient to transform relational judgments into a series of predicative judgments, and comparison will take place, not during the act of attention, but after it. We were able, moreover, to confirm this hypothesis by an examination of the different stages traversed by children from 7–8 up to 11–12 years old in connexion with this comparison test.

But on this hypothesis it still remains to be explained why the child has a narrower field of attention than ours. We showed in the last section of this chapter that the child's awareness of his own thought and reasoning process is fainter than ours. But this is no reason why attention that is directed towards the external world (attention in perception, understanding of language, etc.) should obey the same law. Childish attention might very well, like childish memory or the memory of feeble-minded persons, be more plastic than ours. The difference would then reside in the degree of organization, in the structure of the schema of attention. This is the solution we must look for.

Now it is our belief that childish ego-centrism exerts a profound influence upon this schematism of attention in preventing from adopting the point of view of several different objects simultaneously, or more generally, of objects themselves. The ego-centric way of thinking in relation to one's immediate neighbours (of which we have just been examining examples in connexion with the notions of brother and sister, right and left) brings with it a certain number of habits or schemas which may be characterized as *realistic* in analogy to the many realistic illusions which occur in the early history of science (geocentric hypothesis, etc.) (J.R., Chap. III, §§ 5–7) The child therefore takes his own immediate perception as absolute. Most of the boys in Geneva go on believing till they are 7–8 years old that the sun or the moon follows them on their walks because they always happen to be above them. They are greatly perplexed when they have to say which of two boys walking in different directions is being accompanied by these heavenly bodies. (I was able to make sure that this was due neither to invention nor to deformation of adult talk.) This amounts to practically the same thing as ignorance of relational notions and avoidance of comparison. This is why, in the opinion of young Genevans up to the age of 7–8, wood floats upon water because it is light (in the absolute sense), and not because it is lighter than water. Their language alone is sufficient to make this clear. But what is most significant is that in the presence of equal volumes of water and wood they maintain that the wood is the heavier of the two. This estimate changes after the age of 8–9. In other words comparison and relation, even imagined, have no interest in connexion with natural phenomena before this age. Immediate perception is the measure of all things.

Such habits of thought, acquired as they are over a period of many years, will naturally have some effect upon the schematism of attention. In the first place this realism prevents the child from looking at things as they are in themselves. He sees them always in terms of the momentary perception which is taken as absolute and, in a manner of speaking, hypostasized. He therefore makes no attempt to find the intrinsic relations existing between things. Again, by the mere fact of not being considered in their internal relations, but only as presented by immediate perception, things are either conglomerated into a confused whole (syncretism), or else considered one by one in a fragmentary manner devoid of synthesis. Herein lies the narrowness of the child's field of attention. The child sees a great many things, often many more than we do ; he observes, in particular, a whole mass of detail which escapes our notice, but he does not organize his observations, he is incapable of thinking of more than one thing at a time. Thus he squanders his data instead of synthesizing them. His ' multiple attention,' as Revault d'Allonnes puts it, is out of proportion to his apperceptive attention, just as the organization of his memories is out of proportion to the plasticity of his retentiveness.

Thus, while ego-centrism of thought may hardly be said to involve a narrow field of attention it may yet be claimed that ego-centrism and such an attentional schematism are closely bound up with one another. Both arise from primitive habits of thought, which consist in taking immediate personal perception as something absolute, and both bring in their wake an inability to handle the logic of relations.

§ 4. SYNTHETIC INCAPACITY AND JUXTAPOSITION.—This narrowness of the field of attention in children and the peculiar character of their schema of attention carry yet further consequences. They explain a whole set of phenomena such as the synthetic incapacity which appears in children's drawings, the inability to establish interference between logical classes, the inability to understand partitive relations, etc. all of which, in the verbal sphere, can be brought together under the heading of *juxtaposition* (J.R., Chap. I).

For if things are perceived in the light of the moment, without order or organization, if the work of rational attention is to deal with them one by one and not in groups, then the child will naturally juxtapose things and events in his mind, without achieving their synthesis. M. Luquet has described this phenomenon under the name of synthetic incapacity in connexion with the drawings of children. The child artist will juxtapose pieces of one and the same whole, but will be unable to connect them together. He will draw, for example, an eye alongside of a head, and so on. Now, even in drawing, one realizes that this phenomenon outweighs many technical factors (clumsiness in handling a pencil) and has its roots in the thought of the child. We have published a very clear example of this—the drawings of bicycles between the ages of 5 and 7.[1] In Geneva, 7–8 is the age when the

[1] " Pour l'étude des explications d'enfants," *L'Educateur*, Vol. LVIII, 4th Feb. 1922.

mechanism of bicycles is properly understood by boys. In the earlier stages, even though the child is well aware that a gear, a chain, and pedals are required to make the bicycle move, he is unable to bring out clearly the details of contact and the exact causal sequence between these pieces. Now the age of correct causal explanation given verbally is also the age of correct drawing. But at the age when explanation is fragmentary, drawing is either primitive or accomplished, but always characterized by synthetic incapacity. Thus, between the two big wheels of the bicycle, gear, pedals and two horizontal lines representing the chain will be juxtaposed in complete separation from each other. The synthetic incapacity of the drawing is repeated here in a synthetic incapacity of thought itself.

Synthetic incapacity survives for a long time after this, at least if the concept be extended so as to cover all the similar phenomena which we designate under the name of phenomena of ' juxtaposition.' Thus there is a tendency in childish reasoning to juxtapose classes and propositions rather than to establish their exact hierarchy. We went into this in connexion with the difficulties raised by logical multiplication.[1] The child is given, for example, a test of the form : " If this animal has long ears it is a mule or a donkey; if it has a thick tail it is a mule or a horse. Well, this animal has long ears and a thick tail, What is it." Instead of finding the exact interference of the two classes and saying that the animal in question is a mule, boys, even of 10 or 11 years old, add up the conditions and juxtapose the classes instead of excluding the unwanted elements. In this way, they reach the conclusion that the animal might just as well be a horse, a donkey, or a mule. This shows the true nature of the phenomenon of juxtaposition. The child begins by considering the existence of long ears, and concludes that the animal must be a donkey or a mule. He then considers the existence of the thick tail. If this new

[1] *Journ. de Psych.*, Vol. XIX (1922), p. 222.

condition were made to interfere with the preceding one, the child would eliminate the donkey since it has not got a thick tail. But the child considers this new condition separately, he juxtaposes it instead of contrasting it with the former condition, and he concludes that the animal may be a horse or a mule. Each judgment is therefore juxtaposed and not assimilated to the judgment that precedes it. Finally, the child merges these two judgments into a single whole, but this whole constitutes a mere juxtaposition not a hierarchy. For the child comes to the conclusion that all three cases are possible. He therefore eliminates nothing. He juxtaposes without choosing. In a sense then, this is synthetic incapacity, since all synthesis implies choice and hierarchy, and differs from mere juxtaposition (J.R., Chap. IV, § 2).

This feature of childish judgment naturally excludes any kind of syllogistic reasoning. For the syllogism is a succession of logical additions and multiplications, and the child who is incapable of these operations will by this fact alone remain a stranger to the syllogism. There must therefore be no question of giving children explicit syllogisms to comment upon or to complete. The form given to the syllogisms in logical text-books is one that is of very little use. We think by enthymemes rather than by syllogisms, and, as the method of induced intro-spection has shown, we often think by enthymemes that can be formulated. It is permissible, however, without incurring the charge of artificiality, to give the child tests of the form : " Some of the inhabitants of the town of St Marcel were Bretons. All the Bretons from the town of St Marcel were killed in the war. Are there any inhabitants left in St Marcel ? " [1] Now a large proportion of the boys of 10–11 whom we questioned by means of tests of this kind in Paris failed to perform this logical multiplication. They concluded that there were no inhabitants left in St Marcel.

This test leads us on to the consideration of a second

[1] *Journ. de Psych.*, Vol. XVIII (1921), p. 463.

form under which the phenomenon of juxtaposition may appear. We mean the difficulty which children have in grasping the relation of part to whole[1] and fractional relations in general. These difficulties reappear at various stages, first in the plane of action and perception, then later on that of verbal thought. On the first plane the child (before the age of 7–8) will draw part of an object and will be unable to attribute it to the whole, or more simply, he will forget about the whole (synthetic incapacity) ; or else in attempting to divide 8 or 10 matches into two equal piles he will forget all about the total that is to be divided half-way through the operation. In short, by the mere fact of his tendency to juxtapose instead of establishing a hierarchy, the child is led to regard the parts of a whole as discontinuous fragments independent of each other and independent of the whole. Now once these difficulties have been overcome on the plane of perception they reappear on the verbal plane. On the one hand, when one says to the child "A part of my flowers . . .," etc., the child, in spite of the genitive ' of ' has a tendency not to look for the whole but to consider this ' part ' simply as a small incomplete whole. On the other hand, and in intimate connexion with this capacity for thinking of a part without relating it to a whole, the genitive ' of ' is not taken as partitive. "A part of my flowers" therefore means "a bunch of flowers" (J.R., Chap. III, § 6).

But the tendency to juxtapose instead of synthesizing is not to be found only in the schematism of judgments as in the preceding examples, it also characterizes implication itself. What is meant by this was shown by our study of the conjunctions of logical and causal relation (because) and of the conjunctions of discordance (although) (J.R., Chap. I). In his language, the child frequently omits from between his successive judgments such relations as we would expect to find, and is content to juxtapose these judgments without any conjunctions or simply by

[1] *Journ. de Psych.*, Vol. XVIII (1921), p. 449.

means of the term 'and.' Thus in the explanations that take place between children (L.T., Chap. III, § 1) there are hardly any explicit causal relations. Explanation takes on the character of a narrative. Relations are only indicated by 'and then' even in connexion with mechanical phenomena. This is why, when a child of 7–8 is asked to complete a sentence containing 'because,' he will sometimes do so correctly and sometimes invert the relation indicated by 'because.' For example, " The man fell off his bicycle *because he was ill afterwards*." The word 'because' is often used correctly by the child to indicate psychological relations (such as motivation : " because Daddy won't let me "). But instances of 'because' indicating relations of physical causality or logical relations are almost completely absent from the spontaneous talk of the child, and when their use is induced, mistakes such as those we have quoted tend to occur. For a long time, finally, the word 'therefore' (*donc*) does not exist in child language. It is replaced by the term 'and then' (*alors*) ; but for a considerable period this term only indicates succession in time and not the relation of consequence.

All these facts agree in proving a certain synthetic incapacity in the thought of the child, and show that this incapacity bears primarily upon the schematism of judgment or upon the relations existing between judgments. But does this mean that the mind of the child is peopled with a multitude of juxtaposed ideas and judgments unconnected by any bond, as appears to be the case to an outsider ? In other words, has the child himself a feeling of chaos and discontinuity ? It is obvious that nothing could be farther from the truth, and that for any deficiency in objective relations there is a corresponding excess of subjective relations. This is shown to be the case by the phenomenon of syncretism which seems to be the opposite, but is really the complement of juxtaposition.

There is one particular feature in the structure of childish ideas which serves as a transition between juxtaposition and syncretism ; we mean the relation which unites terms that have been separated by synthetic incapacity. When there is no occasion, such as drawing or language for the child to break up objects by analysis, these are, as will be shown in a moment, perceived syncretically. But once they have been broken up and that synthetic incapacity renders their synthesis impossible, what is the relation which gathers the juxtaposed elements into a group ? M. Luquet has noted with great truth that it is a relation of membership and not of inclusion, by which he means (no regard being paid to the logical meaning of these terms) that an arm drawn alongside of a manikin is conceived by the child as ' going with ' the manikin not as ' forming part of ' his body. We have often come across this relation in the ideas of children, and have given it the name of relation of *property*, so as to avoid confusion with the vocabulary of logic. This is how in the expression " A part of my posy " the term ' of ' indicates neither a partitive nor an attributive relation, but, as it were, a mixture of the two : " the part that is with my posy," such is the translation which a child gave us. And it is in the same way that our young Genevans, though they knew for the most part that Geneva is in Switzerland, yet declare themselves to be Geneva and not Swiss, because they cannot imagine being both at the same time (J.R., Chap. III, § 6). For them, Geneva ' goes with ' Switzerland, but they see no sign here of a part and a whole, and make no attempt to define the spatial contacts. Finally —if comparison may be made between heterogeneous cases—this is how judgments of juxtaposition come to be accompanied by a ' feeling of juxtaposition,' although this feeling never becomes an awareness of causality or of implication. Children who draw a bicycle chain along-side of a gear-wheel and a pedal know that these things ' go together ' ; but if they are urged to be more precise in their statements, they will sometimes say that gear-wheel sets the cogged chain in motion, sometimes that it is the other way about. These two statements co-exist within the same individual, and prove very clearly that in this case the consciousness of causality does not go beyond a simple " feeling of relation."

Juxtaposition and synthetic incapacity do not therefore stand for disharmony. These phenomena are accompanied by relational feelings, either static (relation of property) or dynamic (feeling of causal relation), feelings of which the explanation is supplied by our analysis of syncretism. For they constitute a substitute for syncretism when the unity which the latter supplied has been broken up, and no fresh unity has been built up again.

§ 5. SYNCRETISM.—Syncretism is related to nearly all the phenomena we have been calling to mind. In the first place, as we said a moment ago, it seems like the contrary but is really the complement of juxtaposition. For if childish perception considers objects in their immediate, fragmentary and unrelated aspect, and if either in language or in drawing these objects are simply juxtaposed instead of being arranged in a hierarchy, it is perhaps because these objects, before being broken up by the exigencies of drawing or conversation, were too intimately related to one another, too deeply sunk in comprehensive schemas, and too thoroughly implicated in one another to be broken up with impunity. The reason why this related-ness given in the original perception of objects offers so little resistance to the disintegrating effects of drawing or conversation is perhaps that it was exaggerated and consequently, subjective. Now to say that child thought is syncretistic means precisely this, that childish ideas arise through comprehensive schemas and through sub-jective schemas, *i.e.* schemas that do not correspond to analogies or causal relations that can be verified by every-body. If, therefore, the child possesses neither the logic of relations nor the synthetic capacity which would enable him to conceive of things as objectively related to one another, it must be because his way of thinking is syncretistic. For in the mind of the child everything is connected with everything else, everything can be justified by means of unforeseen allusions and implications. But we have no suspicion of this wealth of relations, precisely because this very syncretism which causes it is without the means of expression that would render it communicable.

This last remark leads one to suppose that syncretism, besides being bound up with the phenomenon of juxta-position and with inability to handle the logic of relations, is also the direct outcome of childish ego-centrism. Ego-centric thought is necessarily syncretic. To think ego-centrically means on the one hand that one does not adapt oneself to the sayings nor to the view-points of other people, but brings everything back to oneself, and on the other hand, that one takes one's own immediate perception as something absolute, precisely to the extent that one fails to be adapted to the perceptions of other people. Under both these aspects the ego-centric tendency leads to the same result, which is to be ignorant of objective relations in favour of subjective relations, to impose arbitrary schemas upon the world of external objects, to be constantly assimilating new experiences to ancient schemas, in a word, to replace adaptation to the external world by assimilation to the self. Syncretism is the expression of this perpetual assimilation of all things to subjective schemas and to schemas that are comprehensive because they are unadapted.

Syncretism therefore permeates the thought of the child. Claparède has pointed out its importance in perception. Cousinet has described, under the name of 'immediate analogy,' the prompt and unhesitating process by which the child identifies new objects with old schemas. In the meantime, we have discovered in the understanding and reasoning of the child under 7–8 and in the under-standing and verbal thought of the child between 8 and 11–12, a tendency which is common to all syncretism. On the one hand, childish understanding undergoes a process which is completely unanalytic. A sentence heard is not broken up into distinct terms, but gives rise

to a general schema which is vague and indissociable.
On the other hand, the child does not reason by explicit
inferences, but by projecting these schemas into one
another, and by fusing images according to laws which
are more often those of ' condensation ' than of logic.
Let us recall quite shortly how syncretism makes its
appearance before the age of 7–8, then what it becomes
once it has been shifted on to the verbal plane between
7–8 and 11–12. Before the age of 7–8, syncretism may
be said to be bound up with all mental events and with
nearly all the judgments that are made. For any two
phenomena perceived at the same moment become caught
up in a schema which the mind will not allow to become
dissociated, and which will be appealed to whenever a
problem arises in connexion with either of these two
phenomena. Thus, when children of 5–6 are asked :
" Why do the sun and moon not fall down ? " the answer
does no more than to invoke the other features appertain-
ing to the sun and the moon, because these features,
having been perceived *en bloc* and within the same whole
as the feature requiring explanation, seem to the child
a sufficient reason for the latter. Such answers as these
would be absurd if they did not point to a reciprocal
implication of features that have been perceived together,
far more powerful than would be the case for a non-
syncretistic mentality. Here are some examples : The
sun does not fall down " *because it is hot. The sun stops
there.*—How ?—*Because it is yellow* " (Leo, age 6). " And
the moon, how does it stop there ?—*The same as the sun,
because it is lying down on the sky* " (Leo). " *Because it
is very high up, because there is no* [no more] *sun, because
it is very high up* " (Béa, age 5), etc. Or again, if one
shows the child a glass of water and if, after putting a
small pebble into it so as to make the level of the water
rise, one asks the child why the water has risen, the only
explanation given will often be a simple description of
what has happened ; but because of syncretism this
description will possess explanatory value for the child.

Q

In Tor's opinion (age $7\frac{1}{2}$) the water rises because the pebble is heavy. When wood is used, the water rises because the wood is light, and so on. Incidentally, these answers, when submitted to analysis, showed that to the child, weight meant something more dynamic than it does to us ; but what is most remarkable is that two contradictory reasons can be invoked by the same subject. Either such facts as these are due to the *n'importe quisme* of which Binet and Simon have spoken (and this would hardly apply to cases where the child is interested in the experiment in which he is taking part), or else description has a greater explanatory value for the child than for us, because features bound together within the raw material of observation seem to him to be related to one another by causal connexions. This immediate relation is what constitutes syncretism.

In all these cases—and they are without number— syncretism seems to describe the following course. First of all two objects or two features are given simultaneously in perception. Henceforth the child perceives or conceives them as connected or rather as fused within a single schema. Finally, the schema acquires the strength of reciprocal implication, which means that if one of the features is isolated from the whole, and the child is asked for its reason, he will simply appeal to the existence of the other features by way of explanation or justification.

This facility in connecting everything with everything else, or to speak more accurately, this inability on the part of childish perception and understanding to isolate the elements of all-round schemas, is to be found again on the verbal plane after the age of 7–8. For after this age perception becomes more analytical, causal explanation begins to play its part in a mentality which up till then was precausal (see § 8) ; in short, syncretism tends to disappear from the subject's view of the external world. But on the verbal plane, which, with the increasing mental intercourse between children and between children and adults, becomes the habitual sphere of reasoning, the old difficulties survive and even reappear in new forms. For sentences and statements heard in the mouth of other people give rise to a mass of syncretistic verbal manifestations which are due, as before, to analytical weakness, and the tendency to connect everything with everything else.

We have already had occasion to publish certain facts connected with the syncretism of reasoning in the child,[1] which show very clearly the child's difficulty in isolating the elements of a schema. Here, for example, is one of Burt's tests which raises insurmountable difficulties : " If I have more than a franc I shall go either by taxi or by train. If it rains, I shall go either by train or by bus. Now it is raining, and I have half a louis (10 francs). Which way do you think I shall go ? " The child cannot succeed in isolating the two elements from one another. Since you take the train or the bus if it rains, you must take the train or a taxi if it does not rain. Of this he feels convinced. Consequently, most of the subjects deem that you will go by bus, since the train is to be found in both terms of alternation, and is bound up with the condition ' fine weather.' Thus syncretism prevents analysis, and prevents deductive reasoning. Such cases also show how syncretism explains the child's inability to perform logical multiplication, and reveal his tendency to put juxtaposition in the place of synthesis.

Another and very different case of syncretism which we discovered is equally suggestive from the point of view of the analytical weakness shown by the child whenever there is any question of connecting propositions or even of understanding words independently of the schemas in which they are enveloped (L.T., Chap. IV). The child is given a certain number of easy proverbs and a certain number of corresponding sentences jumbled together, but each meaning the same thing as one of the given proverbs. He is then asked to find the connexion. Now up till the age of 11-12 the child chooses the corresponding sentence more or less at random, or at any rate by means

---

[1] *Journ. de Psych.*, Vol. XIX (1922), pp. 222–261, *passim* (*op. cit.*).

of accidental and purely superficial analogies. But the significant thing is that at the moment of choosing the corresponding sentence the child fuses proverb and sentence into a single schema which subsumes them both and justifies the correspondence. We have here a syncretistic capacity which at first sight seems due to pure invention ; but analysis shows that it comes from the child's inability to dissociate comprehensive perceptions or to restrain the tendency that wants to simplify and condense everything. For instance, a child of 9 assimilates the proverb "White dust will ne'er come out of sack of coal," to the corresponding sentence, " People who waste their time neglect their business." According to him, these two propositions mean ' the same thing,' because coal is black and can be cleaned. Similarly, people who waste their time neglect their children, who then become black and can no longer be cleaned. The uniformity shown by these answers to which we need not return at this point, excludes the hypothesis of invention. It shows how universal is the tendency of the child to create comprehensive schemas in his imagination, and to condense the various images into each other.

Such, then, is syncretism : immediate fusion of heterogeneous elements, and unquestioning belief in the objective inter-implication of elements condensed in this way. Syncretism is therefore necessarily accompanied by a tendency to justify things at any price. Now this is exactly what the facts show to be the case. The child can always find a reason, whatever may happen to be in question. His fertility in framing hypotheses is disconcerting, and recalls the intellectual vagaries of ' interpreters ' rather than the imaginative constructions of normal adults. The experiment in proverbs of which we have just been speaking bears testimony to this. The same tendency appears very clearly in children's ideas about natural phenomena. It partly explains why the idea of chance is absent from the thought of the child before the age of 7–8, and this constitutes one of the principal reasons for the phenomenon of precausality.

§ 6. Transduction, and Insensibility to Contradiction.—Does reasoning in the child obey the laws of
adult logic ? Above all, does it obey the law of contradiction ? If it be borne in mind, in the first place, that
child thought is ignorant of the logic of relations, that
addition and multiplication of logical classes are unknown
to it (juxtaposition being constantly chosen in preference
to hierarchical arrangement) : if it be remembered,
moreover, that the various relations created by syncretism
are comprehensive and do not admit of analysis, then
nothing will prevent us from concluding that the process
of reasoning in the child is, as Stern has put it, neither
inductive nor deductive, but *transductive*. By this Stern
means that child thought proceeds neither by an amplifying induction nor by an appeal to general propositions
which are designed to prove particular propositions, but
that it moves from particular to particular by means of
a reasoning process which never bears the character of
logical necessity. For instance, a child of 7 who is asked
whether the sun is alive, answers : " *Yes.*—Why ?—
Because it moves [moves along]." But he never says that
" All things that move are alive." This appeal to a general
proposition has not yet come into being. The child seeks
neither to establish such a proposition by means of successive inductions, nor to postulate it for the purposes of
deduction. On the contrary, if we try to make him aware
of a general rule, we shall find that it is by no means the
rule for which we were prepared. In the above example
it cannot be " All things that move are alive," because
certain things " that move " are conceived as inanimate,
as for example clouds (" Because the wind pushes them " ;
they are therefore not self-moving). In a word, the child's
reasoning is concerned only with individual cases and does
not attain to logical necessity. This is why it is transductive.

But Stern's description requires to be completed. For
recent discussions on deduction and induction and M.
Goblot's work in particular have altered these conceptions
in such a way that if we were to accept Stern's definition

of transduction it would be found not to differ from adult deduction that deals with singular cases (as, for example, in mathematics).

What seems to us the distinguishing feature of trans-duction is therefore its lack of logical necessity; the fact that this type of reasoning deals only with individual cases is certainly important, but cannot be said to be fundamental. As a result of his ego-centrism, the child does not as yet feel any desire for demonstration ; he makes no attempt to connect his judgments with bonds that bear the mark of necessity. Childish judgments—of which a chain constitutes precisely what we have called transduction—are therefore connected to each other in the same manner as are our tentative movements, viz. without consciousness of the uniting relations. What welds these momentary judgments together is some one aim, external to the act of judging, or some one action carried out upon the world of reality. But outside such extrinsic systematization there exist between these judg-ments no conscious implication and no demonstrative links. The psychologist will certainly succeed in finding the logical reason for a child's judgment, but the child himself looks for no such filiation between his propositions. At this stage, therefore, implication constitutes a motor rather than a mental phenomenon, and it is no exaggera-tion in this sense to say that there is no logical reasoning before the age of 7–8. For the justifications arising out of syncretism are devoid of logical necessity. As to the motor implications which have produced the reasoning process, they are still below the level of consciousness.

For by the term ' reasoning ' should be understood the work of controlling and proving hypotheses, which work alone creates conscious implications among judgments. Claparède has distinguished with great clarity three distinctly separate moments in intellectual activity : question, invention of hypothesis, and control. Now, the question is only the manifestation of a desire ; the hypothesis is framed by the imagination to fill up the gap created by this desire. Reasoning therefore appears only at the moment when the hypothesis is verified. Up till then there has been no logical activity. How then does the control take place ? To use the current formula, by means of a mental experiment. But this formula is slightly ambiguous and there are, in our opinion, three genetically distinct types of mental experiment: that which we find in the child before the age of 7–8, that which we find between 7–8 and 11–12, and finally, that of the adult. We also believe it necessary to point out that this third type of mental experiment is accompanied by an experiment which might be called ' logical experiment.' Unless this is done there is a certain element of ambiguity in the descriptions of Mach, of Rignano, and even of Goblot. The difference between extreme instances of these types is as follows :

Mental experiment is a reproduction in thought of events as they actually succeed one another in the course of nature ; or again, it is an imagined account of events in the order which they would follow in the course of an experiment which one would actually carry out, if it were technically possible to do so. As such, mental experiment knows nothing of the problem of contradiction ; it simply declares that a given result is possible or actual, if we start from a given point, but it never reaches the conclusion that two judgments are contradictory of each other. Consequently, mental experiment, like actual physical experiment, is irreversible, which means that, starting from a and finding b, it will not necessarily be able to find a again, or if it does so, it will not be able to prove that what it has found is really a and not a become a'. Similarly, if it finds b again after starting from c or from d, and not from a, it will have no means of proving that what it has found is really b and not b become b'. And these defects in mental experiment are the same as those which characterize childish reasoning, for the latter is content to imagine or to reproduce mentally actual physical experiments or external sequences of fact.

The logical experiment which intervenes from the age of 11–12 is certainly derivative from this process and has no other material than that of the mental experiment itself. It also deals mostly with individual cases, and does no more than combine the different relations existing between things, with or without the aid of syllogisms. But this logical experiment which comes as the completion of mental experiment and which alone confers upon it the quality of true ' experiment,' introduces nevertheless, a new element which is of fundamental importance : it is an experiment upon the subject himself as a thinking-subject, an experiment analogous to those which one makes upon oneself in regulating one's moral conduct. It is therefore an attempt to become conscious of one's own operations (and not only of their results), and to see whether they imply, or whether they contradict one another.

In this sense, logical experiment is very different from mental experiment. The first is the construction of reality and the awareness of this reality, the second is awareness and ordering of the actual mechanism of the construction. Now this ordering, which is the mark of logical experiment, has a considerable effect upon mental experiment : it makes it reversible. This means that the subject is led to lay down only such premises as are capable of entertaining reciprocal relations to each other and of remaining each identical with themselves throughout during the mental experiment. (This feature is one whose importance may not be evident to introspection, but is nevertheless fundamental from the genetic point of view, because it appears very late and is in no way implied in the mechanism of mental experiment pure and simple.) Premisses which are the necessary requisite of logical experiment will therefore contain decisive judgments, which means that they will necessitate the use of conventional definitions, of assumptions, and so on, and that they will consequently extend beyond the sphere of mere fact and observation. This is the price of reversibility in mental experiment. Logical experiment is therefore an experiment carried out on oneself for the detection of contradiction. This process is undoubtedly founded on mental experiment, but on mental experiment which it fashions for itself, and which differs from primitive mental experiment as widely as does the work of the physicist from the observations of the man in the street. The necessity resulting from mental experiment is a necessity of fact ; that which results from logical experiment is due to the implications existing between the various operations : it is a moral necessity due to the obligation of remaining true to oneself.

We are now in a position to understand how this first stage of childish reasoning is to be distinguished from logical reasoning proper. We were saying just now that the judgments of children before the age of 7–8 do not imply each other, but simply follow one another, after the manner of successive actions or perceptions which are psychologically determined without being logically necessitated by each other. For transduction is nothing but a mental experiment unaccompanied by logical experiment. It is either a simple account of events in succession, or a sequence of thoughts grouped together by one and the same aim or by one and the same action ; it is not yet a reversible system of judgments, such that each will be found to have remained identical with itself after no matter what kind of transformation.

Here are the proofs. We began by making a verbatim report during certain hours of the day of the spontaneous talk of six children between the ages of 3 and 6 (yielding a total of some 10,000 remarks). Now, in these 10,000 utterances there is not a single process of explicit reasoning. There are either simple isolated assertions, or else sequences of individual statements connected in the two following ways, which are both of them characteristic of pure mental experiment. In the one case, the subject foresees what will happen to him if he actually carries out a given experiment. For example, Lev (age 6½) is making a cardboard desk. *" I can shut it if I want to, that is why I don't make it stick. Afterwards* [if I want to], *I won't be able to shut it any more."* In the second case the subject foresees a sequence of events that is independent of him. Reasoning is then equivalent to a simple description. At the age of 6½ : " Why do balloons go up ?—*They can fly too, they* [people] *blow them up, they* [the balloons] *like the air, so when we let them go, they go up into the sky."* All these transductive reasonings are therefore simply descriptive or explanatory. The logical justification of statements is never given, for it would mean appealing to a definition or a law. Expressions such as " They like the air " appear at first sight to be the equivalents of laws, or seem to show that laws are implicit in the child's mind, and might be made more explicit, but, as we shall presently show, the child's insensibility to contradiction makes this hypothesis untenable. For one and the same statement made by a child may lead, according to the context, to completely contrary results. It is therefore a completely artificial procedure to bridge over the trans- ductions of children by means of implicit demonstrations or definitions. At this stage, mental experiment is still devoid of the element peculiar to logical experiment.

The counter-test of this may be made in the following way. The children are asked to think out little physical problems, such as why a pebble dropped into a glass of water causes the level of the water to rise. It will then be seen that the child reasons about individual cases with- out generalizing. Mull (age 8) tells us that a pebble makes the water rise because it is heavy, and that a piece of wood (lighter than the pebble) does so because it is big.

Why, in a case like this, does the child fail to generalize ? It is because he can handle neither the logic of relations nor the elementary operations of the logic of classes (logical addition and multiplication), both of which are themselves dependent upon the logic of relations. He can find neither the reciprocal counterpart to a relation (if a pebble makes the water rise because it is heavy, then a light object ought not to make it rise at all), nor the element that is common to both relations (if the pebble and the piece of wood both make the water rise, the common element which makes the water rise must be volume).

In short, the mere fact of reversing or multiplying relations, even in a single experiment, leads to the discovery of general laws. Consciousness of the necessity resulting from the reciprocity of individual relations is sufficient for generalization. Transduction does not generalize because it cannot handle relations. This is why it is an irreversible process.

The irreversibility of primitive reasoning may be recognized by the further circumstance (J.R. Chap. VI, §§ 4–5) that the subject cannot keep a premiss identical with itself throughout a mental experiment. This is because while he is 'constructing' by means of this premiss a whole series of new results, he has no means (unless he takes the decisions that regulate the experiment itself) of knowing whether this premiss has varied or not in the course of the mental experiment. Or again, there is no means of knowing whether a concept to which one has been led by different paths is really the same under these different forms, and does not contain any contradictions. In reality, neither of these questions exists for the child before the age of 7–8, and his habit of reasoning only about individual cases, of applying judgments which, though universal in appearance are particular in fact, leaves him in almost complete ignorance of the problem.

Childish concepts bear abundant testimony to this, at least in so far as they are implicit, i.e. such as the child applies before having become conscious of their definition. For instance, we can take a list of objects specially selected so as to avoid suggestion, and ask children of 7–8 whether such and such an object is alive, or has force, and so on. We shall then immediately realize that a concept like that of 'life' is frequently determined by two or three heterogeneous components. For example, the same child will agree that the sun, the moon, wind, and fire are alive, because they ' move,' but that neither streams, nor lakes, nor clouds are alive, because the wind pushes them and they consequently have no movement of their own.   On the other hand, clouds are alive, because they " make rain," the lake, because it ' runs ' ; both, in short, because they perform some activity which is useful to man.   Thus the two components ' self-movement ' and ' useful activity ' define between them the concept of life.   But owing to the schematism of childish judgment which we have described, these components do not multiply, or to put it differently, they do not interfere, but remain juxtaposed without synthesis in such a way that they only act one at a time, and make the child say, for instance, sometimes that the lake is alive, and sometimes that it is not.   The idea of force, again, is defined by movement, by solidity and by activity, all of them components that define the adult idea of force, but which in the child remain thrown together without any hierarchical order.   It is in this sense that childish reasoning is irreversible.   According to the turn taken by the mental experiment, the child will discover on the way facts which will cause him to alter his definitions, modify his premises, and which will completely change the nature of one and the same concept by reason of the path taken to reach it. This, moreover, is only the direct result of the schematism of childish judgments.   On the one hand, the logic of relations is foreign to the child along with all the adult habits of logical multiplication, of hierarchical arrangement of classes and of propositions.   This is one cause of irreversibility.   The child can certainly reach a conclusion from given premises, but he cannot perform the return journey without deviating from his path.   On the other hand, syncretism, which makes the child connect everything with everything else, and prevents him from making the excisions and distinctions necessary to analytical thought, will have the natural consequence of making him concentrate heterogeneous elements within a single word. We have here a second cause of irreversibility. The concepts of children are systems which are not in equilibrium, to borrow a term from chemistry. They have a pseudo-equilibrium, which means that their seeming immobility is simply due to their viscosity. In consequence of this they do not remain identical, but vary imperceptibly throughout a reasoning process.

We can now lay our finger upon the real cause of contradiction in the child. There can be no doubt that up to the age of 7–8, child thought teems with contradictions. This strikes one particularly when the child is asked to explain a natural phenomenon, like the fact of boats floating or of clouds moving. These are not artificial events, *i.e.* such as are occasioned only by the experiment, for it is obvious that the various factors which the child invokes in the course of his explanation were already present in his mind, though without order or connexion. On the other hand, it is certainly at about the age of 7–8 that these mental phenomena diminish in intensity. And as these contradictions to which the child seems completely insensible are of two kinds, it is important to distinguish very clearly between them.

To begin with, there is what may be called contradiction 'by amnesia,' which, incidentally, has no particular interest for us. The child has two contradictory opinions about one object, and hesitates between them. When he is questioned he will affirm one of these, but a moment later he will forget what he has said, and affirm the other, and so on. For instance, a child believes that rivers are dug out and made entirely by the hand of man. Then he learns that the water coming from their sources has been sufficient to produce them. But for a long time he fluctuates between these two explanations, neither of which he finds completely satisfactory, so that when questioned, he will give first one, then the other, forgetting each time what he has previously asserted. This type of contradiction is more frequent in the child than in us, but it does not differ in its nature from the hesitations of an adult in the throes of a problem that has not yet been mastered. It only points by its frequency to greater degree of irreversibility of thought than exists in our minds.

The second type of contradiction, on the other hand, strikes us as peculiarly characteristic of child thought. It is what might be called contradiction " by condensation." The child, unable to choose between two contradictory explanations of one and the same phenomenon, agrees to both simultaneously and even fuses them into each other. Nor must it be thought that this is in any way an attempt at synthesis. The child is never in the presence of two terms which are first conceived as separate and then condensed, *faute de mieux*. It is rather a certain lack of restraint that allows new elements to be constantly heaped on the old ones, regardless of synthesis. Such schemes inherit their character from these syncretistic habits of thought which lead the subject to simply add up and condense his impressions instead of synthesizing them. And this is the immediate consequence of what we were saying just now about the irreversibility of child thought. For one and the same concept being different according to the path along which the child has reached it, the various components of which this concept is the product are bound to be heterogeneous and to lead to incessant contradictions.

Let us recall an example. A boy of $7\frac{1}{2}$ tells us that boats float because they are light. As to big boats, they float because they are heavy. Theoretically, this reasoning is legitimate. In the first case, the water is thought of as strong and supporting the boat, in the second case the boat is thought of as strong and supporting itself. But as a matter of fact, the child is not aware of this opposition. He is subject to contradiction because he is unable to resolve this condensation of heterogeneous explanations.

Such facts as these are extremely frequent. The child either reasons about individual cases without looking for any links between these cases (which in actual fact are contradictory), or else, in his unbridled way, he condenses his statements without attempting to conciliate them.

We may also conclude that transductive reasoning, in so far as it consists purely in mental experiment, is still irreversible and consequently powerless to detect contradiction. The reason for this is quite simple. Consciousness of contradiction arises from an awareness of mental operations, and not from observation of nature, whether this observation be actual or imaginary. Now, up to the age of 7–8, childish judgments entail each other without any awareness of implications. They succeed, but do not justify each other. It is therefore perfectly natural that contradictory judgments should be added straight away to the pile by simple condensation. Only if the child became conscious of the definitions he has adopted or of the steps by which his reasoning proceeds, would these judgments seem to him to contradict one another.

After the age of 7–8, however, comes a stage lasting till about the age of 11–12, and during which the following fundamental changes take place. Little by little the child becomes conscious of the definition of the concepts he is using, and acquires a partial aptitude for introspecting his own mental experiments. Henceforward, a certain awareness of implications is created in his mind, and this gradually renders these experiments reversible, removing at least such contradictions as are the fruit of condensation. Does this mean that these are finally disposed of, and that the child is now fit to reason formally, *i.e.* from given or merely hypothetical premisses? We have shown that this is not the case, and that formal thought does not appear till about the age of 11–12. From 7–8 till 11–12 syncretism, contradiction by condensation, etc., all reappear independently of observation, upon the plane of verbal reasoning, in virtue of the law of shifting. It is therefore not until about the age of 11–12 that we can really talk of 'logical experiment.' The age of 7–8, nevertheless, marks a considerable advance, for logical forms have entered upon the scene of the mind in perception.

Within the sphere of direct observation the child becomes capable of amplifying induction and of necessary deduction.

It is not without interest to recall that these advances in logic are connected with the definite diminution of ego-centrism at the age of 7–8. The result of this last phenomenon is on the one hand to give birth to the need for proof and verification, and on the other to induce a relative awareness of the way thought moves. We have here a remarkable instance of the influence of social factors on the functioning of thought.

§ 7. MODALITY OF CHILD THOUGHT, INTELLECTUAL REALISM, AND INCAPACITY FOR FORMAL REASONING.— The question of reasoning and particularly of contradiction in the child is closely bound up with the problem of modality or of the different planes of reality on which the child uses his thought. For if contradiction ' by amnesia ' is so frequent before the age of 7–8, in other words, if the child has the faculty for permanently hesitating between two contradictory views and of always forgetting the view he held a moment previously, this is to a great extent because he has the power of passing far more swiftly than we can from a state of belief to a state of invention or of play. In thinking about reality, the child has a whole scale of planes which are probably devoid of any sort of hierarchy, and therefore favourable to logical incoherence. We have here at any rate a problem worth discussing.

Before entering upon this discussion, two truths should be remembered. The first is that for ego-centric thought the supreme law is play. It is one of the merits of psycho-analysis to have shown that autism knows of no adaptation to reality, because pleasure is its only spring of action. Thus the sole function of autistic thought is to give immediate and unlimited satisfaction to desires and interests by deforming reality so as to adapt it to the ego. For reality is infinitely plastic for the ego, since autism is ignorant of that reality shared by all, which destroys illusion and enforces verification. In so far then as child thought is still permeated with ego-centrism, the question of modality will have to be embodied in the following somewhat biased formula : Does there exist for the child only one reality, that is to say one supreme reality which is a touchstone of all others (as is the world of the senses for one adult, the world constructed by science, or even the invisible world of the mystic for another) ? Or does the child, finding himself, according as he is in an ego-centric or in a socialized state of being, in the presence of two worlds which are equally real, and neither of which succeeds in supplanting the other ? It is obvious that the second hypothesis is the more probable.

Nay, more—and this is the second truth to remember— there is nothing to prove that the child is any the worse for this bi-polar nature of reality. Seen from the outside his attitude seems disharmonious : at one moment he is believing, at the next he is playing. As Baldwin has said : " The object, therefore, not only exists, but always exists as fulfilling the interest which motives its apprehension." [1] But seen from the inside there may be nothing particularly uncomfortable about this attitude. For us adults lack of harmony and hierarchy between states of belief and play would be unbearable, but that is because of a desire for inner unity which is perhaps very late in appearing. For it is chiefly in relation to other people that we are obliged to unify our beliefs, and to place on different planes those that are not compatible with each other, so that we gradually build up within ourselves a plane of reality, a plane of possibility, a plane of fiction, and so on. The hierarchy of these planes is therefore determined by their degree of objectivity, and the capacity for objectivity depends in its turn upon the socialization of thought, since we have no other criterion of objectivity than the agreement of different minds. If our thinking remains shut up within the ego, if it cannot place itself at the point of view of others, disparity between objective and

[1] J. M. Baldwin, *Thoughts and Things* (London, 1911).

R

subjective will be through this alone seriously endangered. For the child whose thought is still ego-centric there will be no possible hierarchy between these different realities, and this absence of hierarchy will not even make itself felt, for lack of continuous contact on the part of the subject with the thought of others. At certain moments, the child, shut up within his ego, will believe in his fictions, and make light of his previous beliefs, at others, and especially when he resumes his contact with other people's thought, he will forget what he has just believed, and return to the second pole of what for him constitutes reality.

In conclusion, there may be several realities for the child, and these realities may be equally real in turn instead of being arranged in a hierarchy as with us. It may be, moreover, that the disharmony resulting from this fact is in no way a source of discomfort to the child (L.T., Chap. V, § 9). The facts show this very clearly. Four stages can be picked out in the evolution of modality. The first lasts till the age of 2-3, the second extends from 2-3 to 7-8, the third from 7-8 to 11-12, and the fourth begins at this age. During the first stage, reality may be said to be simply and solely what is desired. Freud's ' pleasure principle ' deforms and refashions the world to its liking. The second stage marks the appearance of two heterogeneous but equal realities—the world of play and the world of observation. The third marks the beginning of hierarchical arrangement, and the fourth marks the completion of this hierarchy, thanks to the introduction of a new plane—that of formal thought and logical assumptions.

Stern has noted that round about the age of 3 such expressions as ' to think,' ' to believe,' etc., begin to appear, which indicates that the child has detected a shade of difference between two kinds of existence—what is true and what is simply imagined. And as a matter of fact, from this date onwards children distinguish better

and better between ideas that are believed *pour de vrai*
as the young Genevans say, and ideas that are believed
pour s'amuser. But we must not allow ourselves to regard
this as indicating two hierarchical planes. When the
child is directed towards one of these poles, he turns his
back on the other. Until he reaches the age of 7–8, the
question of modality very rarely occurs to him at all. He
does not try to prove whether such or such of his ideas
does or does not correspond to reality. When the
question is put to him, he evades it. It does not interest
him, and it is even alien to his whole mental attitude.
The rare cases when he spontaneously asks himself such a
question ("Do they exist sometimes?" etc., 5 cases out
of 750 questions asked by a boy of 6) are due to necessary
friction with the thought of others. Outside circumstances such as these, the child from 2–3 to 7–8 is certainly
acquainted with two planes, or two orders of reality, that
of play and that of observation, but they are juxtaposed
and not hierarchisized, in the sense that when he is in
the presence of one it seems to him the only true one, and
he forgets the other.

In consequence, these two planes, that of play and that
of sensuous observation, are very different for the child
from what they are for us, and in particular they are less
distinct. This probably explains the lack of hierarchy;
for two still partially indifferentiated elements obstruct
one another far more than when a clear differentiation
has shed light upon their opposing qualities. In the
first case the contradictions involved by the lack of
differentiation produce antagonism, in the second case, the
oppositions make synthesis possible.

For, for us, play rests on fiction. But for the child it
is something much more. It is not enough to say, with
Groos, that it is a 'voluntary illusion,' for this attitude
presupposes in the child the power to resist illusion,
or rather to contrast certain beliefs that are voluntary with certain others that are necessary. As a

matter of fact play cannot be contrasted to reality, because in both cases belief is arbitrary, or rather devoid of logical reasons. Play is a reality which the child chooses to believe in by himself, just as reality is a game which the child chooses to believe in with grown-ups and with anyone else who believes in it. In both cases the belief is either very strong or very weak, according as it is characterized by its momentary intensity or by its duration, but in neither case does it require any intrinsic justification. Childish play may therefore be said to constitute an autonomous reality, by which we mean that ' true ' reality to which it stands in contrast is far less true for the child than for us.

Thus, sensible or ' true ' reality is also quite different for the child from what it is for us. To us, this reality is given by experimentation, and its laws are submitted to incessant control. For the child, sensible reality is observed and experimented upon to a much lesser degree, and its laws are hardly submitted to any control whatsoever ; it is made up almost in its entirety by the mind and by the decisions of belief.

We are dealing here with the phenomenon of ' intellectual realism,' as studied by specialists in children's drawings and by M. Luquet in particular, and which we have extended to cover the concept of child thought in general.[1]

For we have already seen (L.T., Chap. V, § 3) that in consequence of his ego-centrism, the child's picture of the world is always moulded on his immediate, sectional, and personal point of vi w. Relations between things will therefore not be what is yielded by experimentation or fashioned by comparison of view-points ; they will be what child logic, and especially what syncretism makes them. By reason of the same cause which prevented him from adapting himself to other people, the child will fail to be adapted to the observation of the senses. He does not analyse the contents of his perceptions, but weighs it down with a load of previously acquired and

---

[1] *Journ. de Psych.*, Vol. XIX (1922), pp. 256–257.

ill-digested material. In short, he sees objects, not as they really are, but as he would have imagined them, if, before seeing them, he had *per impossibile* described them to himself. This is why the early stages of children's drawings are not characterized by visual realism, *i.e.* by a faithful copy of the model in question, but by intellectual realism, such that the child draws only what he already knows about things and copies only an ' inner model.' Childish observation follows the same lines. The child often sees only what he already knows. He projects the whole of his verbal thought into things. He sees mountains as built by men, rivers as dug out with spades, the sun and moon as following us on our walks. The field of attention seems wide in this sense that things are observed in large numbers, but it is narrow in the sense that things are schematized in accordance with the child's own point of view, instead of being perceived in their intrinsic relations.

Intellectual realism is the picture of the world that is most natural to ego-centric thought. It points, on the one hand, to an incapacity for objective observation (visual realism). On the other hand, it is realism none the less, for the child is neither an intellectualist (his disregard of logical system is complete) nor a mystic. His ego-centrism is, moreover, perpetually leading him into realistic delusions, such as confusing words and things, thought and the objects of thought, etc. ; in a word, he is conscious of nothing but his own subjectivity.

In conclusion, there exist before the age of 7-8 two planes of reality—play and the reality of ordinary life, but they are juxtaposed instead of being compared and ordered in a hierarchy, and each taken by itself is different from what it is for us. But at about the age of 7-8, certain changes take place in the modality of childish judgment which are in close relation to the appearance of a desire for a system and non-contradiction. This stage is characterized on the one hand by the beginnings of a positive observation of the external world, and on the other by an awareness of the implications contained in such reasoning as is connected with actual observation. These two facts tend to make the child dissociate objective reality from verbal reality, to dissociate, that is, the world of direct observation from that of stories, of fantasies, and of things conceived or heard of, but never seen. This is therefore the decline of intellectual realism, so far as actual observation is concerned.

But in virtue of the law of shifting, all the phenomena which up till now have stood in the way of complete adaptation to the external world (inability to handle relations, syncretism, juxtaposition, etc.), are shifted on to the verbal plane, and stand in the way of the child's awareness of his own reasoning process. This gives rise to two consequences which are closely bound up with each other, one being concerned with modality, the other with the structure of the reasoning process.

Here is the first. As regards the faculty of perception, the different planes of reality, stand in hierarchical order. The categories of the possible and of the necessary in particular (which alone enable the different orders of reality to be grouped in relation to each other) appear in the conception of nature, and allow the child to conceive of some phenomena as due to chance (for this notion first appears at the age of 7–8), and of others as bound by a necessity that is physical and not moral. But as regards the verbal faculty, these different planes have not yet come to be distinguished, so that the child is incapable of conceiving on the one hand of a purely logical necessity (If we say that . . . then we must say that . . .), on the other hand of a plane inhabited by pure hypothesis or by logical assumption (Let us say that . . .).

Childish reasoning between the years of 7–8 and 11–12 will therefore present a very definite feature (J.R., Chap. II) : reasoning that is connected with actual belief, or in other words, that is grounded on direct observation, will be logical. But formal reasoning will not yet be possible. For formal reasoning connects assumptions—propositions, that is, in which one does not necessarily believe, but which one admits in order to see what consequences they will lead to.

At about the age of 11–12, on the contrary, modality in the thought of the child becomes more or less what it is with us, or at least, with the uneducated adult. The various planes of reality—play, verbal reality, observation are set in a hierarchy that is defined in relation to a single criterion—experience. And this hierarchy is possible, thanks to the notions of necessity and possibility which are now extended to verbal thought.

This evolution in the structure of childish reasoning has very important consequences. We have already[1] put forward the view, which has since been confirmed by a more recent study, that formal thought does not appear till the age of 11–12, at the period, therefore, when the child comes to reason about pure possibility. For to reason formally is to take one's premisses as simply given, without enquiring whether they are well-founded or not ; belief in the conclusion will be motivated solely by the form of the deduction. Previous to this, and even in the minds of children from 7–8 to 11–12, deduction is never pure, by which we mean that belief in the validity of the conclusion is still bound up with belief in the validity of the premisses. For before the age of 7–8, there is no awareness of logical implications. Thought is still realistic, and in reasoning, the child looks always to an ' inner model ' which is considered as true reality, even when his reasoning bears upon it all the marks of deduction. This is mental experiment pure. The pseudo-assumptions of children of 6–7 are of this type. (" If I was an angel and had wings and if I flew up into the fir-trees, would the squirrels run away or would they stay . . ."). Between the years of 7–8 and 11–12, there is certainly awareness of implications when reasoning rests upon beliefs and not upon assumptions, in other words, when it is founded on actual observation. But such deduction

---

[1] *Journ. de Psych.*, Vol. XIX (1922), p. 222. (" Essai sur la multiplication logique et les débuts de la pensée formelle chez l'enfant.")

is still realistic, which means that the child cannot reason from premises without believing in them. Or even if he reasons implicitly from assumptions which he makes on his own, he cannot do so from those which are proposed to him. Not till the age of 11–12 is he capable of this difficult operation, which is pure deduction, and proceeds from any assumption whatsoever. Take, for instance, the absurd-phrase test which Binet gives as one for 10 years, but is really an 11- or 12-year-old test : " If one day I kill myself from despair, it will not be on a Friday, because Friday is an unlucky day, . . . etc." Before the age of 11–12 the child cannot make the assumption. He either accepts the data and fails to see the absurdity, or else he rejects them as absurd and fails to see the formal absurdity of the argument.

11–12 is therefore the age at which we must situate the appearance of what a little earlier we called ' logical experiment.' Logical experiment, in conclusion, pre-supposes and may be defined by the two following con-ditions : 1° A ' mental experiment ' carried out on the plane of pure hypothesis or of pure possibility, and not as before on the plane of reality reproduced in thought ; and 2° an ordering and awareness of the operations of thought as such, as for example of definitions or assumptions that one has made and has decided to retain identical with themselves.

It is not without interest to note that this new aware-ness is once again under the dependence of social factors, and that conversely, incapacity for formal thought is very directly the result of childish ego-centrism. For what prevents the child from reasoning from data that he does not agree to but is asked simply to ' assume,' is that he is untutored in the art of entering into other people's points of view. For him, there is only one comprehensible point of view—his own. Hence the fact that up till the age of 11–12, physical reality is not accom-panied by subjective reality (the child being unaware of the personal character of his opinions, his definitions, and even his words), nor, consequently, even by a logical reality in which everything conceivable would be possible. Previous to this, there is only the real and the unreal. There is undoubtedly a plane of physical possibility, but there is no plane of logical possibility. The real alone is logical. At about the age of 11–12, on the contrary, social life starts on a new phase, and this obviously has the effect of leading children to a greater mutual understanding, and consequently of giving them the habit of constantly placing themselves at points of view which they did not previously hold. This progress in the use of assumptions is probably what lends greater suppleness to the child's conception of modality, and teaches him the use of formal reasoning.

§ 8. PRECAUSALITY IN THE CHILD.—We have now reached the end of our outline of child logic. We must nevertheless recall in a few short words a certain question which so far we have asked rather than answered. What is the picture of the world which goes hand in hand with such a logic ? What are the notions of causality which the child constructs at his different stages of development ? We ought perhaps to have begun with this. But by making a direct study of children's talk about the phenomena which surround them, we would have exposed ourselves to the risk of either taking them literally or of deforming them, for lack of having analysed their logical structure. We consider ourselves to be now sufficiently armed against this danger.

How, then, are we to formulate the problem of causality in the child ? Undoubtedly, by a study of his spontaneous questions and especially of his ' whys.' To this end we collected during ten months 1125 questions from one and the same child of 6–7 years old (L.T., Chap. V). The results of the analysis and classification of these questions were as follows. The desire for causal explanation proper was found to be extremely weak, and the ' whys ' pointed to a sort of indifferentiation between physical causality and logical or psychological justification, which character of indifferentiation is precisely what we shall select as the distinguishing feature of precausality.

Let us recall the facts. Out of 360 ' whys,' there were found to be only 5 "whys of logical justification," and 103 " whys of causal explanation." But of these 103 ' whys ' the greater portion showed signs either of animism, of artificialism, or of finalism ; only 13 of them could be interpreted as pointing unambiguously to a desire for mechanical explanation by means of spatial contact. It is possible, therefore, to foresee that childish explanation will be equally far from constituting a proof or a logical deduction as it is from appealing to spatial insertion with regard to things that are set in motion. Childish explanation is neither logical nor spatial. In addition to this, a large number of these questions showed us that the idea of chance is absent from child thought before the age of 7–8. Before this date, the world is conceived as an assemblage of willed and well-regulated actions and intentions, which leave no room for fortuitous and, as such, inexplicable events. Everything can be justified ; we need only appeal to an arbitrary factor, which is not the equivalent of chance but resembles rather the whim of all-powerful wills.

This, then, is the sense in which we can speak of pre-causality : indifferentiation between physical causality and psychological or logical motivation. What are the roots of this precausality, whose dual fruit is childish animism and artificialism ? Once again, we believe the answer to be : ego-centrism and the resultant intellectual realism which it brings in its wake.

Ego-centrism helps, as we saw, to make the child unconscious of himself. But this unconsciousness goes far beyond the difficulties in introspection which we described ; it goes so far as to prevent the child under 7–8 from being aware of the phenomenon of thought as a subjective phenomenon, and even to prevent him from establishing the exact limit between his own ego and the external world. Baldwin has laid great stress upon this

' adualistic ' character of primitive thought. We have ourselves described a very definite phase (about the age of 7) during which the child knows that his dreams are subjective (a person standing beside him could neither see nor touch them), and nevertheless locates them in front of himself in the room.[1] A large number of facts of this order has led us to admit that the child is ignorant of his own thought, and projects it in its entirety into things. He is therefore a ' realist ' in the sense in which one talks of the realistic illusions of thought. But this realism keeps its possessor in ignorance of the distinction between the physical and the psychical, and consequently leads him to regard the external world as endowed with both these qualities at the same time. Hence the tendency to ' precausality.'

On the other hand, and for the same reasons, childish realism is intellectual and not visual (see preceding paragraph) ; the child only sees what he knows, and sees the external worlds as though he had previously constructed it with his own mind. Childish causality is therefore not visual, in other words is not interested in spatial contacts nor in mechanical causation. It is intellectual, that is to say, full of considerations that are foreign to pure observation : justification of all phenomena, syncretistic tendency to connect everything with everything else (see § 5), in short, confusion of physical causality with psychological or logical motivation. Hence, once again, pre-causality.

In this sense, then, precausal mentality, as we defined it above, will be seen to be the type of mentality most in agreement with ego-centrism of thought and with all the logical peculiarities which this ego-centrism entails.

But once again, we must remind the reader that we have just raised an enormous problem by drawing attention to these few characteristics of childish causality, and that we are still very far from guessing its solution.

[1] See *Arch. de Psych.*, Vol. XVIII (1923), p. 288.

CONCLUSION.—On the other hand, we believe that we have solved the problem which we set ourselves at the beginning of our enquiry. The features of child thought which we have described really do constitute a coherent whole, such that each of its terms partially implies a portion of the other terms. To be sure, child thought cannot be isolated from the factors of education, and all the various influences which the adult exercises upon the child. But these influences do not imprint themselves upon the child as on a photographic plate; they are ' assimilated,' *i.e.* deformed by the living being who comes under their sway, and they are incorporated into his own substance. It is this psychological substance (psychologically speaking) of the child's, or rather this structure and functioning peculiar to his thought that we have tried to describe, and in a certain measure, to explain.

It is therefore our belief that the day will come when child thought will be placed on the same level in relation to adult, normal, and civilized thought, as primitive mentality ' as defined by Levy-Bruhl, as autistic and symbolical thought as described by Freud and his disciples, and as ' morbid consciousness,' in the event of this last concept, which we owe to M. Ch. Blondel, being eventually identified with the former. But we must beware of the danger of drawing parallels in which functional divergencies are forgotten. Moreover, we have already taken our stand on the subject of the relations which exist between the thought of the child and symbolic thought; though perhaps we did not at the time sufficiently emphasize the differences which separate these two kinds of thought.[1] Let us therefore not be in too great a hurry to follow a path so full of the pitfalls of Comparative Psychology. Patient analysis of the child's mentality keeps on safer ground, which though not yet thoroughly cleared, offers so sure a realm of investigation that wisdom forbids us to leave it forthwith.

[1] " La pensée symbolique et la pensée de l'enfant," *Arch. de Psych.*, Vol. XVIII (1923).

APPENDIX

NOTE ON THE COEFFICIENT OF EGO-CENTRISM

Since the publication of our first volume (L.T.) we have continued our collection of remarks made by various children in the *Maison des Petits* in order to establish how the coefficient of ego-centrism varies with age. Here are the results which we have obtained up to date, including the coefficients of Lev and Pie, which have already been published.

Subjects.	Age.	Number of Remarks Classified.	Coefficient of Ego-centrism.
Dan	3 years	1500	0·56
Jan	3 years	1000	0·56
Ad	4 years	1500	0·60
Ad	5 years	800	0·46
Pie	6 years	1500	0·43
Lev	6 years	1400	0·47
Clau	7 years	800	0·30
Lev	7 years	600	0·27

It can be seen at once that round about the age of 7 ego-centrism diminishes rapidly after having gradually decreased up to that point. The mean variations continued to be weak ($\pm$0·02 as a rule). We found nothing particularly significant in the details of the categories of language as they developed with age.

We wish to express our warmest gratitude to Mlles Berguer, Fiaux, and Gonet, who were kind enough to undertake the thankless task of collecting and classifying, which enabled us to carry on our research.